HANS URS VON BALTHASAR

YOU HAVE WORDS OF ETERNAL LIFE

Hans Urs von Balthasar

YOU HAVE WORDS
OF ETERNAL LIFE

SCRIPTURE MEDITATIONS

Translated by Dennis Martin

IGNATIUS PRESS   SAN FRANCISCO

Originally published in German as
Du hast Worte ewigen Lebens
© 1989 Johannes Verlag
Einsiedeln, Trier

Cover by Roxanne Mei Lum

With ecclesiastical approval
© 1991 Ignatius Press, San Francisco
ISBN 0-89870-308-5
Library of Congress catalogue number 90-85062
Printed in the United States of America

When Hans Urs von Balthasar died on June 26, 1988, he had finished editing these texts. He projected one hundred meditations; in the end there were 101. He personally read proofs for a third of them.

Copiously, in a final effort, he scatters once more the seed of God's word. He does this in the way he has always done it in the communities he founded: in trusting faith in the vitality and healing power of this word.

The author expressed the urgent concern and purpose that inspired this book with words once uttered by Saint Seraphim of Sarov.

All Saints' Day, 1988

"In our day holy faith in our Lord Jesus Christ is so slack, and indifference and lack of passion for communion with God loom so large, that one really must say: we have almost completely abandoned true Christian living. Many passages of Holy Scripture have become completely foreign to us. Some people label them 'incomprehensible', asking how it could be that men could see God in such concrete fashion. But that is not hard to comprehend; that we no longer understand things stems from the fact that we have departed from the original simplicity of Christian understanding. Through what was supposed to be an enlightenment we have stumbled into ignorant darkness. We think incomprehensible what the ancients saw with such clarity that they could converse about the revelation of God to men as an obvious fact."

Then I asked the Abba Seraphim, "How can I know whether I am in the grace of the Holy Spirit?" "That is very simple, my friend of God", answered the staretz, "for that is why the Lord says that everything is simple for those to whom understanding is given. That is why the apostles write in their letters: 'Submit to the Holy Spirit in us.' For this reason alone they let their letters be sent out as an eternal truth for the benefit of all believers, because they sensed themselves to be filled with the Holy Spirit. See now, my friend of God, how easy it is?"

Saint Seraphim of Sarov (1759–1833)

CONTENTS

1. IMAGE–FILLED AND IMAGELESS CONTEMPLATION

In this much-discussed matter all depends on whether the contemplator is a Christian or not. If he is not a Christian, he will from the beginning strive for imageless contemplation, wishing to free himself from the daily assaults of a world overwhelmed by sensual images, shapes, and outlines, hoping to gain the quiet and personal depth that lies behind or above it all. Such a quest can range from simple psychological therapy to a philosophical and religious contemplation and experience of the depths of the cosmos beyond all appearances, phenomena, and concepts.

For the Christian all is different. For him the Absolute is the God of love, who merits this name only because within God is both a lover—one beloved from his origin in God and become beloved in God's bosom—and their mutual love. The beloved of the "Father" is called "Son", radiance, reflection, Word, Image. His imageness is just as absolute and eternal as the primal Source that generates without images. Both are identical in essence and one in their love, which is the fruition and evidence, the overflowing, the "Holy Spirit" of this love. We know about this fullness in God only because the eternal Image has entered the multiplicity of our world of images, portraying and explicating the imageless Father, immersing us in the Divine Spirit so that we gain access to the divine world of love.

If that is so, then the incarnate Son lives out before us, in images perceptible by men (individual deeds, words, actions), that which belongs to him alone, as the eternal, suprasensible image of the Father, to reveal to us of the Father. He does this so that, graced with the divine spirit of love "poured out into our hearts", we might sense something of the unimaginable Source of all love. Thus the path of all Christian contemplation is prefigured in the essence and purpose of the incarnate "Word" (or Image) himself: because God and man are not two different persons but one and the same person in the Word, the path of contemplation moves from a comprehension of the world's image to the Divine Image that is expressed therein. Because of the unity of the Image's "person", there is really no path to follow; rather, the divine "meaning" lies directly in the human "sign" (*semeion*), or "expression". Our sole aim is to view the sign in the manner in which it seeks to reveal itself. For example, if one reads properly one of the stories of physical healing, it is directly apparent that the incarnate Son is the real and divine healing One, the saving One. His way of speaking ("never has a man spoken like this one" [Jn 7:46]) itself announces directly that he speaks with a "completely new", truly divine "authority" (Mk 1:27). Jesus continually emphasizes that this transition from surface to the depths takes place right in his being and acting. Everything else depends on whether men have eyes to see and ears to hear, on whether they have the purity of heart to see the divine in the human (Mt 5:2ff.).

Yet with that we have merely passed from one image to another. Is not the thrust of all contemplation to arrive beyond all imaging? In a Christian sense it is impossible to arrive at the Divine "Image", or "Word", or "Son" without also directly "seeing" in him his imageless Origin. "Show us the Father", one of them begged. Jesus answered, "Have I been among you so long and you have not yet known me? He who has seen me has seen the Father. Don't you believe that I am in the Father and the Father is in me?" (Jn 14:9–10). It is no rational conclusion that leads from the Son to the Father but rather faith in God's perfect unity, in which Image and Imagelessness, Birth and Birth-giver are simply integrated. The Son is so much a pure expression of the Father that one cannot encounter him without being addressed by the Father. His human, and thereby divine, love is purely and simply the Father's word of love spoken to us.

Thus, in a Christian view, nothing in any height or depth of contemplation surpasses the limits of simple Christian faith: the faith that God and man are one person in Christ, the faith that the Persons of Father, Son, and Spirit are not three gods but a single God. Contemplation simply realizes what was always present in Christian faith (which itself is a gift from God). This realization is something that the Christian himself, trusting in God's grace, can attain, even when grace freely moves beyond the contemplator's active possibilities to make him passively experience (*pati divina*) divine truth more than actively attain it.

Such exuberance is always the deepening of what begins in the simple occurrences of the gospel, even when our gaze has slipped away from earthly image to the eternal Image. There is no other door to the imageless: "He who denies the Son has not the Father" (1 Jn 2:23), for otherwise the contemplator would slip past absolute love into absolute emptiness. To be sure, one can describe the Father as "empty" of every image, since he lives in "inaccessible light" (1 Tim 6:16), but he is the actual superabundance of every image because he is, all in all, self-giving Love that eternally begets his Beloved, his Image.

2. God Is Limitless and Defined

For men everything that is defined has borders; where the boundaries disappear, things become vague. For that reason the idea that God is three in one seems to contain a contradiction: if the Son is not the Father and the Spirit is neither Son nor Father, we think there must be a boundary between the Divine Persons. Can this appearance of contradiction be resolved?

It is a tenet of Faith that God the Father has perfectly expressed himself in his Word and Son. God has reserved for himself nothing that he is or can or knows or wills, for, as Father, he is fully this self-expressing, communicating action. Were this not so, the Son could not be of the same being as the Father, and we would all be Arians. That no creature can be self-expressingly, self-generatingly, self-birthingly identical with its own act of expression, generation, and birthing is clear. God must be identical with his action if he is not merely to have love, like the creature, but really is love.

If the Father gives to the Son all that he is, then all that the Father is and can and knows and wills is in the Son and, naturally, vice versa, even though the Son is the Word of the Speaker and not the Speaker himself. Yet it bears repeating: if the speaker expresses himself completely and thereby places into his word all that he is, leaving nothing unexpressed behind the word, then the speaker and the spoken are of the same extent, are of the "same substance". Nonetheless, the infinitely birthing one is not the infinitely birthed one.

In this act of endless birthing there necessarily must be a departure, if the birth is to take place at all: if the giver were not separated from his gift, there would be no giving. Now this cannot mean that the self-giver holds something back, for that would nullify his innermost purpose; yet, if he is to put all of himself into the gift, he must be the giver and not the receiver. The distinction becomes most tangible where the giver wishes to express with his gift nothing other than himself, namely, his love.

If God the Father is the unlimited self-giving that generates the Son, then Father and Son are identically limitless and unbounded, without—insofar as they are giver and receiver— coinciding. There can be no suggestion that the Son is the antithesis of the Father (Hegel), for to be the opposite of the Father he would need to be limited, and we would once more be Arians. And thus the Holy Spirit, who belongs to both Father and Son, cannot at all be the synthesis in which their differences are suspended (even in the ambiguous meaning of *suspension* as the word was used by Hegel).

How, then, are we to imagine the being of the Holy Spirit, if the Spirit is supposed to be neither the Father nor the Son, and if all things have attained their (endless) end through the selfless self-giving of the Father? The only way to understand this is that the Spirit, as the spirit of love, rests perfectly in the self-giving of the Father and perfectly in the receiving love of the Son. (The latter is necessary, for otherwise the Father would not have given his entire love.) Yet the necessary distinction between giver and gift (gifted) transcends itself, without blurring itself, in the mutuality of the love, a mutuality that makes something new and complete out of the distinction.

Men and women can experience the newness of this reciprocity at the instant when lovers realize not merely that one loves the other but also that their love is a common, mutually reciprocating love. Thus the act of sexual union is a testimony that merely incorporates the body to produce naturally the newness (the child) that already lay in germ in the merging of mutual love.

Now God the Father focuses on this mutuality already in the act of generative self-giving, and the Son, in the completeness of received love, belongs limitlessly to this mutuality. Such reciprocity does not set up a kind of recompense. Instead this mutuality reveals the miracle of love that pervades all things; reveals that love exceeds all calculating, that it is more than one plus one (selfless love simply cannot count); reveals itself as the exuberant boundlessness that defines in itself the divine. In the creaturely experience of mutual love, too, an unbounded space for possibilities opens up to the lovers, a realm of freedom. For that reason it is appropriate to attribute absolute freedom and love to the Holy Spirit in God.

Unity and distinction in God so far transcend what can be calculated with the limits set by numbers, so far transcend the sequence of time, that both the responsive love of the Son and the mutuality of the Spirit are perfectly "simultaneous" with the generative act of the Father. Thus both the responsive love of the Son and the mutuality of the Spirit continue eternally to affect the very act of generation that is the eternal Source of all.

3. GOD'S WILL IS DEFINITE

God's will is defined by his being: limitless Goodness. Likewise, in God's variously limited creation, God's all-encompassing will is always limitless. His will is to let the world participate in his unbounded kindness, a participation that means joyful fulfillment for all creatures. To the extent that this comprehensive, limitless, yet defined will of God enters into the individual situations of free and rational creatures, it appears to limit its content. Yet it only appears to do so—it is the situation, not the divine will, that is limited.

In the light of the Father's boundless, comprehensive will Christ was able to carry out a definite commandment (*mandatum*) of the Father as an action of unlimited love and also to make the same equation the norm for his disciples: "As the Father has loved me, so have I loved you. Abide in my love; when you keep my commands, you abide in my love, as I have kept the commands of my Father and have remained in his love. That is my command, that you love one another as I have loved you" (Jn 15:9–10, 12). This command (in the singular) contains all commandments relating to particular situations: "Love is the fulfilling of the law" (Rom 13:10).

This glimpse of God's inclusive will bursts through all apparent impediments, obstacles, and incomprehension: death, incurable illness, suffering, and experiences of injustice and humiliation. These things are not simply to be endured passively. A commensurate reaction may be called for out of love of neighbor or in view of one's own mission: Jesus obscures himself from his enemies, either because his hour has not yet come or because it is part of his mission to reprove them and reject their excuses. There are times, however, when he does not defend himself against attacks and simply lets scorn and mockery descend upon himself. In both instances he is following the Father's will, not by virtue of his own decision but rather in obedience to the Divine Holy Spirit, who makes the Father's will clear to him in each setting. The Father's absolute will, which seeks the salvation of the world, is known to the Son without needing to be explained. The Spirit's leading has to do solely with the form the Father's will takes in a definite situation.

If men seek to understand the definite will of God in a particular instance, the first thing they learn is that they already know the comprehensive and limitless will of God. They can also remind themselves that God's will as such is identical with God's absolute freedom and that carrying out the divine will is always liberating for people, no matter how difficult the situation. The second thing is learned from Christ: God's will is always love, and one thus always seeks God's will in concrete instances by orienting oneself toward the greater love—whether God's good pleasure becomes apparent to me or to my neighbor. What pleases God does not necessarily involve something inconceivably difficult for me, nor is it fixed legally or literally in such a way as to rob me of my freedom as a child of God to function within a range of options and to make my decision in a free, rather than servile or timorous, glance toward God.

The only exception is if I have freely offered up my range of options in ecclesiastical obedience to God in order to submit to the instructions of an ecclesiastically confirmed superior, whom I then follow unless something "obviously contrary to God is commanded" (Ignatius). This superior then shows me renewed freedom to maneuver with my own decisions within the context of ecclesiastical obedience.

This unlimited-in-itself-yet-defined will of God can reveal itself through many layers of created reality. At bottom we find natural and common sense, whether in personal or in social settings, which requires an intelligent and courageous weighing of the alternatives ("Should I ask Mother to come and live with us, even though I know that my husband can't stand her?"). Even here the deliberation can most helpfully take place in God's presence, that is, in a prayerful attitude, even if one expects no direct "voice from heaven".

Other basic decisions take place at another level, where the endless loving will of God seems to focus like a spotlight on one's specific existence. These are the life-changing decisions that make up the core of the Ignatian Exercises. In which form do I offer my life to God: In a commitment to the evangelical counsels (chastity, poverty, obedience), in the priesthood, in marriage? Here too God's will seems to be directed toward the person as a whole but not thereby limited: it denotes to an individual the place that this one should occupy in the universal scheme of salvation. Because this will requires the entire person, no breadth of ability to choose is conceded here: here we must "see how we ought to prepare ourselves to arrive at perfection in whatever state or way of life God our Lord may grant us to choose" (*Spiritual Exercises,* 135). Such a choice cannot be made on the basis of general principles but rather only in a face-to-face encounter between God and the individual. Yet this has to do not with private perfection but with the place to be filled within God's comprehensive program of salvation. That one's natural, deliberating reason plays a role is obvious, but the decision itself can take place only in prayer and under the assurance and enlightenment of prayer. Human freedom offered completely to God thus encounters the freedom of God that is poured out in this way and in no other.

4. No Sign but Jonah

For "this evil generation" Jesus has no sign except the "sign of Jonah". Matthew and Luke differ in their interpretations of this sign, and exegetes tend to prefer Luke's version: "For as Jonah became a sign to the people of Ninevah, so the Son of Man is to this generation"—the Ninevites recognized God's sign in the prophet and were converted; thus they shall "arise in judgment against this generation and condemn them, for they repented", whereas those listening to Jesus failed to repent, even though "something greater than Jonah is here" (Lk 11:29–32). In Matthew's account, Jesus alludes to the first episode in the book of Jonah: "This adulterous generation demands a sign, but the only sign that shall be given it is that of the prophet Jonah. For as Jonah spent three days and three nights in the belly of the sea monster, so the Son of Man shall spend three days and three nights in the bosom of the earth." As in Luke, the condemnation by the Ninevites of this generation and "something greater than Jonah is here" follow (Mt 12:38–42).

It cannot be proven that Jesus was not referring to the second point, which, like the first, is the opposite of the vision-sign demanded by the "evil generation". An "experience" is necessary if one is to open up to faith. "Unless you see signs and wonders, you will not believe me" (Jn 4:48). The disciples too desired a sign so that they could orient themselves toward Christ's return: "What will be the sign of your coming?" (Mt 24:3).

The sign of Jesus' Resurrection is his death. Precisely in this apparent contradiction the faith Jesus demands gives proof of its victory over the world. What sign did Jonah make when he proclaimed to Ninevah her own destruction? Certainly no miraculous vision. Yet there must have been an incomprehensible power in his preaching if the whole city, including its king, believed him. It must have been the character of his word, embedded in the word itself yet reaching out beyond it to the hearts of his hearers.

All that this reaching out required was that they not shut themselves up against the power and character of the word.

"No other sign", Jesus says. It is as if he thereby sweeps away all his healings and exorcisms, all his multiplication of loaves and calming of storms, as if all these "works" were invalid as signs, as if in the ultimate decision he was confining himself to himself, who surpasses Jonah in signification. He transcends Jonah's sign through the insignificance ("even to death on the Cross") of his three days spent hidden in the bosom of the earth. Those demanding a sign receive nothing but the character of the (incarnate Divine) Word in its mundane, humiliated form. This, and only this, is believable — every ostentatious sign would be incredible and would point only to a power opposed to God (Rev 13:3–4, 13–15).

That Jonah was spit out onto the dry ground on the third day, that Christ arose on the third day, is not given as a sign to "this evil generation". Unlike the healing of the mortally wounded beast in Revelation, the resurrection is no spectacle upon which belief focuses. Nowhere is it called a "sign", and Thomas was explicitly instructed: "Blessed are those who have not seen, yet believe" (Jn 20:29). The witness must be believed; just as Jonah testified to his mission from God, so Jesus is the testimony of the Father, and the disciples are Christ's witnesses (Acts 13:31; 10:41). They will have both Cross and Resurrection to bear witness to, but the Cross is the visible sign, and the Resurrection is the invisible sign. The Cross shows itself as a defeat; the Resurrection victory is invisible.

Therefore, Christ's Church shows herself to the world as a sign of humiliation, persecution, and death. Her rising again is indeed real but hidden. The world will always wonder why the Church is not finished and done for. And the Church cannot precede herself with a triumphantly proclaimed Cross. The Cross she preaches says only one thing: it is something to die upon. The Church can proclaim only one Christ, the one for whom one loses one's soul in order to gain it by virtue of losing. And, if she is granted miracle-working power (which has been promised her), her miracles are not visible marvels but almost always quiet ones with little public relations value. Church history has seen thousands of miracles, but they have always been easily questioned, quickly forgotten, or simply ignored. Paul mentions only in passing the miracles he performed in Corinth (2 Cor 12:12)—the powerful evidence that he valued from beginning to end was his life crucified with Christ, subject to all manner of scorn, devoid of all status. People demanded proof of his authenticity, just as they had demanded it of Christ: "You require proof that Christ speaks through me?" (2 Cor 13:3). He can and wishes to point to nothing except his visible humiliation (at the hands of people and of God himself), for through this humiliation the hidden power of the resurrected life expresses itself.

The world is not likely to abandon its demand for a sign from God, from Christ, from the Church, promising to believe when it is given—especially if Christians themselves continue to seek such proof. If only the Church can keep from disguising herself in such a sign.

5. GOD IS OUT OF TOWN

"Men say to me continually, 'Where is your God?'" (Ps 42:4 [3]). He has taken a trip. "A nobleman went into a far country to receive a kingdom and then return" (Lk 19:12). As he tells the parable about this man, Jesus is planning to journey into the Cross and death. He cannot give the date of his return because only the Father knows that date (Mk 13:32). It is useless to stare at the place from which he disappeared: "You men of Galilee, why do you stand there gazing up into heaven?" (Acts 1:11).

Before he departed, the "nobleman" called together his servants and "entrusted to them his property" (Mt 25:14)—apparently in its entirety, for there is no mention of any limits, and the text says that he gave them *exousia* (full authority) over it (Mk 13:34). To each one, however, he gave according to his "ability". "Then he went away" (Mt 25:15).

To entrust to men what he possesses is an incomprehensible act of trust on God's part. As he places into their hands all that he has—he can do no more—they receive God himself together with all that he has. They receive it both as truly theirs yet also as his, given into their stewardship. And since they can expect nothing more from him, he disappears behind the gift.

Whoever recognizes the giver in the gift knows immediately that the gift can be utilized and administered only in the spirit of the giver. In the original act of giving lie a generosity and fruitfulness to which one can reply only with a correspondingly generous and fruitful stewardship. It is important that the servants see the unity between the gift and the requirement found within it, for the expectation of fruit bearing is part of the generosity of the gift. Servants dare not make distinctions between what is "truly given" and what is "merely loaned". This becomes absolutely clear when we use the parable as a window to view the truth it intends: what God has entrusted to us—our existence, with all its possibilities—is truly entrusted to us, given to us with such finality that it cannot

23

be taken away again, yet this gift is a loan to us from the treasury of God (who is all being). From that follows the realization that the gift must be dealt with in keeping with its character as gift.

Whoever understands that his existence is both true gift and loan in an inextricable unity will recognize the nature of the "departed" giver who makes himself scarce so that we might recognize him in the given-ness of our existence. It is in the given-ness of our existence that he is present, for "he is not far from any one of us" (Acts 17:27), "his invisible nature is clearly seen in the things he has made" (Rom 1:20). Others, who fail to grasp the vision of the invisible in the things that are made, may indeed cry continually, "Where is your God?" Failing to find him (because they are shouting so loudly), they construct a substitute God in the realm of what they are able to perceive: "futility" (Rom 1:21).

In the parable, the man who received only one talent failed to catch sight of the unity of gift and loan. He could not see the gift's mercy, only its requirements, and he then found himself trapped in obvious contradiction. When called to account, he confessed, "I knew that you are a stern man: you reap where you do not sow and gather where you have not scattered", and "because I was afraid, I buried the money in the earth. Here, you can have it back again." One might think that he would have worked with all his might to please such a stern master, but no, he "was afraid". He received his existence under his cloud of anxiety—a paralyzing fear—and accomplished something that corresponded to the meaning with which he received the gift. What he buried was the sense for gift and fruitfulness, and thus the gift itself became meaningless to him. He does not return the gift with the fruitfulness it possesses; rather, he throws it back at the giver like Judas threw down the silver pieces in the temple, since neither he nor the high priest had any more use for them (Mt 27:5). The "lazy servant" is deprived of what he had without depriving it of any value, and it is given to the one who recognizes the essence of gift. "From him who has not, even that which he has will be taken away" (Mt 25:29) means that whoever fails to recognize in the "God who has gone away" the one who is present in his gift, despite his ability to do so (as his self-contradictory words make clear), considers the existence "he has" to be so worthless that he no longer possesses anything in the existence he has.

6. "Dead to the Elemental Spirits of the Universe"

For Paul the "elemental spirits" (Col 2:20) are cosmic powers that would gladly appear to be divine, holding out to men an apparent transcendence of created things so that they might be worshiped by men. But they have been "disarmed by Christ, made into a public spectacle in his march of triumph" (Col 2:15). They have thereby lost even their apparent divine attraction for Christians, who, if they have been "crucified with Christ to the world and the world to [them]" (Gal 6:14), have certainly also been crucified to the cosmic "principalities and powers". They owe no veneration to the powers, and the powers can ultimately do Christians no harm. "Neither angels nor principalities, neither powers of heights nor of depths nor anything else in all creation can separate us from the love of God in Christ Jesus" (Rom 8:38–39).

People stumble over and fall into the hands of these elemental spirits if they refuse to believe that Christ has triumphed over the "principalities and powers". All these elements, without exception, belong to this world, even when they claim to offer a secret path to escape the realm of the mundane. Their chief characteristic is that they require some form of initiation involving something like a paranormal experience before one may approach them. Once one has been "initiated" into their sphere, one is permitted to see something "fascinating". Paul describes this initiation into what he elsewhere calls "worldly wisdom" (2 Cor 1:12) most concretely when he talks about "subservience" as a consequence of "the visions granted upon entry [into the sect or secret society]", visions that "puff one up in the sensuous mind" (Col 2:18).

This fascination takes various forms, but only externally, since the same elemental spirits always lurk underneath, merely changing their disguises. First "primitives" perceived hidden forces in all of nature, forces one had to appease through magic rites. Higher cultures were built entirely on ancestor worship and the mysterious power and presence of predecessors. Then ghosts and sprites of all sorts became significant, conjured up and employed by witches for evil purposes. Then the souls of the dead were turned into "poor souls" surrounded by all manner of superstitious practices—alongside all of these contacts with the otherworld were actual satanic cults: "To sound the depths of Satan" was enticing already in Thyatira (Rev 2:24), and it has remained enticing to the present, through all the variants, from witches' brooms to Baudelaire and Lautréamont, although Satan worship seldom actually produces anything more fantastic than a bit of boring fornication.

How modern all of these ancient attempts to expand consciousness into regions of the supra- and subconscious are! In them one not only encounters more-or-less living archetypes and theosophical-anthroposophical principles but also meets oneself in an alien form that one supposedly possessed as a wandering soul in an earlier existence. Or one might hear and see spiritist voices and materalizations from a supposed otherworld who then, usually in mockery of Christian fear of God's judgment, reveal how happy things are in the paradise of light beyond this earthly world. Materialists carry on research into these "elemental spirits" today for scientific and, for all one knows, political purposes. One ought to prepare oneself to see these various quests for transcendence coalescing in the near future to confront powerfully in the name of a "new age" of "total humanism" the shabby faith of Christians. Mankind's most ancient efforts to break free of the earth (reaching as far back as animism) constantly parade themselves in new fashions; indeed, they have no qualms about invoking the legendary antiquity of their always secret wisdom to heighten their claims to relevance.

Today, Christians who are bored with a Church that never "puts on a show" drift in large numbers into worship of the "elemental spirits". This involves a remarkable step backward from the freedom of being children of God into the subservience of pre-Christian law, from the solid embodiment of Christ and his Church into a shadow world (Col 2:17). Above all, the secret of all these realms and powers remains hopelessly confined within the universe, trying with all its might to break free of it. That much-desired freedom is given only to the one who has "died to the powers of this world". "You are dead; your life is hidden with Christ in God. When Christ your life", (Col 3:3–4) "with whom you have been raised up from the beginning" (Eph 2:6) "appears, you too shall appear with him in glory" (Col 3:4).

7. THE BAPTIST

The Bible gives us no figure more isolated than John the Baptist, who does not quite fit either the Old Testament or the New. The fragmentary reports about him frustrate anyone who would assemble from them a full portrait. The task seems to have been impossible even for John himself. Three times he sidestepped questions about his identity, leaving his listeners with the metaphor of a less-than-tangible voice crying in the wilderness (Jn 1:19–23). Jesus described John, as had John himself, as a watershed: on the one hand, John is the greatest of those born of women; on the other hand, the least in the Kingdom of heaven is greater than he is (Mt 11:11). John is "more than a prophet" (Mt 11:9)—in the Old Testament, what can be greater than a prophet? John is the preparatory "messenger", the "Elijah of the end times", who proclaims the coming of someone greater than himself yet is unable to identify that Greater One across the yawning chasm between the two dispensations: "Are you the one who is to come, or should we look for another?" (Mt 11:3). In order to proclaim the coming of this unimaginably greater One, John had to imagine him, and he did so by contrasting the water with which he baptized with the "Holy Spirit and fire", a fire very close to the "unquenchable fire" that will consume everything unprepared (Mt 3:11–12; Lk 3:16–17). Yet what concerns him most is the unbridgeable distance. We see this not only in his threefold "No" that rejects any attempt to confuse him with Christ but also in his attitude of prostration, insisting that he is unworthy even to kneel down and undo Jesus' sandals (Mk 1:7). The negative character of his mission is emphasized in his abstinence: "John came neither eating nor drinking" (Mt 11:18), and in the way he shrank from Christ's request to be baptized: "It is I who should be baptized by you, yet you come to me?" (Mt 3:14).

That John, in his humility, placed himself within the old dispensation that must necessarily decline (Jn 3:30) says nothing about

Jesus' verdict on where John belonged. It is not possible to decide the matter on the basis of Jesus' comments about "taking heaven by storm" (Mt 11:12; Lk 16:16), since Luke's version has the "law and prophets" lasting "to John", from which point onward "the Kingdom of God is preached", while Matthew's account places John in the new era: "From the days of John until now the Kingdom of heaven has suffered violence, and men of violence take it by storm. For all the prophets and the law prophesied toward John" (Mt 11:12–13). Yet even if one decides that Luke's version captures the original meaning more precisely, one dare not forget that according to the infancy narrative the one who came after sanctified his precursor—that is, equipped him for his task—already in his mother's womb. We glimpse here an event that applies throughout the entire Old Covenant. After all, according to Paul, we see Jesus accompanying his wandering people as a spiritual rock offering water in the desert (1 Cor 10:4), and, according to the Letter to the Hebrews, Moses preferred the humiliation of Christ to the riches of Egypt (Heb 11:26). Yet the calling of John in his mother's womb takes place explicitly at a specific event—when two women met—and was expressed in equally concrete terms: "You, child, shall be called the prophet of the Most High and shall go before the Lord to prepare his way" (Lk 1:76). Without question John was aware of his personal vocation as he grew up, and it is out of his awareness of having been called that he discovered his ineluctable symbol—baptizing in the River Jordan.

With that we have approached the image of John the Baptist found in the Gospel of John. This cannot have been superimposed later, because, in all likelihood, the disciple telling the story had himself been a follower of John the Baptist (Jn 1:35–36). Here, in John's Gospel, we find the herald's apocalyptic portrait of the Coming One giving way to a deeper understanding in spirit and in fire: "He upon whom the Spirit descends and remains, he is the one" (Jn 1:33). Somehow he seems to have perceived that the divine fire would consume like a sacrificial lamb the one drawing such a conclusion. From that point on the "voice in the wilderness" becomes a pointing finger: "Behold, the Lamb of God." John releases his followers to follow Jesus; he does not begrudge them their larger following (Jn 3:26–27); indeed, he rejoices that his task declines while the Coming One's grows.

And thus the manner in which he belongs to the Old Covenant by disappearing from the scene also belongs fully to the New Covenant. He himself must have understood something of that, since he developed the metaphor of being unworthy to kneel at Christ's feet into the metaphor of a friend who rejoices when he can entrust to the bridegroom the bride he has led to the wedding, when he can yield to the "voice of the bridegroom" his self-image as "voice". The Baptist's "joy which is now full" (Jn 3:29) shows how much he belongs—precisely as the one who lets go—to the wedding festivities of the New Covenant.

Yet he himself never situates himself anywhere. For him it is enough to be purely transitional (Passover, Pascha).

8. Presentation in the Temple

The events are presented in an obviously stylized manner. The account begins with a threefold mention of the "law", whether as the "law of Moses" or the "law of the Lord" (Lk 2:22–24), and it concludes with yet another mention of the "law of the Lord" (2:39). The point of departure is the law's requirement that the new mother be "purified" on the fortieth day after the birth of a boy, because she is "unclean" as far as worship is concerned. Thus "every male that opens the mother's womb" (Ex 22:28–29) must be presented as an offering to God and thereby "redeemed". The Gospel writer redirects attention from this motive to the presentation of the child Samuel, whose mother dedicated him to God for his entire life. Finally he mentions specifically the purification offering of the poor (according to Lev 12:8): "A pair of turtle-doves or two young pigeons". And so "all has been done according to the law"—the "custom of the law" (fifth mention of the law, Lk 2:27) is fulfilled.

Such a focus on obedience is confronted by an equally strong emphasis on the spirit. The Holy Spirit is mentioned three times in connection with the actions of the venerable Simeon. The Spirit "is upon him" and present to him, revealing to him that he will see the Messiah before he dies; ultimately, "inspired by the Spirit", he "comes to the temple" at precisely the moment when the parents carry the child in. His entire song of thanksgiving directed to God with the child in his arms, no less than the prophecy that follows, is obviously delivered in the Spirit, just as were the words of the prophetess Anna, although the latter are not reported to us.

The astonishing thing about this story is that the minutely described obedience of the New Covenant is directed toward the Old Testament law, obscuring the distinction between old and new completely. It is as if the child, who like no other comes from God and belongs to God, must still be "presented" and handed over to God; as if the one who conceived immaculately and gave birth virginally requires a purification. No thicker veil could be drawn over the mystery of mother and child than this. On the other side of the line, the ancient people of God sparkle in the light of the Holy Spirit, who had promised in advance a vision of the new and brings about an encounter with the new at the first possible opportunity. The prophet and prophetess draw back the veil that obscured the mystery and reveal to the whole world the divine plan of salvation.

This is the "light of revelation for the Gentiles", "salvation in the presence of all nations", but it shines from the "redemption of Jerusalem" (2:38) and is thus "a glory to your people Israel" (2:32). "Salvation comes from the Jews" (Jn 4:22), but "the hour comes in which you shall no longer worship the Father on this mountain and in Jerusalem" (Jn 4:21). How this expansion of something Jewish into something universal will take place the prophet tells directly to the Messiah's Mother, who in that role is the inclusive representative of Israel. The one who obeyed the law of Moses and through it obeyed God, even to the point of denying herself, is the one to experience the universalization of the Jewish law.

Her child is "established for the fall and the rising of many in Israel", but not for both to the same degree. The "sign that is contradicted" will be the significant one, the dominant one. "His own received him not" takes the spotlight (Jn 1:11); he comes to bring not peace but a sword, "so that the thoughts of many hearts might be brought up into the light", and the "whitewashed tombs" might be "opened" (Mt 23:27; 27:52), so that the promised "light of revelation" might penetrate to the ultimate depths until "everything lies bare and uncovered before the eyes of him before whom we must give account" (Heb 4:13). The child of praise is "the true light that enlightens every man" (Jn 1:9), a light that is both salvation and judgment at the same time, depending on whether the enlightened one opens himself up to the light or shrinks from it (Jn 3:19–21).

Yet the sword that this child carries (simply by existing) will "also pierce your heart" (Lk 2:35), a heart that is incapable of division, whose obedience is perfected beyond any concern for itself, yet a heart that, as the Mother of men (and especially of

33

Israel), must share the pain of the judgment. As the Mother of the Son, she feels the sword that the Son must wield for the "healing of the nations" slice through her heart.

9. "As One Who Had Authority"

Jesus' first sermon (mentioned in Mk 1:22–28), combined with his having cast out a demon, puzzled his listeners mightily. He taught "differently than the scribes", with an authority never before encountered, even though he taught nothing different from the scribes. The scribes serve the authority of the law that they expound. The tone of Jesus' preaching makes clear that he is master of the law he explains. This is audible in the resonance of his voice itself, and behind the voice is found the speaker with his entire personhood: it is as if the word of the Lawgiver himself rings forth. For that reason it seems to the listeners, who, after all, are hearing an exposition of words very familiar to them, as if "a completely new teaching is being proclaimed" (Mk 1:27). The doctors of the law expound the word of God as it has been written down, and its carefully formed letters are holy for them. What is "completely new" now is that God's living Word takes physical form in human sounds and letters before the eyes and ears of Jesus' audience. It is not a matter of "Scripture" but of the original Event that was once—subsequently—written down in "Scripture" but that seems to have been slumbering so lightly in Scripture that it can suddenly spring alertly into Event again. Sometimes people ask if Jesus preached anything really new that was not already in the Scripture. Irenaeus' answer to that question has never been superseded: "[He revealed] himself, who, as speaking Word, unveiled God's depths of power and glory in a deeper way than legislators and prophets were capable of hearing and squeezing into words."

These depths revealed themselves in what followed, as the deed of authoritative speaking became the deed of authoritative acting. The slumbering abyss stirs itself because the word of authority has penetrated into its depths. The "precursor" character of the Old Covenant's words is evident in the fact that the demonic had not yet made its appearance. Sins there were in great abundance—

adultery and murder (David), doubt about God's power and mercy (Moses, Jeremiah), betrayal of the Lord of the Covenant (the whole people of Israel)—all of these were common. Yet all of these could be accounted for within this world and its history. Now, when Jesus' "completely new teaching" sounds forth, a completely new head rears itself, that of the apocalyptic beast. The Word has reached the demon, has called it by its name. Knowing that it is now known, it thus knows the One who knows it: "I know who you are, the Holy One of God."

Yet it is decisive that no titanic battle ensues. There is to be no wrestling between God and Satan, but rather simply an overpowering command: "Be silent and come out of him", out of the afflicted one. Never, not even in the wilderness, does Jesus struggle with the devil, although Satan's temptation is a genuine temptation that can work its fascination upon him, that even employs Holy Scripture in the process. Yet where the words cross like fencers' blades, Jesus' word has already conquered the word of temptation. Likewise, in the story of this healing, the demon must depart, but not before he displays himself in a farewell seizure of his victim. According to the Church Fathers, all the persecutions of the Church since the time of Christ are part of this tantrum thrown by the devil on his way out: the head of the serpent has been crushed underfoot, but the body thrashes about in a desperate wrestling with itself. It is important to see that the essence of Christian salvation is symbolized in Jesus' first healing: the man is freed from the demon who has held him in thrall. The demon cannot be redeemed, but the man is torn from his grasp.

Yet this first scene, like those that follow, already points to the Cross, which is subsumed under the word *authority* from the start. "I have power to lay down my life." "I offer it up of my own accord." "That is the charge that I have received from my Father" (Jn 10:17–18). Power, authority is at once permission, free decision, and commission, all of which merge into an inexorably superior capability. Even on the Cross no struggle with the devil takes place; rather, Christ disappears beneath all the powers, including demonic powers, in the powerlessness of being ultimately nailed fast and motionless, in the greatest conceivable contrast to all that we understand by the word *power*. He does this to demonstrate the all-powerfulness of the love of God, which, stretching its own capacity to its very end, unmasks by its inability all the powers it faces.

10. "What Do You Have That You Did Not Receive?"

Paul admonishes the Corinthians (1 Cor 4:7) in order to call to their senses those who had "become puffed up" against another (leader of a faction). Paul likes the phrase, because "puffing oneself up" demonstrates an inner vacuousness that can burst open (1 Cor 4:18-19). Reality, which is love, does not "puff itself up" (1 Cor 13:4); only self-deceiving knowledge does (1 Cor 8:1). Knowledge that holds itself accountable to love exhibits no such empty space because it is filled with the humility of having received.

This begins at the most fundamental level. The self, which admits to having received many things, often enough forgets that it has received itself. Not too long ago it was itself nothing. As a prerequisite for all further receiving it was given itself. By whom? Its parents' union was certainly a cooperating cause, but a free, responsible person must find a deeper source for himself, or he will thoughtlessly underestimate himself. Through a "Yes" and a "No" he is able to engage himself ultimately—and "ultimately" does not mean merely until death or until "reincarnation".

Everything else is constructed upon this first receiving. Had I never received human love, I would never have become a person—I would be at most a wolf child. That I received a spiritual life is something for which I must be forever grateful; it is pure gift, and it is upon that gift that I can boast of having a father and a mother, brothers and sisters, and friends. I was fed, cared for, and taught, at first at home, then in school. I learned to comprehend what my senses gave to me and was introduced to language that mediates, until I grasped and mastered it. In the course of time countless cultural traditions filled me from the outside, portrayed themselves to me, and shaped and formed me in themselves. Mastery became ability to make: I stood awed by all that people had already learned to make and forgot that all making derived from an original receiving. Our civilization, built as it is entirely on the making of things, on techniques, has forgotten this, so much so that it dares to intrude its techniques into the sacred realm of the original reception.

Now it is self-evident that the original receiving consists of taking hold of a gift that has been given me for my use. The person receiving it is no lifeless trunk into which everything is deposited but is rather a plowed furrow in which seed is supposed to grow. If the field is a living spirit, the parable of the talents becomes relevant: that which has been entrusted to me must be "administered" and made fruitful in a spiritual sense. As it is given to me, it is mine in the expectation of its yielding something, a harvest for which I am to give account. One can thereby judge how much weight the current expression *self-realization,* or *self-discovery,* might have in the scale of truth—about as much as *self-redeeming,* in other words, about as much as Paul Bunyan's blue ox. Anyone who really wants to search for himself would have to find the giver of himself.

We can see this most clearly in the Church of Jesus Christ. In the Church there can be no forgetting of the original gift. Here no one helps himself to something unless it has been given to him. No one goes to confession and helps himself to absolution from his sins. No one goes to baptism and pours water over his own head. No one enters the Church intending to help himself to a host from the tabernacle. Even more important: no priest ordains himself; rather, he must be consecrated by someone who himself has received consecration. If one follows the long chain of "apostolic succession" back, one comes to the first ones, the ones who received authority from Christ to "do this in remembrance of him" and, having received the Holy Spirit, to forgive sins in the Spirit, or, when necessary, to "bind" sins for the sake of a future better forgiving. Nothing in the Church is made; everything is granted as a gift, a gift that should reproduce itself in faith thirty, sixty, even one hundred times over. And none of that for itself but rather for the wholeness that Jesus called the "Kingdom of God". One cannot even help oneself to prayer. In response to the disciples' request ("Lord, teach us to pray" [Lk 11:1]), prayer was placed in their mouths and then enjoined on them as a duty (Lk 18:1). The receiving that makes us fruitful presupposes open willingness, which is the opposite of busyness: "Unless the Lord builds the house, those who build it labor in vain. Unless the Lord guards the city, the sentries stay awake for nothing. It is in vain that you rise up early and go to bed late at night, eating the bread of anxious toil; for he gives to his beloved sleep" (Ps 127:1–2). Children sleep a lot and are dependent on gifts: "Unless you become like little children". They are like the "lilies of the field that neither toil nor spin" but "grow" (Mt 6:28).

The best is always given; things made are of lesser quality. We think that we can make children, but "sons are God's free gift; the fruit of the womb is 'a reward'" (Ps 127:3), and the same applies to the fertility of human minds (the best they have is given to them, is inspiration), above all, to spiritual fruitfulness, when, "cooperating" (1 Cor 3:9, etc.) with God's grace through love, devotion, repentance, and intercession, it is permitted to become "Father" (1 Cor 4:15) and "Mother" (Gal 4:9). Such a one knows that nothing is more of a gift than such a work.

ii. "He Is Brother, Sister, and Mother to Me"

Although his physical family stands outside and demands a response (Mk 3:31–35 and parallels), he will not be taken in by them. He has set about the task of founding a new family. One should not limit one's interpretation of the new relationships he announces in this passage to a conventional, horizontal explication—as a description of the new community in the Church. That would be inadmissible simply because the early Christians never had the audacity to call the person they worshiped as their Lord (*Kyrios*) by the fraternizing name of "Brother", to say nothing of "Son". (From that perspective alone it is impossible to insist that Jesus' words were the product of a "communal imagination".) Instead, one must take seriously the realization that Jesus' words about a common doing of the "will of God" (Mk 3:35), "my Heavenly Father" (Mt 12:50), and a common "hearing and doing of the word of God" (Lk 8:21) allude to a common parentage in the Father. For his own part already as a twelve-year-old Jesus had undertaken to distinguish between his being an earthly child and his being a heavenly child, to the uncomprehending astonishment of his earthly relatives. The Father confirmed this unique, vertical form of Jesus' childhood at his baptism in the Jordan. The angel of the Annunciation first proclaimed him the "Son of the Most High" and only then added the prophecy that God would give him "the throne of his father David" (Lk 1:32). His Messiahship remained subordinate to his Divine Sonship. Jesus obscured the former from view because his contemporaries misunderstood it, commanding them not to proclaim him the Messiah; yet he spoke frequently of his unique Sonship: "No one knows the Father but the Son and the one to whom the Son reveals it" (Mt 11:27 and through the Gospel of John). It is this divine Sonship alone that matters if one wishes to become Jesus' relative, a possibility to which he alludes in the scene at hand. He thus has in mind a colossal and incomprehensible reality that is called "being born from above", "from God", "from the Spirit" who is God (Jn 3:3, 6). The prerequisite for this incomprehensible reality is expressed with simplicity: to do the will of God, the Heavenly Father—but, of course, to do it as does Jesus, who lives from and feeds on the will of God with his whole being, his humanness included. "I live from food that you know not" (Jn 4:32). This means to live with a radicalness that does not refuse the food even when it is a cup of hemlock offered as "the cup of Yahweh's fury and wrath" (see Is 51:22; Jer 25:15). "Shall I not drink the cup that my Father has given me?" (Jn 18:11). There is thus no reason to put a great gulf between "your Father" and "my Father" in Jesus' instructions on prayer ("your will be done on earth as it is in heaven"). Already before the Resurrection Jesus includes the new brothers and sisters in his own prayer; immediately after his Resurrection he expressly unites "my Father and your Father" (Jn 20:17).

Yet, at the moment we are observing, a diverse crowd of listeners surrounds Jesus as he casts his gaze "round about" before speaking the word about a new kinship. Perhaps this gaze searched out among those present the ones to whom the phrase referred— either now or later.

Jesus talks as naturally about his sisters as he talks about his brothers. This means that his own Sonship relation to the Father has nothing to do with the difference between the sexes. The same applies to the divine childhood of all those born together with him from God. His reference to motherhood, which comes first in the first listing ("they are my mother and my brothers" [Mk 3:34]), cannot point exclusively to Jesus' eternal parentage since nowhere does he apply a feminine name to God. Instead he is hereby drawing Mary into the causing of his coming. He does this indirectly, since he does not even permit his physical Mother to appear in the scene at hand, but he does it just the same so that, however hidden, his birth from her, from her perfect assent, becomes a cocondition for his brothers' and sisters' own birth from God. They cannot bypass the condition on which his own Incarnation was based if they are to participate in his own divine birth. Later the Fathers of the Church would say that no one can have God for a Father who does not have the Church for a mother—likewise in an obscure manner uncomprehended by the child who is born. At heart this Marian-ecclesial relationship seems natural for someone who has grasped that she owes her divine birth to no one else but the incarnate Son of the Father.

12. CHRIST OUR BROTHER

From what point onward is Christ our brother? Is he our brother because we men are offspring of God just as he, as the eternal Son, originates from the Divine Father (Heb 2:11)? Or is he our brother because, "assuming flesh and blood" (Heb 2:14), he who was so unlike us sinful creatures subject to lifelong fear of death (Heb 2:15) made himself "like us in all things" (Heb 2:14), in temptation (18) and in suffering of death (9), and thus "unashamedly" "calls us brothers" when he says, "I will tell of your name to the brethren; in the midst of the congregation I will praise you" (Ps 22:22), and, "Behold, I and the children whom God has given me" (Is 8:18; Heb 2:12–13)?

In the first instance the brotherhood comes from our creation, which may have a certain similarity to the generation of the Son, for both point to an originating; both, as different as they are, "have one origin" (11) in God, who as Father is also the Creator. In the second instance it is the difference, the distance, that is prominent. To become our brother the eternal and holy Son has conquered this distance, making himself like us unholy mortals subject to "the power of death", even to "the devil" (14), "so that through [his] death he might destroy the one who has power over death, the devil, and deliver all those who through fear of death were subject to lifelong bondage" (14–15).

One might ask whether these two are mutually exclusive. They seem to be, since the eternal Son is called "the Sanctifying One", and we creatures and sinners are called "the sanctified ones" (11). Yet this contradiction (which is a lasting one) is superseded in the same breath through the all-encompassing saving plan of God, "for whom and by whom all exists" (10), a plan that "shall bring many sons to glory". This takes place through the "leader of their salvation", who, having become one with them, leads them on the path to the Father, the path he pioneers for them. Thus the original, infinite difference between the eternal Son who sanctifies and the temporal creatures who so greatly need sanctifying and deliverance would be placed in doubt by an even more original saving will of God, the origin and end of all that is within God and of all that is created. But the questioning does not level all distinctions: the "Sanctifying One" is God in his work of grace; the "sanctified ones" are we, the ones upon whom this power of grace works without our help. We thus remain children given to the Son by the Father, who is willing to call us his brothers: "Behold, here am I, and the children God has given me" (13); "I will proclaim your name to my brethren" (12).

The Son alone is exalted above everything: "For to what angel did God ever say, 'You are my Son, today I have begotten you'?" (Ps 2:7; Heb 1:5). Nonetheless this Son is "the one through whom he has created the world, whom he appointed the heir of all things" (Heb 1:2), and therefore God has entrusted to him "purification from sins" (1:3). Thus has this Son exalted above all things the "image of the glory" of the Father and has become the "merciful and faithful High Priest" (2:17). He exercises this priestly office solely on the basis of his Sonship and solely for the purpose of leading his brothers into participation in his Sonship. He did not "take the honor of this priesthood upon himself" (5:4); indeed, it belongs to him not merely by virtue of the fact that he is the Son; rather, he was appointed for it by the Father, set apart for a priesthood that is unlike any human priestly office. It is limitless in keeping with his eternal Sonship: "You are a priest for ever" (5:6). It is also, again in keeping with his Sonship, a completely personal priesthood that consists only in a perfect self-sacrifice "through the eternal Spirit" (9:14). It is equally unique and unrepeatable (6:4, etc.), just as his Sonship remains incomparable.

Yet how can we be granted the title of brothers if this Sonship and priesthood are so unique? If he is to be the "pioneer" ("of salvation", 2:10; "of faith", 12:2), then it must be possible for him to have followers. Thus are we encouraged to an equally personal self-sacrifice that must constitute the core of all "priesthood" of the brothers of Christ: "Let us look to the pioneer and perfecter of our faith, to Jesus, who, for the joy that was set before him, endured the Cross, despising the shame" (12:2–4). The path of this priesthood leads both to the same goal: for the Son it leads to the "throne at the right hand of the Father" (12:2); for the brothers it leads "to the city of the living God" (12:22). As the Son exercised his priesthood "outside the gate", so "let us go forth to him outside the camp and bear the abuse he endured, for we have no lasting city here; rather, we seek the city that is to come" (13:12–14).

Here, in this common striving for the eternal day of rest in God (3:7–4:11), we travel as brothers of the Unique One toward the same goal as he, a goal that God has always had in view, a goal at which we humble and endangered creatures become sons in the Son and brothers in the Brother.

13. OCCUPATION AND VOCATION

"For they were fishermen. Jesus said to them, 'Come, follow me, and I will make you fishers of men'" (Mk 1:16–17). Both continuity and sudden change make up the path from an occupation to a vocation. The suddenness is visible when they jumped up and "left everything and followed him"—without it there would be no discipleship. "Whoever treasures something more than me is not worthy of me." The sudden change also involves no expectation whatsoever that what has been abandoned will ever be resumed. Yet despite this, there is continuity: the fisher of men already knows something about his task because of his former occupation. He needs a net, a boat, and knowledge of when to fish and when not to fish, of winds and weather, and of how to handle a boat in a storm, to list only a few things.

For years Jesus was a carpenter, and the beginning of his public life represents a big change from that. But he knows what a good foundation for a house is—rock, not sand; he knows that one must sit down before starting to build a house and estimate what it will cost, that one must ask whether or not one has put aside (stored up with the Father in heaven) enough to finish the job. He lived like every other person; yet in a single leap the twelve-year-old moved to a different house, insisting that he "must be in that which is my Father's". Every person must eat (and Jesus even comes under the banner of "eating and drinking" [Mt 11:19]), but suddenly Jesus had "food to eat that you know not; my food is to do the will of him who sent me" (Jn 4:32–33)—he lives "from every word that proceeds from the mouth of God" (Mt 4:4–5). Every person has a mother, but the mother-son relationship changed suddenly for Jesus: "Whoever does the will of my Heavenly Father, he is my mother" (Mt 12:50).

All conceivable occupations are mentioned in the Gospels, and all of them are a launching pad for something that has to do with being called. There is the farmer who sows his seed in the field:

"And he lay down to rest and got up again, night after night and day after day, and the seed grew he knew not how. The soil produces fruit of itself, first the blade, then the ears, then the full grain in the ears. When the grain is ripe, he applies the sickle, for the harvest has come" (Mk 4:26–29). The "leap" launches human effort into a seemingly idle sequence of time and thus into the "spontaneous" (*automate*) fruit bearing of the soil, within the earthly mystery of the simultaneity of the useless and the purposeful that characterizes the Kingdom of God. What the farmer tosses on the ground multiplies of its own accord—because it was tossed away. But only patience can span the gap: "Behold, the farmer waits for the precious fruit of the earth; he stands firm in patience; in like manner be patient with each other" (James 5:7–8). The Gospels also mention work in the vineyard—hauling manure for the vines. We also encounter the art of medicine: Jesus heals the sick, but not without the great change of the forgiveness of sins, something that can be granted only to those who know they are sinners, for that is the only way the doctor's skill makes sense to Jesus (Mk 2:17). We also find the administration of the assets of someone who has diversified his investments and disappeared— for there are, in both earthly and supernatural arenas, a right way and a wrong way to administer that with which one has been entrusted. We encounter the art of strategy: a king must deliberate carefully to discover a way to counter with his army of ten thousand an opposing force of twice that size. If he can master tactical skills, he will succeed; otherwise, he must ask for peace terms. As far as Jesus is concerned, there is only one strategy for victory: to "renounce all that one owns" is the right tactic (Lk 14:31–33). Women know how to mend clothes—it does no good to sew a patch of new cloth on an old garment. They know that one must simply keep searching for a lost coin until it is found, even if it means moving all the furniture. Likewise, the shepherd knows that he cannot overlook a missing sheep but must leave the others where they are and go off in search of the lost lamb.

We can find similar examples in Paul's writings. He knows about planting and watering and only mentions it because he has already taken the great leap into caring for the Lord's garden (together with Apollos). He took the step from natural conception and motherhood to a spiritual fatherhood and birth pangs for the Church. And he knows with complete clarity that he possesses the strength for both solely from God (not to mention his supernatural warrior's art [2 Cor 10]), yet he possesses it only by having renounced his ability to do anything of his own accord.

The leap from earthly occupation to a supernatural calling must always be an indivisible whole—otherwise one disappears into the abyss that lies between them. Jesus is not interested in striking any deals—they are unworthy of him. But there are behaviors and circumstances that scarcely change when transferred from the earthly to the heavenly Kingdom—for example, fasting, or the continual admonition to be alert, to stand watch, to stand ready with torches and rolled-up sleeves, to do one's sentry duty. Viewed from the outside, the attitude both here and yonder is most similar when a professional element is involved (for example, a physician who is constantly on call, even at night). The leap, the transformation, takes place inside, in one's motives. Much of what one possesses on earth *can* already be very close to what Christ requires.

That is why, after the leap has been taken, earthly things—reassessed and reinvigorated from above—can be entrusted again to someone who has left it all behind to follow Christ. It seems odd that, after the Cross and the Resurrection, the disciples should be sent back into the mundane life of Galilee in order to seek the Lord *there*. It seems strange that Peter and his friends find themselves fishing again at the end of the Gospel just as in the beginning. But then the carpenter from Nazareth also took up again the objects of his craft—when he lifted the heavy beam of the Cross.

In the secular institutes this is the rule.

14. "You Who Have Persevered in My Temptations"

The words that Jesus spoke to his disciples at the Last Supper (Lk 22:28) refer to "temptations" in the plural. After all, it is Luke who closes his account of the temptation in the wilderness with the phrase: "After concluding all [these] temptations, the devil departed from him until the [next, opportune, particular] time" (4:13). Does that refer to the time of the Passion? We find no direct mention of temptation by the devil in the accounts of the Passion, except perhaps the statement that Satan entered into the betrayer (Lk 22:3; Jn 13:27). Furthermore, Jesus' words to his disciples refer not to his imminent Passion but to the entire time that they have persevered with him in his temptations.

To take these words to heart, it will not suffice to note that Jesus continually dealt with people possessed by evil spirits, with those whose mouths the devil employed to cry out, "We know you", and, "Don't torment us" (Mk 5:7). Nor did Jesus deal only with the Pharisees, who, having accused Jesus himself of being possessed by evil spirits, were on the receiving end of his statement about the unforgivable word spoken against the Holy Spirit (Mt 12:24, 32). Nor is it adequate to realize that Jesus was accompanied by a "devil" within his own group of disciples (Jn 6:70), who apparently pursued him with growing suspicion and mistrust. His disciples were all very much aware of all these encounters with evil powers, yet these do not exhaust the meaning of his words at the Last Supper.

Far more significant is the realization that immersion in the realm of constant temptation is part of the nature of our existence ("A man's life on earth is like the hard service of a wage laborer" [Job 7:1]). Immersion in temptation must be considered a mark of and cause for joy (James 1:2; 1 Pet 1:6). Paul had to endure temptation constantly "in humility and with tears" (Acts 20:19). If we take the humanness of the Son seriously, our knowledge that constant temptation is central to human existence can reinforce the assertion that Jesus "helps those who fall into temptation, since he himself was tempted and suffered" (Heb 2:18) and that we have "a High Priest who is able to sympathize with our weaknesses" because he "was tempted *in all things* just as we are, yet without sinning" (Heb 4:15). The phrase *in all things* goes a long way and can comfort and strengthen anyone who feels he can no longer resist the weaknesses of his flesh and spirit.

The Gospels only occasionally illuminate Jesus' experience of continual temptation. For instance, we glimpse his patience with his disciples' slowness to grasp his teaching: "They understood not a thing [of the multiplication of loaves]" (Mk 6:52). "Are you that dense?" (Mk 7:18). "You still understand nothing and comprehend nothing! Your hearts are hardened! You have eyes and see nothing, ears and hear nothing!" (Mk 8:17–18). Not merely stupidity but also ungodly thinking hides here under the guise of humanness: "Get behind me, you Satan, for your thoughts are the thoughts of men, not God" (Mk 8:33). The futility of his whole mission must have become steadily more obvious to him. And the devil most certainly would not have failed to taunt him with such an obvious realization: "There you are! Don't you wish you had listened to me back there in the desert!" The tears he shed over Jerusalem were an open admission of his defeat. Where was the "fire" that he had wanted to kindle upon the earth (Lk 12:49)? And was it not something very much like a temptation when, having realized his lack of success, he wished he could escape his imminent suffering? "I must undergo a baptism, and I am in great distress until it is finished" (Lk 12:50). Indeed, this baptism was so horrible that he "offered up prayers and pleas for help, with cries of anguish and tears, to the one who could save him from this death" (Heb 5:7). In it, his real baptism, he finds shelter from an existence immersed in temptations. In it he is protected from Satan, who is now out of the picture—the one who bears all human guilt deals only with the Father from this point onward. He must drink the cup. Yet, because of the human frailty that the tempted One has taken upon himself, the last temptation becomes the fiercest of his whole life.

Christ is a man like us "in all things except sin". And only for that reason can we endure "all things" that men face, not only all manner of suffering but also all manner of temptation, without having to surrender to sin. He told his disciples that, having persevered in Christ's temptations, "therefore I assign to you the Kingdom, just as my Father assigned it to me" (Lk 22:29).

15. The Toughest Task

Although the rules of the historical-critical method incessantly warn against attempting to write a life of Jesus or to meddle with his self-understanding, the Gospel writers are not afraid to show us that he undertook the most difficult mission imaginable. After all, it was his undertaking to convince men, by using all the means of thought and evidence available, of something that lies beyond all the categories accessible to men: that God is triune love. This could be demonstrated only through Christ's word, work, conduct, and suffering.

Recognizing the impossible mission required of him, Jesus could have conceived of his earthly activity merely as propaedeutic, thus postponing the convincing proof for his death or, even better, for the Holy Spirit, who was to come and enlighten hearts for the first time, shedding light on that which he had accomplished. But that would misconstrue the Holy Spirit's method, which is not to make ultimate sense out of fragmentary beginnings but rather to expound what has already been "completed" in the work of Christ (Jn 16:13–15)—completed, even though before the coming of the Spirit no one was able to glimpse the seamless whole in the scattered pieces.

Thus Jesus had to use as well as reject the available content, which offered a preliminary understanding; he had to practice both affirmative and negative theology with these fragments. Yes, he is the Messiah, the promised Son of David, born in the city of David, descended from David through Joseph, the one who would gather together the lost sheep of Israel. Yet no, he is not the Messiah expected by the people and even the disciples, and he must tell people not to apply that title to him. Yes, he is the prophet prophesied by Moses, who shares the prophet's fate of being scorned in his own country, who must be murdered in Jerusalem like all the other prophets. Yes, he must be addressed by the people as a "great prophet" (Lk 7:16), recognized as "the

Prophet" (Jn 6:14). But no—if John the Baptist was already "more than a prophet" (Mt 11:9), then even the disciples had to realize that he must be something other than what the people think he is (Mk 8:28–29). So he chooses a name that cannot be pinned down: Son of Man means every man born of woman, but it also can mean that unique one who, according to Daniel, descends from heaven on the clouds (Mt 26:64).

Jesus must have had the hardest time of all with miracle working. As long as the miracles were infrequent, as is the case with the "signs" found in John's Gospel, as long as they created a shock effect that confronted people with the distinct either-or of faith and disbelief, vision and blindness, they served their purpose. But what happened when the masses turned him into a medicine show miracle worker, when people surrounded him with vast collections of the infirm and suffering (as the Synoptic Gospels report collectively)? Here he faced a dilemma: where he perceived genuine, though muted, faith, he could not refuse to heal; but where he found nothing but faithless hunger for wonders, "he could do no miracles" (Mt 6:5). The entire problem of the "secret Messiah" lies within the orbit of this dilemma. That he forbids the demons to call him "Son of God"—no one would have believed the sick who screamed that out anyway—is understandable, since people still lacked an adequate bridge to such faith. That he told the disciples not to tell anyone about his Transfiguration before he had risen from the dead likewise makes sense, since the purpose of the Transfiguration was to prepare the three disciples who witnessed it for their night of testing on the Mount of Olives (Mk 9:9). Yet Jesus also forbids talk about individual healings, and, when his prohibition is ignored, he gains the reputation of a completely secular miracle doctor, a reputation he then has to try to escape, often without success. Had he been confined to this level, his true task would have been completely lost. How many of his healings were forced upon him in the confusion of the crowds is hard to say, but precisely these scenes are the ones that remained vivid in people's memories and then were written down individually or in collections of stories. Fortunately the Pharisees accused him of black magic (Mt 12:24), giving him an opportunity to situate his miracles within his larger mission. Healing on the Sabbath also, fortunately, gave him a chance to proclaim his superiority to the law.

Much has been said about the contradiction between the disciples' lack of understanding, underscored by Mark and especially by Luke (18:34), and their relative insight into Jesus, in Matthew's account (see 14:33). This contradiction is visible again in the disciples' uncomprehending protests during Jesus' farewell discourse. By the very nature of things, their insight can be no more than a dawning in comparison to the noonday light of Jesus' words. The relationship between Father and Son (both within the Godhead and in divine activity) cannot be expressed in words more clearly than it is in the discourses in John's Gospel, but Jesus cannot expect to find people comprehending this during his life on earth. Thus he can only assert: "It is good for you that I depart, for if I did not, the Paraclete would not come to you" (Jn 16:7). All that he had done on earth was in vain as long as the focal point upon which it all converged was not visible. Taken in itself, it was nothing but failure. And most significantly, it is precisely his ultimate failure, being rejected by his own, being crucified by Christians, Jews, and Gentiles, that brought about the decisive breakthrough: "Truly, this man was the Son of God" (Mk 15:39).

According to Luke the Resurrected One introduces his disciples to the "law, the prophets, and the Psalms" (24:44), primarily simply through his appearance to them. Now such titles as "Messiah" (Acts 2:36), "Son of God" (Rom 1:4), "Servant of God" (Acts 3:13), and "High Priest" (Heb) can be understood in their true meaning: something all surpassing to which human preunderstandings can ascend only if one simultaneously crosses them out. Crossed-out language (the *via negativa*) points upward to the *eminentia,* and this lofty language shines its invisible light on all images, making them capable of serving as signs.

16. ST. JOSEPH

On many Christmas icons Joseph sulks in a corner, far from the action. An ascetic figure, obviously the prophet Isaiah ("the virgin shall bear a child"), stands in front of him and tries to make clear to him that he has not been cuckolded. Is not the same message, expressed in icons with great candor, clearly hinted at in many of our modern pictures, where the husband has nothing better to do than to hold up a stable lantern or to usher in the shepherds? What other job can the fellow be given?

His work is more profound and deeper than a painting can portray. One must see him as the overshadowing counterpart to Abraham, as the concluding summit of the series of patriarchs, prophets, and priests who, each in his own way, symbolize the Covenant between God and his people. At the age of one hundred, Abraham laughs because God promised him a son, "for he said to himself, can a hundred-year-old conceive a son? Shall Sarah, who is ninety, bear a son?" (Gen 17:17). But he laughs not out of unbelief; rather, he laughs because "he believed God, who gives life to the dead and calls into existence what does not exist" (Rom 4:17). Abraham thus becomes the lasting symbol of the Covenant: God alone accomplishes the impossible, but not without human involvement, which itself is God's greatest gift. Woe to him who, like Zacharias, refuses the gift in unbelief (because, after all, God does it all by himself): he is struck deaf and dumb. In the Covenant it will not do to declare that God does everything and men do nothing; rather, it is far more important to realize that God can be everything in and with human nothingness. If Abraham lets God be everything in his physical procreative power, and if that is "reckoned to him for righteousness" (Gen 15:6)—that is, considered a proper covenant action—then this act of giving way to God is not something passive but the most active thing a man can accomplish. What this act of letting God hold sway brings forth, when taken to its ultimate, becomes visible in Mary, Joseph's wife: it generates a claim on the entire human person, spirit, soul, and body. And that could not have happened had not Mary's husband responded to the same challenge to give way to God. The only difference is that, instead of making room for God in the limited area of sexual fecundity, Joseph must give way completely. Thus, in a secondary way (since God has already acted), he permits the all-encompassing activity of God to take place. God's plan regarding the Incarnation of his Son cannot be split into pieces, and Joseph's acquiescence plays an integral part in carrying it out.

This represents more than just the prelude to the New Testament fecundity of male celibacy that God sometimes asks of man ("not according to the will of the man" [Jn 1:13]). Rather, giving way to God becomes an indispensable part of the fecundity of the Mother and Bride of Christ. It is indispensable also, indeed, precisely because, a time of anxiety and fear precedes it all, and Joseph appears to have been left behind like a useless, antiquated tool. (The Church's celibates also have to walk this path.) Only when an explanation comes from on high does Joseph see how essential his cooperation was to the accomplishment of Mary's mystery. It does little good when a man thinks he is indispensable from the very beginning.

When Joseph does take up his assigned role, which in the view of the world still seems rather contemptible, he is handed an unexpected great gift: he is the one who gives the child the Messiah's name, something that he did not himself possess, not even as a descendant of David, yet something he is authorized to grant. Let us take careful note—we are dealing here with more than a mere juridical formality or fortunate coincidence but rather with an essential aspect of God's single and integral plan of salvation. A complex web that has been spun for many centuries here receives its finishing touch from a man who has been specifically foreseen for the task. In the fact that Jesus must be the Son of David *inwardly* and knows and comprehends himself as such (Mt 22:41–46) we realize how fundamental is Joseph's contribution to the completion of salvation history.

And it is good that Joseph adds not a single word of self-expression to the clear profile of his character in the story. The word that God speaks through Joseph needs none of that.

17. "No Forgiveness without Shedding of Blood"

The axiom announced in Hebrews 9:22 surrounds itself with a detailed set of proofs. First, we are reminded of the great ceremony on the Day of Atonement when the High Priest dare not enter the Holy of Holies "without taking blood that he offers for the sins of the people" (9:7). Behind that lies the Mosaic Covenant commitment, which likewise could not take place "without blood" (9:18), since Moses sprinkled the book, the people, the tabernacle, and its vessels with blood and spoke words that point forward to the Eucharist: "This is the blood of the Covenant, which God has offered to you." And even further back lies God's instruction forbidding the eating of blood (Gen 9:4), because God has placed the living soul in circulating blood. Only at the altar may blood "be shed as atonement for your life, because blood atones for life" (or "through the life" that it contains) (Lev 17:11).

This thoroughly buttressed axiom serves to clarify the mystery of the Cross, which in turn thoroughly explodes the axiom. The Old Testament principle of "nothing without blood" was valid yet powerless at the same time. How could "the blood of rams and bulls" (Heb 9:13) that "annually recalls sins anew" "remove sins" in the conscience (10:4)? Yet priests were limited to the sacrifice of animals because human sacrifice was forbidden in the law, and they could not kill themselves. No one could see a way out, a way to overcome the old futility, because the new and ultimate Covenant was to be new and at the same time a fulfillment of the old one. One requirement stood relentlessly unfulfilled at the end of the Old Covenant, and the Covenant itself shattered in its collision with this wall of unfulfillability. The Letter to the Hebrews struggles to illuminate from all sides this unresolvable contradiction.

It describes the work of Christ as a resurrection out of this logical death. Between the "symbol" (*parabolē*, [9:9]), that is,

59

the "image and shadow" (8:5), and its fulfillment stretches an unbridgeable chasm. Across it strides the One who says in his incarnateness to the Father: "You have no pleasure in burnt offerings and sin offerings, but you have given me a body. Behold, I come to fulfill your will." On the basis of this will we have been sanctified once for all through the offering of the body of Christ once for all (10:5–10), through the One who, "taking his own blood, once for all entered the Holy of Holies", through the One who "by the power of the eternal Spirit offered himself without blemish to God" (9:12, 14). God gives the body made alive by its blood, and the living Son, Priest and Victim brings it to the altar in the eternal Spirit, even though mortal men perform the ritual slaughter.

Therefore devotion to the "precious blood" is not something that can be abandoned to popular piety. The true High Priest comes before the Father "once for all", meaning "always now", "with his own blood" that was shed in the "eternal Spirit", thereby "winning for us an eternal redemption" (9:12), "so that we henceforth might serve the living God" (9:14). "This is the blood of the New and eternal Covenant", presented to us daily in the Eucharist, whose flowing, life-giving power circulates through the body and members of Christ and imparts to all parts a single, unified life. Any speculation that a resurrected body can no longer bleed is futile. It is useless to accuse the Doctor of the Church Catherine of Siena of exaggerating when she sees the living blood of Christ continually washing the Church and the world clean. After all, the saints in the Apocalypse have also "washed their garments white in the blood of the Lamb" (Rev 7:14; cf. 1:5).

Catherine has an unusual thought. She asks the Lord why, after his death, he permitted his heart to be pierced through. The answer she received was: "My yearning for the human race was limitless, but my temporal work of bearing suffering and torment was limited. Therefore I wanted you to see the secret of my heart by opening it up and offering it to you. In this way it should be clear to you that my love was greater than what I could reveal by my limited suffering. That is the way it is when the power of the divine and infinite nature united with a human and finite nature suffered in me, the Word clothed in humanity. Yet because the one nature was immersed in and mingled with the other, the eternal Divinity took to itself the suffering I accepted with burning love. Thus one can call this work an infinite work. Had it not been limitless, the entire human race—those living now as well as those who have died and those who are yet to come—could not have been restored. Fallen men could never have arisen from their guilt if this baptism of blood had not been given without limit. That is what I revealed through the opening of my side" (*The Dialogue,* II, 2, 78 [= chapter 75 in Cavallini edition (Rome, 1968) and Noffke translation (New York, 1980), p. 139]).

Decisive here is a final, limitless, divine wound, a bleeding that pulses with life from the other side of death. We can understand why Catherine's stigmata remained invisible. In this light the phrase "not without blood" has the following Christian meaning: nothing bears fruit without being pierced open—an organism with inward circulation closed in upon itself accomplishes nothing; rather, life must make its way outside, and it flows best out of the center that keeps life circulating. How else could the mystical body of Christ come into being?

18. GOD'S WRATH

What are we to make of the hundreds of places in the Old and New Testaments that speak of the wrath of God? It would be dishonest and dangerous to perform a sleight-of-hand maneuever to explain it away through sociology (Girard), history of religions (by reference to the many wrathful deities grinding their teeth in anger), or religious evolution (arguing that only traces of a wrathful God remain in the New Testament). What would we then do with the many scenes in which Jesus breaks out into undisguised wrath? (The book of Revelation even refers to the "wrath of the Lamb" [6:16].) We see Jesus' anger directed not only toward the evil of the Pharisees (Mt 18:34), who are hypocrites (15:7) and who tip the scale as sons of the murderers of the prophets (23:31–32), but also toward the demons of leprosy (Mk 1:25 and elsewhere; Mk 1:41 should read "enraged", not "moved by compassion"), "hissing" at the sick man (Mk 1:43; cf. Mt 9:30) as he commands him not to tell anyone about the healing. In the synagogue Jesus gazes "angrily around himself, sorrowful over the hardness of heart" of his audience (Mk 3:5). Twice he slips into angry agitation at Lazarus' grave (Jn 11:33, 38), presumably aroused by death's tyranny. In his parables he has no qualms about the wrath of God: the irresponsible servant (Mt 18:34), the unprepared wedding guest (Mt 22:11–14). Jesus himself is capable of swinging the lash at those who desecrate the temple (Mt 21:12–13) and of cursing the fig tree that bears no fruit (Mk 11:14).

Paul is thoroughly acquainted with talk of the wrath of God. The last judgment is as terrifying for him (Rom 2:5: "By your unrepentant heart you pile up for yourself wrath at the day of wrath") as it was for the people of the Old Covenant, for the Baptist, for Jesus himself (see Lk 21:23). Yet even now "God's wrath from heaven above reveals itself" without restraint "against all godlessness and unrighteousness of men, who suppress the truth in their wickedness" (Rom 1:18). We find the same lack of restraint elsewhere: the Gentiles to whom Paul writes were, together with "us" (the Jews), "by nature children of wrath" insofar as we lived according to the "lust of the flesh" (that is, egoism) under the dominance of the "spirit of this world" until God's deliverance came (Eph 2:3; cf. 5:6). One need not extend the list of citations.

We need to be clear about one thing: if we are going to dismiss language about the wrath of God as "anthropomorphism", then the language about God's "mercy" or "patience" also must disappear for the same reason. We would then be left with nothing but a concept of God as the "Absolute" transcending all concrete and realistic relationship between God and men. Instead, let us ask what God's wrathful reactions visible in Jesus' anger have to say about the moral chaos of the world. They enunciate quite simply God's relentless "No" to anything irreconcilable with his purity and holiness. God's "Yes" can be nothing but a "No" in response to everything that rears itself up against his Positiveness. "The nations raged, but your wrath came" (Rev 11:18). The same thing is expressed by the images of consuming fire and the "living and powerful two-edged sword that penetrates even to the division of soul and spirit" (Heb 4:12). To that which is loveless God's eternal "pleasure in loving" can only seem to be displeasure and resentment. Once more we see how correct Anselm was to understand righteousness as an inner characteristic of love that would be merely flaccid without God's angry displeasure toward the unloving.

Yet "God's weakness", which, according to Paul, is "stronger than men" (1 Cor 1:25), has nothing to do with that kind of flaccidity. God's weakness is much more the form that his relentlessness takes in order to deal with the world's defiant "No". If God were not prepared to stand firm through all the consequences of the absoluteness of his love, would the feeble world, with its readiness to compromise, ever have been confronted with the unyielding love of God? The Son's Cross, an act of the Father's ultimate love, is the unsparing (Rom 8:32) revelation of a love that knows no moderation. "Hard as death is love" (Song 8:6).

One can view the Cross as a battle between an enraged humanity and the wrath of God (along the lines of the book of Revelation). But the Crucified One does not fight; instead, the battle rages around him. The lance thrust may symbolize the victory of worldly wrath ("Proud and precisely landed thrust between rib and hip, driven through to the intertwined Trinity" [Claudel]), but the flood of water, blood, and spirit is the triumph of God, whose loving wrath delivered the Son to take the place of sinners.

When the book of Revelation portrays the "Word of God" riding out to "war" wearing "bloodstained garments", he rides not to the decisive battle but already in triumph, for he has already "trod the winepress of God's fierce anger". When he rules the people "with iron scepter" (Is 11:4; Ps 2:9 in the Septuagint; Rev 2:27; 12:5; 19:15), the metaphor tells us that Jesus' demand too is a relentless one, that anyone who prefers the world is not worthy of Christ. On the Day of Judgment no one will be able to smuggle into the Kingdom of God anything fashioned of "wood, hay, and straw", for "his works will be burned up, and he must suffer their loss"—he will be happy to save himself, but only "as through fire" (1 Cor 3:15).

19. Magdalen

At the Cross she learns how much it cost him to deliver her from seven demons. Even before that she was certainly filled with nothing but gratitude and had placed all she had at the disposal of Jesus and his followers. Freed from a sevenfold servile bondage, she had entered a freedom unknown to her like one who steps out of a gloomy dungeon into the open air. Everything within her was drawn toward her liberator, to whom she owed a completely new existence exceeding all her hopes. For these reasons what she experiences at Golgotha cannot be put into words. Her liberator cruelly nailed up in a tortured death agony and she, the one he set free, unable to do anything at all to free him. Moreover, she knows, unbearably, that her freedom to love him is purchased by this torment. She cannot return to her prison and thereby set him free; she must simply endure having her freedom paid for with this breathtakingly high price. She realizes that her offer of love can do nothing now to brighten the dark night of his abandonment by God. She cannot offer her suffering as a balm for his. He is alone, on the other side of a broken bridge.

She cannot make herself useful in any way. She hears the death rattle, sees the blood run from his open side, but it is the men who take the corpse down after Joseph of Arimathea finally returns from seeing Pilate and buying linen. They may have laid his body on his Mother's lap, but certainly not on Mary Magdalen's. She is an observer and remains one while the corpse is prepared for and finally placed in the tomb, which is then sealed. "Mary Magdalen and the other Mary stayed there, sitting down across from the tomb" (Mt 27:61). Behind the stone that cut off her line of vision lay what had once been her life. For the entire following day the stone of the Sabbath weighed heavily upon her existence and robbed her of all action. "On the Sabbath they rested according to the law" (Lk 23:56).

Then comes the report of a Resurrection morning that cannot

be entirely reconstructed with certainty: carrying their spices, the women find the open tomb; Magdalen runs to the disciples to give the news (before or after the angels' proclamation in Mk 16:5–7?) and then finds her solitary way back to the grave for the great scene reported by John (20:11–18). Neither the gaping emptiness nor the conversation with the two angels who sit at the head and feet of a missing corpse, not even her words to the supposed gardener, can drive the opaque darkness of Good Friday away from the woman's soul. Only with the name "Mary" does the whole light of the Resurrection flood into her. And therewith the heavy rock that separated her from her Master under the Cross is pushed aside: "Mary—Master" is a pure merging of love. Yet in the same moment a new curtain of separation falls: "Don't hold on to me."

The woman must hold. The man holds not: he takes hold and lets go; he goes his own way, does his own deeds. But in his taking hold he forces the woman to hold, and she will hold the child in a completely different way than he. And, if the man holds her not, she has a deep desire to hold God, to present herself to him as a "bride" whom he cannot leave behind. The same applies if Mary is *personam Ecclesiae gerens,* that is, playing the role of the Church, as the Church Fathers say: the Church must also grant freedom to her Bridegroom ("If it is my will, what does it matter to you?" [Jn 21:22–23]). For that is the only way she receives the freedom of Easter. As she lets go, she can receive Jesus' message for his brethren; had she clung tight in spirit, she would never have been able to carry it out. The Lord granted the woman—both as the Church and as an individual—freedom to say nothing of her experience with him and rather simply to pass on his message. "Mary Magdalen went thither and announced to the disciples: I have seen the Lord, and that is what he told me" (Jn 20:18).

The men—who dismiss the women's message as "empty talk" (Lk 24:11) and receive a scolding from Jesus for having done so (Mk 16:14)—take over the proclamation of the Resurrection, with Peter at their head (Lk 24:12; 1 Cor 15:5). The message of the women disappears behind them (in Jewish law women were not legitimate witnesses). But this message dare not be forgotten, for it is the message of that Church who was present to the end at the crucifixion and the first to be granted a glimpse of the Resurrection.

20. To Worship in Spirit and Truth

"For such worshipers the Father seeks" (Jn 4:23). They alone respond. They respond to what the Father is. Worship can go wrong in two ways. The first occurs when a man, dwarfed and overwhelmed by God's majesty, feels crushed to the ground. The more abstractly one imagines and experiences the relation between the finite and the Absolute, the more powerfully a terrifying dissimilarity makes itself felt, often leading to sensual portrayals of a fierce God with fangs bared in anger. One should not underestimate the religious value of these portrayals of the *maior dissimilitudo* [greater dissimilitude] between God and man, as repulsive as they may be to us. For the other failure in worship lies in the would-be worshiper's inability to dissociate himself from his own person and its concerns.

The Hebrew language lacks the word for *thanksgiving,* but its content lies embedded within the Hebrew concept of *praise.* Gratitude, an attitude indispensable to a relationship with God, holds the received gift in the hand and recognizes the gift's source. If the giver is God, then the cord binding the Giver and the gifted one is plaited from nothing except free, undeserved mercy. This gratitude can root itself so deeply in the receiver that he thanks God no longer for a specific gift *he* has received but rather for *himself,* who receives himself from God as a pure gift given for no reason at all. The person praying Psalm 139 is overcome by realizing that he was given himself long before he was aware of it: "My frame was not hidden from you when I was being intricately wrought in the depths of the earth; I thank you that I have been so marvelously made." We find echoes of our initial theme in the middle of all this—the sense of being completely surrounded by an Infinitely Greater—but that awareness brightens into gratitude for the marvelousness of such a perfect gift of being, a gratitude that undergirds one's entire existence.

Thus, as the Psalms illustrate, expressions of gratitude and prayers of petition continually intertwine themselves at this level—at the point where one realizes one's total dependence. Just as one can only be thankful in response to all that one has received, so too one can only continually ask the free and merciful Source for everything one needs.

Worship hitches a ride on this running board yet also leaps lightly off of it. The receiver's tiny vessel forgets itself and sees only the boundless stream pouring into it. That the receiver himself comes from this overflowing—indeed, the "yield" of this outpouring, the outpoured, never leaves its source behind—all this fades from view. All of the self that the stream has yielded up disappears into the self-giving one. I am preoccupied no longer with the fact that I am loved but rather with the fact that love *is being given.* If we continue to speak of gratitude, then it is simply a gratitude for the fact of love. One no longer glimpses the giving in the thing given or the existence in the thing existing; rather, one sees only the giving, the existing of love. Thus "love" and "giving", that is, love and love's being, are the same. The saints find themselves at this level of worship. This is precisely the point Ignatius of Loyola was aiming at with his phrase *de arriba* ("from above"): "All blessings and gifts [descend] from above. Thus my limited power comes from the supreme and infinite power above, and so, too, justice, goodness, mercy, etc. descend from above as the rays of light descend from the sun, and as the waters flow from their fountains, etc." (*Spiritual Exercises,* 237). St. Francis' "Canticle of the Sun" rings out from the same level, for he is not praising the sun, fire, wind, earth, and death that stream from the Divine Source; rather, together with all the creatures he attributes all blessing (*omni benedictione*) to the Source of all. The great Psalms of praise attain this vision: mankind may be ever so transitory; how good it is that God *is* in eternity.

Yet it is the Son who penetrated deepest into the worship of the Father in spirit and in truth, in the prayer that he taught us: "Hallowed be thy name", we pray. But who is holy, and who can make holy except God himself? Thus we are really praying, "Father, make your name holy" (Jn 12:28), that is, praying that he radiate his inner holiness within himself and, if he so wills, into the world. The entire carrying out of salvation is God's self-sanctification insofar as he is the unpreconceivable outpouring of love. The Son does not call himself the eternal product of this outpouring; rather, he is within it, and he himself pours out—his outpouring is the "truth" that reveals the Father's outpouring, and it is the "Spirit" in which Father and Son are the same outpouring of love. The Father's outpouring is his "Kingdom" that will "come" without being wished into existence by human agency, and the Father's outpouring is his "will" to be love himself as unimpeded on earth in heaven.

The Son is not the Father, and, in the Son, we remain creatures—we do not become God. Yet we worship God not in order to fortify ourselves over against God as his counterpart (nor do we worship in order to be suffocated by his contrasting immensity); rather, we worship in order to flow into the source from which we flow together with him. We worship God not in order to be a separate and stagnant pond but to let ourselves be channeled into the place where his Kingdom has need of us and his will makes use of us.

21. THE WIDOW'S MITE

Jesus sits across from the temple treasury (Mk 12:41). This "across from", the position from which he observes what people decide to contribute to the temple, to worship, to God, is first of all God's own position. God's Son represents God in this position. Objectively seen, his view of the people making their offerings is one of appraisal and thus judgment. Simultaneously he sees both the amount they are prepared to give up and the motivation from which the giving proceeds. "Many rich people put in large sums" is the first observation made. But, Jesus adds, "They all gave merely from their abundance." That is the second observation. They give without giving up anything; they won't miss what they have offered. Thus they in fact offer up nothing, regardless of what may have motivated them to give. Perhaps they hope people will think they are generous. Perhaps they hope that God will consider their donation a sacrifice. Perhaps they are moved by a certain humanism that desires balance between rich and poor; through a "large" gift they quiet an uneasy conscience. None of that is of interest to Jesus.

Then the interesting thing happens. "A poor widow tossed in two tiny coins." Jesus had been sitting by himself but now calls his disciples to him. The decisive event has happened, the focal point of his entire gospel. In Mark and Luke it is the last scene before the eschatological discourse that introduces the Passion narrative. A summary of the good news Jesus offered people is here put into action. What Jesus says about this deed no longer challenges, but recognizes with astonishment and wonder a response. What he observes corresponds to what he expects at the end, but what scarcely seemed possible to expect of people. "All the others contributed out of their surplus, but out of her poverty she has given up everything she had, her whole livelihood."

The difference, the distance, between the two is immeasurable—

from too much, from too little; the superfluous, the indispensable; the carefully calculated (to avoid running out), the uncalculated (because the difference between too little and nothing has become meaningless). No one asks whether the woman knew Jesus' teaching or not, for Jesus had already often found greater "faith" outside rather than within the circle of his preaching. No one investigated whether she gave her last half-penny simply because she wanted to give something to God and his temple or because, less likely, she hoped to receive some kind of compensation from God for her gift. Certainly she does not intend to do some heroic deed but intends, rather, simply to give God what belongs to him. Perhaps she is embarrassed to be able to give so little; perhaps she fears being despised or rejected by the priest who receives the offerings and places them in the appropriate collection boxes. It makes little difference—she wants to give what she can, even if that means she will no longer have the means to go on living. The difference between the almost nothing of the offering and the absolutely nothing that remains is infinitely small, scarcely observable. But for Jesus it makes the greatest possible difference, incomparably greater than that of any of the other givers.

It might be enough to have pointed out that Jesus is able at the end of his career as a teacher to show his disciples a perfect response to what he requires of them. But we would then overlook that what Jesus requires more than anything else of his disciples is that they follow him, a total abandonment of everything, which could only be a following of him if he himself totally abandoned everything. Otherwise, as Irenaeus (who died ca. 200 A.D.) points out, Jesus would be demanding of his disciples something he is not ready to do himself. Is Jesus then the model for the poor widow? According to his categorical challenges, it could not be otherwise: whoever does not abandon everything but instead keeps something for himself, even if only his own self (Lk 14:26), "is not worthy of me". "For he who would save his life must lose it" (Mk 8:35; Lk 9:24; 17:33). Beyond one's life, there is nothing more to lose, not even for Jesus. The poor widow freely gives her livelihood away—she has the power to do that. Jesus too has "the power to lay down my life", and for the sake of this self-surrender the Father loves him

(Jn 10:18, 17). Such self-abandonment is a reckless and vulnerable act that makes no calculations about what one will have "tomorrow" (Easter), for "this day" (Good Friday) "has cares enough of its own" (Mt 6:34). His shed blood stays shed in eternity (Catherine of Siena knows that); it is not gathered up again. Just as the poor widow receives her penny back only in the form of one of the sacrificial animals offered to God, so Jesus can receive back his blood in the form of those who bring this "sacred cup" to the Heavenly Father and receive it back from him to drink.

Whoever volunteers, "I will follow you wherever you go", receives the answer, "The Son of Man has nothing on which to lay his head" (Lk 9:57–58). If, at the outset, he had food "that you know not"—"to do the will of my Father" (Jn 4:32–33)—at the end this food, this livelihood, persists only in the form of deprivation, or, better said, in the form of the cup of Yahweh's wrath over the world's sins. Live from that, if you can; otherwise, die.

22. "I Have Become All Things to All Men"

Some have mocked this "diplomatic" adaptability of Paul (Voltaire calls the Jesuits *"Pères tout à tous",* that is, "fathers all to all"), but for Paul it is no expression of his ability to juggle roles; rather, it is the direct outgrowth of the paradox of the Cross of Christ by which God consigned all to disobedience "in order to show mercy to all" (Rom 11:32). It is through the Crucified One, who became all things to all men—Jews, Gentiles, and Christians—that the disciple can pursue such catholicity. The Cross does not make sinners unrighteous in God's eyes; rather, it becomes "justification, healing, and salvation" for them (1 Cor 1:30). It does this not by covering evil with a blanket of good but by identifying with a tiny bit of good and expanding it to full validity. "Forgive them, for they know not what they do" (Lk 23:34). As Paul says, it is a "becoming weak with the weak" (1 Cor 9:22) motivated by love alone.

Paul does not give up his "freedom in all things" to make himself a "servant of all" for the sake of appearances alone. He wants to have "a share in the gospel" in the same way that the "Lord and Master" has already made himself a servant of all. Not for appearance alone, then, does Paul become "to the Jews a Jew, in order to win the Jews" but rather because the One who "is subject to the law" finds himself where God has placed him, and the law is good and holy in and of itself. The Pharisees believe in the Resurrection, which permits Paul to call himself a Pharisee (Acts 23:6); he can have Timothy circumcised (Acts 16:3) and participate in Jewish ceremonies in the temple (Acts 21:21–26). All of these things are neutral things for him (*adiaphora*). He makes this clear to the Gentile Christians (at the same time that Timothy is circumcised) by announcing to them the decisions of the apostolic council that met at Jerusalem (Acts 15:4). Born a Jew, Paul here becomes "like a Jew" for the Jews, even though he "no longer falls under the law"; yet he stands in solidarity with "those who fall under the law", stands with them where they are in order to lead them from within to the fulfillment of the law in Christ. Making connections where a possibility of understanding exists is what Christian Aggiornamento means.

But how can Paul "become lawless like the lawless"? His response: "Insofar as I am not lawless before God" because "I have been legitimized into Christ" (*ennomos Christou*) (1 Cor 9:21). In the "law of faith" (Rom 8:2) we are "freed from the law of sin and death", thus "lawless" in an objective freedom that can become a connecting link for the Gentiles outside the law. They thought they were free, but in Christ they should realize a much more complete freedom, the freedom from sin and death, a freedom "to which Christ has delivered us" (Gal 5:1).

Both those bound by the law and those outside its bounds are the "weak", because they know the fullness of neither the law nor freedom, both of which coincide in Christ. Yet neither Christ nor the apostle fetches these weak ones out of a sense of superior power; rather, both of them take them up by becoming "weak to the weak" in order to "win the weak". They do this through neither condescension nor professorial superiority but rather on the basis of the inscrutable decree of God that seeks to show that what is fundamentally "scorned and counted for nothing in the world", that is, the "foolishness of God", is "wiser" and "more powerful" than men (1 Cor 1:21–25). This happens not out of a desire to display a paradoxical test of human power but rather out of the most mysterious law: the principle that a loss of power on the divine and God-Man side becomes a gain in power on the human side. Impossible to measure in any scientific cause-and-effect manner, it takes place in the orbit of the exchange of life within the Trinity, something of which overflows into the world by virtue of the Incarnation of the Son.

This law is universally valid in God. Thus God can say that he has imprisoned everything in disobedience so that he can show mercy to all (Rom 11:32). Elevated upon the Cross, Christ can proclaim that he will draw all men to himself (Jn 12:32). The disciple arrogates to himself no power over God's law of love;

rather, he contents himself with the statement: "I have become all things to all men that I might by all means win some" (1 Cor 9:22).

23. "Each in His Own Place"

"Now do you believe? Behold, the hour is coming and is already here when you will be scattered, each in his own place, and you will abandon me" (Jn 16:31–32). In his farewell discourses Jesus continually looks beyond the gaping chasm of the Cross and death, and the total picture appears as an integral glorification of the Father. Since he paints this larger picture to console and fortify his disciples, they now feel they can also leap over the distance between the present and that which is to come. They tell Jesus: "Look, now you are talking clearly instead of in parables."

Not only is Peter's consolation put off until the future ("later you will follow me" [13:36]), but also he has to accept—precisely as he is impulsively declaring himself ready to leap to the other side—the distressing news that he would presently plunge into the abyss ("you will deny me three times" [13:38]). And then all the disciples have their thoughts brought back to the present, to an hour certain to come precisely because they cannot conceive of it in the midst of their conviction that they have already reached the other side. Indeed, their perverse certainty means that it has already arrived.

"You cannot follow me now", Peter was told (13:36). All of them now hear in utter clarity: "You will be scattered, each in his own place." When their shared commonality with Jesus breaks up, they lose every kind of community. They are unable to distance themselves from Jesus in concert; each follows his own path, a direction whose meaning and content are characterized precisely as "my own". No other content is to be had, as Peter realized when he responded to Jesus' question, "Are you also going to leave?" with the words, "To whom could we go?" (Jn 6:68). Since there is no "who" that could compare with Jesus, all that remains is "one's own", forcing them into a dispersal in which each one's "own" has nothing in common with another's.

"One's own" is the only alternative to unity in the one Word of

God: "I have come in my Father's name, but you do not receive me; if another comes in his own name, you will accept him." Jesus calls this a mutual admiration society, which makes receptiveness to faith impossible (Jn 5:43–44). The "each his own" expands into a doctrine, into a system that seems plausible and credible enough but whose irreducible core remains "his own" and "his own honor", diametrically opposed to the core of Jesus' word: honoring the Father. To speak "one's own" is the same thing as lying, and that is anti-Christ and demonic. When the devil "lies, he speaks from himself" (Jn 8:44)—one could invert this: because he speaks from himself, he lies.

Only at this point do we realize how ominous is Jesus' comment to the disciples: "Do you now believe?" Do you think you now have arrived at unity and truth in faith in me? You are still on this side of the abyss, where you have already begun to disperse from unity into your own places. You are still basing your faith in yourselves, not in me. You still seek in yourselves your own certainty, your own satisfaction, your "self-fulfillment", and, since each of you is incomparably different from the other, there will be as many sects ("scraps") as there are individuals with their individualities. To think that you can merge into a unity through agglomeration is simply one more lie that corresponds to the self's self-importance but inwardly contradicts itself.

This scattering into individual selves would lead to a hopeless dead end were not the Lord's solitary suffering a trinitarian solitude. "You will abandon me. But I am not alone, for the Father is with me" (Jn 16:32). With me even in, indeed, precisely in, my being forsaken by the Father. The Son has nothing of his "own" that does not simultaneously belong to the Father in the Spirit, so that "all that the Father has is mine" (16:15). True faith therefore consists in abandoning all of one's "own" to receive in its place the "gift of grace" intended for me, a gift whose meaning and being consists in being present for all. "For every one must keep in mind that in all that concerns the spiritual life his progress will be in proportion to his surrender of self-love and of his own will and interests" (Ignatius of Loyola, *Spiritual Exercises, 189*).

24. The Son as the Father

"He who sees me sees the Father" (Jn 14:9). Jesus puts it so plainly. He does not say something like "he who sees me guesses that I am the Son of the Father". Yet we know that he calls himself and the Father "one" (10:30), not "one person", and that he says that the Father is greater than he (14:28). Despite that, their identity is perfect—one can "know and understand that the Father is in me and I am in the Father" (10:38), that the Father thus is "seen" only in the Son, not beside or behind him. "In" cannot mean that there are certain places in the Son where the Father is; rather, the Father is in the entire Son. Nor can *in* mean that the Son is some kind of transparency that disappears to permit the Father to be visible in its place. That would render meaningless the *we* that Jesus uses to speak of the joint advent of Father and Son to those who believe.

The Council of Nicaea declared that the Son is just as much without beginning as the Father. Thus, like the Father (Rev 1:8), he may call himself "the Alpha and the Omega, the first and the last, the beginning and the end" (Rev 22:13). If everything, absolutely "everything has been given him by the Father" (Mt 11:27), this certainly includes being beginning and end, in order that "all might honor the Son as they honor the Father" (Jn 5:23). The prologue to John's Gospel insists on this origin of the Son: "Without him not a single thing was made that was made" (Jn 1:3). Does this mean that the Father also gives his Fatherhood—in some mysterious way—to the Son?

One of the royal titles of the Messiah is "Everlasting Father" (Is 9:5[6])—*Pater Futuri Saeculi* according to the Septuagint. The Messiah might be Yahweh's viceroy on earth. But in the early Church as well it was not uncommon to refer to Jesus as Father. Was he not, after all, the Divine Bridegroom of Mother Church? The marvelous "Rule of the Master" (fifth century) explains the entire Our Father as a prayer to Christ, and Benedict's Rule, which drew heavily on the Rule of the Master, gives the head of the monastery the title "abbot" because he stands in Christ's stead and is addressed as "Abba" (that is, Father, Papa).

This kind of thinking seems strange to us because it seems to obscure the core mystery of the Trinity; indeed, it seems to contradict Christ's own words: "You have one Father, who is in heaven" (Mt 23:9). It is indeed true that the innermost mystery of salvation is expressed in our being embraced within the eternal begetting of the Son from the bosom of the eternal Father (Jn 1:13)—through the eternal Divine Spirit who brought forth the birth of Jesus.

However, we would fall far short if we glimpsed in Jesus merely our "older Brother" without realizing how much he makes the Father present to us in his entire work of salvation. The authority he claimed and possessed is not an authority different from the Father's; rather, it is the authority given him on earth by the Father so that "all will honor the Son as they honor the Father" (Jn 5:23). When the Son dies for us on the Cross, he wants to bring home to us how much the Father loves the world (Jn 3:16). No one can delude himself into thinking he has the Father if he denies the Son (1 Jn 2:23). Our becoming children of God, that is, all our salvation from on high, we owe entirely to the Son, which indicates how much creative power the Father gives the Son. That the conclusion to Matthew's Gospel, as well as Paul's hymns, portray him as *Pantokrator* (ruler of all); that the hymns of praise in the book of Revelations are directed both to the Father "sitting on the throne" and to "the Lamb"; all this makes tangible the degree to which what belongs to one of the Divine Persons belongs fully to the other: "All that the Father has is mine" (Jn 16:16). Thus, in the intratrinitarian exchange the Persons do not give each other "something of themselves"; rather, they continually give themselves over and are different only in this intertwining.

"He who sees me sees the Father" need not mean merely that whoever truly recognizes Jesus as Son grasps that he comes from the Father. Rather it also means that whoever recognizes in faith the going forth of the Son out of the Father "sees" in this act of generating the Father who simply is this fathering and is nothing behind or beyond it.

"Now I understand why Christ died for me: because he loved me as a father loves his son, and that not merely as a human father but as the eternal Father loved his eternal Son" (Newman).

25. SAINT IGNATIUS

He has described for us his vision at the river, a vision in which God's saving plan for the world appeared to his eyes in such indivisible unity that, as he tells us, he basically no longer needed Holy Scripture. At La Storta God the Father entrusted him to the Son so that he might give his new foundation the unheard-of name "Society of Jesus". One Jesuit father witnessed his face shining during prayer; Nadal reports that he always obtained whatever he desired in prayer. He burned all his other notes recording mystical experiences, wishing to appear to his own and to the world merely as the intelligent founder and administrator. Few aspects of his constitutions for the society, which in turn became a model for nearly all the subsequently founded religious orders, have become obsolete in the course of 450 years.

He remains a most vividly present reality to the Church in his rather awkwardly edited, unliterary *Exercises*. Who could count how many hundreds of thousands of vocations were inspired over the centuries and continue to be inspired by this book? There are no substitutes for the event it describes, even though many alternative systems have been proposed.

By their relentless practicality the Exercises shove the searcher into the center of the gospel and leave him alone there with Christ, with the triune God who speaks to him. In this way the book sweeps away the hundreds of pious "manuals for perfection" that abounded during the high and late Middle Ages. I used the word *shove* deliberately, for, in order to be sure to arrive at the center, one must first be stripped of his illusions about himself, his fantasies and sins, so that "naked he can follow the naked Christ", so that God's Word—Christ—can confront him personally, nose to nose. This happens not somewhere at the edges but in the center of his existence, so that the call becomes a turning point in his life. "Being called" constitutes the sole center, meaning, and purpose of the whole book and is surrounded with much prudent advice ("pertaining to a proper carrying out of one's call"). The rest of the Exercises merely have to do with sharing Christ's path: Incarnation, birth, hidden and public life and work, Passion, Resurrection, and the founding of the Church.

What is supposed to happen is the same thing that happened long ago on the bank of the Jordan. "As Jesus was passing by" (and Ignatius emphasizes that Jesus is not stationed somewhere but rather is always passing by), "John looked at him and said, 'Behold the Lamb of God.' The two disciples heard what he said and followed Jesus. But Jesus turned around and, seeing them following him, asked them, 'What are you seeking?'" When they reply, "Rabbi, where are you staying?" he answers, "Come and see" (Jn 1:36–39). Make up your mind to come (which means "drop everything" [Lk 5:11]), and you shall see. "And they went along and saw . . . and stayed." What happened back then is not merely a model but is exactly the same thing that happens today, in the here and now, just as the sacrifice of the Cross is present in this Holy Mass, just as the Resurrection Day's remission of sins takes place in each true confession.

Ignatius is not concerned with a "path to perfection" that one can read about in books and follow step by step. He is not concerned with that because, in the first place, no one can determine in advance on which path the call of Christ in the Church and the world will place a particular person. Thus the Exercises cannot outline a "[more] perfect" path. The Lord alone decides what path he has chosen for you—and his choice makes it the best path for you. You can get your marching orders only from him, if you are ready to walk any path that God might choose, if you stand where the boy Samuel stood: "Speak, Lord, for your servant listens" (1 Sam 3:10)—or, better yet, if you, like the Virgin as "handmaid of the Lord", are prepared for anything, for the most burdensome and most beautiful. She appeared to Ignatius on his sickbed and visibly placed her own "Yes" in his heart.

A seeking, groping life: The Carthusians? An itinerant preacher? Alone or with companions? A crusader fighting Islam at the Holy Sepulchre? The Inquisition insisted that he squeeze himself, already full grown, into a schoolchild's desk and learn Latin, philosophy, and theology in the midst of a thousand setbacks: shortage of money, sickness. On the outside he was always the confident leader of ever-growing numbers; inwardly he was the ever-open seeker always praying for guidance. And then in Rome he was the focal point around which everything swirled, whose existence and functioning were taken so much for granted by everyone that, once more in Nadal's words, "in his manner of death he exhibited a marvelous humility, as if he completely ignored himself and was ignored by all others" (*quasi qui se negligeret perfecte, et ab aliis negligeretur omnibus*) (P. Nadal, *Epistolae,* vol. 4, 697).

26. Going Home

It seems to us to be nothing but a pious exaggeration when Christians are told that God "has raised us up with him and made us sit with him in the heavenly heights in Christ Jesus" (Eph 2:6) or that "you have come to the heavenly Jerusalem, to the city of the living God, to thousands of angels, to the festal gathering and to the company of the firstborn" (Heb 12:22–23). Is it not equally true that we "live far away from the Lord in alienation" (2 Cor 5:6), since we are only "saved in hope. . . . But if we hope for what we see not, we hold out for it with patience" (Rom 8:24–25).

Yet are not both contradicted when we discover that "your life is hidden with Christ in God" (Col 3:3)? For we would then be truly, even if in a hidden way, in heaven, and the patience of hope and distance would refer only to our waiting for the hidden reality to be unveiled. Then the description of us as "strangers on earth" (1 Pet 2:11) would also be shown to be true, for our "legitimate citizenship", our "homeland" (Phil 3:20) would be heaven. It is hard for us to fathom how realistically this is meant, because nothing seems more tangible to us than the contrast between an existence on earth and the existence in heaven that we hope for after our death. It may be that a connection exists between the two; after all, we are members of the body of Christ, and Christ certainly is in heaven. But the appearance of our earthliness, better yet, of our sorrowful and guilt-laden existence, is so obvious that heaven fades into the future.

Yet will the appearance hold up when we consider that the Son of God never left the "bosom of the Father" in becoming incarnate (Jn 1:18)? When we consider that he assured us that the Kingdom of God remains "in our midst" (Lk 17:21)? That the will of God happens in him "on earth as in heaven"—not in a vague approximation but in complete identity?

If we think now about Mary, we know that she has a place in God's saving plan, a home, where she was "chosen before the foundation of the world" to be the Savior's Mother, "to be holy and blameless before him" (Eph 1:4). Surely she never left that place as she became a person in time and lived out her entire existence on earth. When she comes to God on the day of her assumption, she simply returns home to the place that was hers from the start, a place so familiar to her (for it is the revelation of her real being) that she instantly knows "this is where I have always been". And this takes place not merely as an idea or divine intention is finally realized; rather, it is because the deepest being of the Virgin Mother was always identical with this idea, and she thus experiences in her assumption: this is where I always was. To what degree she experienced this in her life of faith in the world makes no difference here.

We are not Mary. We do not yet correspond in this "foreign land" to God's conception of us as his child. Yet at the same time something of the completed mystery of Mary is already present in us. We do not know how deep a truth lies in the statement that Christ "gave those who received him the power to become children of God" (Jn 1:12), not in a vague and figurative sense but in the fact that we are born by grace with him from God the Father. Nicodemus found this to be simply incredible, and the Lord scolded him for his unbelief—as a teacher in Israel he should have known about this elementary truth. For elements of it are visible already in the Old Testament. Jesus quoted the words of the Psalm, "I said, you are gods" (Ps 82:6), and applied it to all "to whom the word of God came" (Jn 10:34-35). He means that it came not merely outwardly into their ears but rather deep "into their hearts" so that "all know me, great and small, says Yahweh" (Jer 31:33-34). Already here the chosen ones are carried over into the realm of God through the word God inserts into their hearts. How much more, Jesus says, will it be true of the One whom "the Father sanctified and sent into the world" (Jn 10:36) and thus also of those whom this Sanctified One brings with him back to the Father as the children of God: "Behold, I am here, with the children God gave me" (Heb 2:13). Because we are already children of the Father and members of Christ and have the Holy Spirit in our hearts calling, "Abba, Father" (Rom 8:15), just as the Son called to the Father (Mt 14:36), our homecoming to the conception God has of us eternally is an arrival at the place from which we originated, at the place in which we have been eternally in our own most intimate truth and reality. Only from that place can we measure how far away we were while we wandered sinful and imperfect like the lost son of the parable, who finally set his sights on his father's house and was received therein by his father.

27. "No One Lives to Himself"

We are all dispossessed of ourselves from the outset. Yet initially the opposite seems too obvious: nothing seems to belong to one so inalienably as his own self. To deny this would seem to reduce a person to a commodity—whether in slavery or in serfdom, whether in the old or new form of communism, or wherever the individual (in Sparta as well as in today's totalitarian countries) is taken away from the family and bought and sold as property of the state.

But Paul puts it even more radically: "None of us lives to himself, and none of us dies to himself" (Rom 14:7). A man reduced to a commodity at least dies for himself insofar as in his dying he ceases to have any commercial value. And yet according to Paul he is claimed even in death. Paul abruptly names the real owner and tells why he owns us: "For Christ died and rose again for this reason—that he might be Lord of both the living and the dead" (Rom 14:9). The conclusion follows: "If we live, we live to the Lord; if we die, we die to the Lord" (Rom 14:8). The deed of ownership is based on a principle of dogma: "One has died for all; therefore, all have died. And he died for all, that those who live might live no longer for themselves but for him who for their sake died and was raised" (2 Cor 5:14-15). The force of this claim rests on its double *for*—one for all so that all are for the One. One can, of course, ask whether this *for* provides a basis for ownership. For the Lord, who "dies for" and "rises for", it might at first seem to be an expropriation, or at least a transfer of what is most intimately his own (his life) to those for whom he sacrifices it—a sacrifice that he makes with no thought of taking his life back again ("for himself"). When he does receive it back again, he lives as the one who "died for". Because he was "commissioned" by God to do it, he lives forever "for God" (Rom 6:10), and because this commission has no limit within time, the one who carries it out is the one from God who is timelessly "for us".

All of this makes sense and has significance only if it is interpreted from the center of Christian teaching, from the Trinity and the Incarnation of the Son of God.

The perspective of the Trinity has meaning because in God there is absolutely no "for oneself"; rather, eternal life—absolute life—takes place in self-giving for each other. One might object that one must first be for oneself before one can give oneself up. Not at all: the *self* must be dropped from the *for.* Self exists totally within self-giving; otherwise, there would be not one God but three, mythology. In the human sphere we have no analogy to this except that no one owes his own physical and intellectual existence to himself; rather, all exist "whence". Anyone who wants to attribute his existence to himself discovers, when forced to reflect on it, that his "for himself" is an anticipated "for others". In creatures a "for oneself" exists only as a transition between "whence" and "where to". But then one must realize that this cessation implies, because God is God, God's perfecting sovereignty and freedom—exactly the opposite of an object or commodity.

It is from God's integrated form (*Verfaßtheit;* literally, "composedness"), which we, of course, know only through the Incarnation of the Son, that the possibility of Christ's "forness" arises. It has no other goal than to free men from the prison of "for self" and to introduce them to the shape of divine freedom. It is not enough that men as creatures are from God and toward God, passing through the midpoint of "for self" on the way from the first to the second. Rather, they must be bound up more intimately with the being of God in order to reach the sovereign lordship of God over all things through radical deconstruction of the self: "All things belong to you ... whether of the world or life or death or present or future, it is all yours, but you are Christ's, and Christ is God's" (1 Cor 3:22–23). And, although nothing surpasses God, still God does not belong to himself; rather, God the Father belongs to the Son and the Son to the Father and the Spirit to both.

Christ's life for us and death for us are the priestly work of redemption, a bearing for us of the guilt of the world that is possible only because of his existence as a Son "for the Father". It leads from the first (the Son) to the second (the Father).

A nonbeliever might well be outraged that a Christian puts up with being uprooted from himself and "transferred" (Col 1:13) "into the Kingdom of the beloved Son" of the Father—all without warning. Far from being violated, however, the person is thereby transplanted into the best place possible, a place foreseen already at his creation. By bursting his boundaries in "being for", he gains a share in the fullness of divine and cosmic being, being that comes from the center of the One who is at once both God and man.

28. "The Inscription Was Written in Hebrew, Latin, and Greek..."

... so that the three peoples of the world could read and understand that "this is Jesus, the King of the Jews"; so that they could understand what was incomprehensible to them, what lay on the other side of the threshold to which their understanding could and would reach. For it reaches a good way along the road to Calvary, but a crater abruptly appears in the road. One cannot step across it; one can merely leap across with a faith that is certain only on the other side.

"In Hebrew": "King of the Jews". Here is where most precautions are taken in order to make the unavoidable leap predictable, practiced, and accomplished. The first of these was the faith of Abraham, whose dead body was promised a son so that Abraham might "believe in God who makes the dead alive and calls into existence the nonexistent" (Rom 4:17). Paul may insist that the Mosaic law "intervened", but he emphasizes at the same time that precisely for that reason it is unable to overturn the ancient promise made in faith (Gal 3:15–18). In God's instructions in the Torah he merely declared more clearly how one might live legitimately within the Covenant of promise. Plenty of open questions remained in this Covenant, keeping alive the expectation of something exuberantly fulfilling—questions posed by Job, the preacher of Ecclesiastes, the book of Lamentations. But Israel turned the law into a contract, replacing humble people of faith with self-satisfied Pharisees who want to prove to God that they are perfect business partners. In this way the symbolic signs that God gives are no longer understood as pointers but are mistaken for the thing itself. And then the expectations are politicized—the realization of all that is known and hoped for on earth, and the "fulfilling of the law to its last iota" ought far to "exceed" the existing understandings by leaping over the chasm (Mt 5:17–20).

Yet because the meaning of the law had become restricted to the law itself, whoever wanted to reach its fulfillment in Christ through faith had to "die through the law to the law", thus arriving at precisely the point where the "King of the Jews" was crucified by the law. "I am crucified with Christ . . . what I live now on earth I live by [Abraham's] faith in the Son of God, who loved me and gave himself for me" (Gal 2:19–20).

"In Greek": "The Greeks seek wisdom" (1 Cor 1:2), and they too walked the path that led to Golgotha. They understood many things. Greek writers of tragedy understood that men's lives, precisely great men's lives, are under the direction of the gods, that one comes up against insoluble situations in life, that extreme suffering can become a blessing. At their best they understood that a man must obey God more than men, even when men establish political laws. "The just man" faces the choice "to be scourged, tortured, bound, and in the end, after all torments, to be crucified" (Aristotle, *Politeia Athenaion* [Constitution of Athens], 362A) precisely when "the pure essence of justice without regard for reward, in contrast to the pure essence of injustice without regard for punishment" (ibid., 612C), is at issue. The Greeks understood that a magnanimous man might put his life on the line for his city or his fellowmen. They had deep insights into the nature of human virtue and justice. Yet between all of that and the idea of the substitutionary suffering and death of the One whom God has established as King of the world yawns an impassible chasm, on the other side of which one must start all over again ("God's foolishness is wiser than men" [1 Cor 1:25]). On the other side the earlier insights can be incorporated, but only after they have been completely reassesed.

"In Latin": Here the leap is longest. For Rome rules the world by might, and in Rome one can only display magnanimity and gentleness, the virtues of intellectual superiority, where might is adequately shored up. Rome is the Western superpower to which Jewish political lust for power had to surrender and against which Greek greed for power shattered, mangling Hellas in the process. Rome places all the virtues in the service of power, a point made persistently by Sallust and Augustine. An abyss stretches between this power and the complete powerlessness of the crucified King.

Yet how can that be, if the Resurrected One possesses and grants to his disciples "all power in heaven and on earth"? And how can there be a great abyss if those disciples settle on Rome as their headquarters, if Caesar becomes a Christian and moves his headquarters to the New Rome in the East, leaving the pope in charge in the West, ordering and giving orders? How can this be if eventually new emperors let themselves be crowned by popes and receive their temporal power from the pope's hand? How difficult the necessary leap from Roman power into the Kingdom of the Crucified One then becomes. Can the symbol of powerlessness ever become a sign of worldly victory (*in hoc signo vinces*)? Does Christian mission ever dare follow in the wake of secular conquest? Is a *siglo d'oro* (golden age) possible after all? If anything has triumphed in the Cross—the inscription does mention Kingship—then it can only be a triumph of incomprehensible love whose power cannot be confused with any earthly power. The image of the One who suffered "the most cruel and loathsome torment", that of the Cross (Cicero, *Actio in Verrem,* II.5) must constantly warn us against that sort of confusion.

29. FAITH AND WORKS

The difference between Paul and James seems at first to be merely one of terminology. Where Paul says that Abraham was justified on the basis of faith and not of works (Rom 4:1–12), James emphasizes that Abraham's faith was completed only through his work of sacrificing Isaac (James 2:22). Yet what else can faith mean for Paul except the surrendering of one's entire existence to God, from whom alone one can hope for the grace of justification? And does not Abraham's perfect surrender turn out to be, for James, Abraham's returning to God of the most precious gift God ever gave him, the son of the promise?

The only work that God requires of men is blindly trusting self-abandonment. This is exactly what Paul describes when he says that the only response he can possibly make to the loving self-abandonment of the Lord is faith: "The life that I now live in the flesh I live by faith in the Son of God, who loved me and gave himself up for me" (Gal 2:20). Here he has no desire to divvy up this total life of faith into his various deeds and trials, which he enumerates elsewhere, for example, in his "fool's discourse" (2 Cor 11). Even these are not some sort of keeping of the law by which one responds to certain legal requirements with precision; rather, they are merely episodes of a unified self-abandoning devotion.

God's perfect self-giving on the Cross for the sinner was an indivisible act, and the perfect self-giving of a believer who has received God's self-giving is an indivisible act of grateful response to the Giver on the Cross. The Cross is the action and work (praxis) of God, and faith is the action and work (praxis) of men. The only relation (reason, logic) connecting the two is that faith-practice inwardly presupposes one has realized and recognized God-practice. It cannot be otherwise, for even God's word, the "theo-logy" that precedes his suffering, is already itself a part of God's acting, his praxis. The covenants with Abraham and Moses,

94

God's speaking through the prophets, the Incarnation of the Son and his public life are all episodes of a single Act, and in this action he says exhaustively all that he can and will say about himself (John of the Cross, *Ascent of Mt. Carmel,* II.22).

If men attempt to construct a "theology" in response to God's, there can be only one meaningful point of contact between divine and human praxis. This is no "Lord, Lord" talk (Mt 7:21), no matter how detailed; rather, it is an expression of a faith that understands (through God's grace) itself and the requirements of love of God and neighbor contained in that faith. Intelligible preaching is an aspect of the command to love one's neighbor; ecclesial worship and the personal liturgy of one's daily life are required by love of God.

A word, a "logy", must precede potential practice for the man coming to faith: "How shall they believe in him of whom they have not heard? How shall they hear without a preacher?" (Rom 10:14–15). However, justification says out of faith: "The word is near you, on your lips and in your heart" (Rom 10:8), which means that preaching says nothing that is completely foreign or strange to the world ("Do not say in your heart, 'Who will ascend into heaven?' [that is, to bring Christ down], or 'Who will descend into the abyss?' [that is, to bring Christ up from the dead]" [Rom 10:6–7]). What is preached is ultimately that which is closest to the human heart, that which more completely satisfies its yearnings than the human heart ever dared hope for. A man wants to be justified, but having sunk into the depths of guilt, he sees no possible way out, because he knows deep down that all the exits he has explored are illusions. In the end everything in him is ready for a work, an act, of complete trust, if he could only be assured that such an act is possible, meaningful, indeed, the only act required.

With that we have said all there is to say about theology.

30. Transfiguration and Resurrection

There must be some connection between the two, since Jesus told his three disciples, as they were coming down the mountain after the Transfiguration, not to tell anyone about what had happened "until the Son of Man has risen from the dead". "These words preoccupied their thoughts, and they asked each other, 'What can it mean, "to rise from the dead"'" (Mk 9:9–10). They are far removed from drawing any advance understanding of the Resurrection out of the Transfiguration.

And so it is indeed. If the Transfiguration is to shed any light on the Resurrection, it will do so in a manner that defies expectations. When Jesus walks as a stranger with the disciples on their way to Emmaus, he gives off no brilliant light that would make his identity obvious. The same is true of all his post-Resurrection appearances. Not until the incident on the Damascus road is someone thrown to the ground by a "powerful light from heaven" (Acts 22:6) "boundless as the sun" (Acts 26:13), yet without revealing a shape visible to the one blinded by it. Such is the heavenly glory of the One who has returned to the Father.

The light of Mount Tabor is a descending light, just as the entire trinitarian epiphany serves God's descent into Passion and death. The Transfiguration was preceded by Jesus' first prediction of his Passion and his words about discipleship on the path of the Cross (Lk 9:22–26). Significantly, his conversation with Moses and Elijah had to do with the imminent end in Jerusalem (Lk 9:31). The Father's voice reinforces both themes from highest heaven: "This is my Son, my Chosen [for the work of salvation]; listen to him" (Lk 9:35). The overshadowing cloud from which the voice resounds and which enfolds the overpowered disciples is a form of the Holy Spirit. But the Church that is thus drawn into the events is unable to grasp the meaning of the challenge embedded within them: instead of walking along the path of suffering, the Church wants to persist in ecstatic misunderstanding. Should one say, as a few of the Church Fathers and the Eastern Church say, that Jesus' humanness was constantly bathed in this light from Mount Tabor, even though the disciples did not perceive it day by day? It is not so much the phenomenon of the light that is important as the realization that Jesus' humanity, immersed as it was in day-to-day human dullness, was nonetheless always ready to respond to the Father's good pleasure and was transfigured by it, as if by an invisible glory, into an ever more profound form of a servant. When Jesus then asks the Father, just before his Passion, to glorify his fatherly name, the answer comes from heaven: "I have already glorified it and will yet glorify it" (Jn 12:28).

These words make it possible to endure the paradox of a Resurrection light that breaks forth from the uttermost depths of suffering, of death; the paradox of "love that endures to the end", from the sealed tomb and its corpse bound up in graveclothes, a corpse that needs no external light from above in order to spring back into the light of life. "I have the power to lay down my life and the power to take it up again" (Jn 10:18). Because the extremity of this death was the extremity of divine love, so the life of absolute love was present in the actual physical death itself. The description of the scene ("in the midst of a powerful earthquake an angel of the Lord descended and rolled away the stone: his appearance was like lightning and his garment white as snow" [Mt 28:2–3]) simply puts imaginative clothes on the invisible Resurrection's reality. The utter darkness of Good Friday reverts of its own accord into the pure light of Easter; the concave revolves in a flash to reveal an identical convex.

Because the Resurrected One has now become the "life-giving Spirit" (1 Cor 15:45), he needs to manifest no externally visible Transfiguration. With his bodily breath he can breath into the Church the Holy Spirit and grant his apostles the authority to resurrect those who are spiritually dead: "If you forgive the sins of any, they are forgiven" (Jn 20:23). Jesus' Spirit-breath hovers over the Church now, so that her members inwardly share in it without cowering in fear like the disciples in the midst of Tabor's cloud (Mt 17:6). Christian faith's steady gaze upon Jesus transforms us here and now because "the Lord is the Spirit" "in the glory of the Lord"; indeed, we are conformed to him "from glory to glory, for this comes from the Lord, who has the Spirit" (2 Cor 3:18), yet without this having to turn into a "Mount Tabor experience". The light of Resurrection is something different from Tabor. It turns us into "light in the Lord" and calls on us to "walk in this light as children of the light" (Eph 5:8).

31. The Pharisee and the Tax Collector

The parable of the two men praying in the temple (Lk 18:9–14) has nothing to do with rich and poor, since the tax collector may well have piled up much money. Its point is not about giving away what one owns, for that is precisely what the Pharisee is proud of having done. He even gives away more than he has to. He adds yet another work of giving to the twice-weekly fast, itself not mandatory according to the law: he gives a tithe not only of what is required but also of everything he acquires. There is no hint that he gained it through fraud, whereas the tax collector probably has not the slightest thought of giving away his ill-gotten assets out of a spirit of penitence. But none of this is of concern to God in this story, which has to do instead with the attitude with which the Pharisee's good works exceed the law's demands.

One cannot measure God's good pleasure by applying a standard based on how many or few of one's possessions are given away. "Many rich people threw large sums into the offering box", but "they all contributed from their abundance" (Mk 12:41, 44). Nor is it decisive that the giver's sacrifice costs him some effort and pain—the Pharisee's twice-weekly fasting certainly was not done casually.

Yet the answer to the riddle posed by the parable must be sought not on the asset side but on the debit side, on the giving side. As the tax collector beat his breast and begged as a sinner for God's mercy, he cannot simultaneously have been planning to continue his fiscal frauds. Otherwise he could not have returned "home justified". The key must lie in the giving.

This parable is as relevant to Christians of all ages as it was in the time of Jesus. Christians know that they must give, that they possess nothing they have not first received (1 Cor 4:7). Like the

Pharisee, they could thank God with rectitude for what they have received: "O God, I thank you that I am not like other men" but have instead been chosen from among the mass of ignorant, unbelieving men mired in vices to "shine as a blameless and innocent child of God in the midst of a crooked and perverse generation like lights in the darkness of the cosmos" (Phil 2:15). Moreover, in contrast to their surroundings, they pursue spiritual growth by acquiring virtues that guarantee them "treasures in heaven" (Mt 6:20). They are to be a "city on a hill that cannot be hidden"; they should let their "light shine before men, so that they may see your good works" (Mt 5:14–16). How scandalously perilous all of these instructions are—instructions not just to amass spiritual goods but also to distribute them while conscious of one's own generosity and selflessness, doing so with explicit instructions to be seen and admired in the process. What a temptation for individual Christians and their charitable organizations.

Recipients perceive the dangers better than givers—if the former refuse to be bought off with donations, if they refuse to be the collection plate into which "many rich people generously" toss their money. With all of today's talk of the "option for the poor", it is necessary to look more closely at what Jesus' parable really says. It certainly has to do with attitudes. For the talk of "being seen of men" is confronted by another instruction: "When you give alms, let not your left hand know what your right hand is doing, so that your alms may be in secret" (Mt 6:3). The "being seen" can have only one purpose—that "the Father who is in heaven" (Mt 5:16), not the Church, be praised. Occasionally this can happen even among the most suspicious people if the charitable societies' workers are humble and selfless enough. What may seem at its source to be a welfare industry can at the other end of the pipeline, where individuals devote themselves to other individuals, to their brothers, turn out to be an expression of a genuine Christian spirit. What may at first seem closer to the Pharisee's mind-set may in the end take place in the spirit of the tax collector who beats his breast in penitence because he knows he does no "good work" in giving away what he possesses illegitimately in the first place.

This applies not only to material gifts to poor and "underdeveloped" countries; it applies equally to all intellectual and spiritual possessions: intellectual advantages that we gained through our social and educational environment do not belong to us and must be placed at the service of society; spiritual goods are good only when they draw us deeper into the inner spirit of the tax collector. Progress in this area can come only through a regression from oneself, from every self-possession and self-awareness, into the gospel poverty that was the first object of Jesus' praise in the Sermon on the Mount. One can no more pile up riches of poverty than one can be proud of humility.

32. "Mary Kept All These Words and Pondered Them in Her Heart"

Here we have an important and scarcely noticed word about Mary. Why should this keeping and pondering be mentioned specifically, indeed, singled out a second time in regard to the twelve-year-old whose words puzzled her (Lk 2:19, 51), if it has no specific import for the Church that took shape after Easter? Both are significant — the preservation, which makes her heart and memory into a treasure chest, and the pondering, which suggests something more present and dynamic, more life giving, than a mere mental warehousing of words. When the time comes for Mary's treasure box to be opened or to open itself, it will contain nothing stale and musty but will be filled with things that through constant movement have stayed as fresh as the day they were put away.

First, the preservation — keeping things in herself. She has space to store all the words of God, the words that the angel spoke to her, then the words with which the shepherds narrated what they had been told about the Child. The words agree with each other, for ultimately they are all words of God that are gathered together in the Child that Mary carried and who now lies before her as yet incapable of speech. The words of God that she stores up in her heart are at one with the Word of God that she brought into the world. After giving birth she has not stopped bearing the word within her. And yet she has brought forth from within her what she lastingly stored up — she has brought it forth as at once the Word of God and as her word. Thus it would be surprising if, when the time was right, she did not relate many of the words she had preserved within her to the Church, perhaps by way of John, in whose household she lived and with whom she certainly must have often talked about her Son. Where else would we have learned so many details about Jesus' childhood?

The other word, captured here with *ponder*, really means to collect, confront, encounter, compare. The term *symbol* comes from the Greek word *symballein*, which refers to the sign of recognition between two guests — two pieces of the same object must be matched in order to make the symbol a mark of recognition, a point of connection, a form of evidence. In similar fashion the Latin word *con-ferre* means "bring together", draw together for comparison, bring into relationship. We find a singular passage in Paul (according to the Vulgate), where he says he compares the spiritual with the spiritual (*spiritualibus spiritualia comparantes* [1 Cor 2:13]). Many Church Fathers applied this to the dynamics of Christian contemplation and theology: a spiritual word of the Scripture is brought into relationship with another word, and behold, out of their mutual approach a new understanding dawns, a third word, as it were, that proceeds from the union of the two. If Christ calls himself the light and in another place calls himself the way, so arises the thought that we need his light to walk the way he is. The Bible is a totality, and no single word dare be expounded by itself without comparison to others. Christian contemplation thus opens itself to an unlimited field of activity; God's words reflect as in a hall of mirrors in which meanings multiply into infinity.

Mary wants to hold in her heart and rock back and forth precisely the ungrasped, uncomprehended word of the twelve-year-old. She lives in faith whose very essence is expansive, a seeking faith that finds much without ever concluding its perusal. With God a final vision is never possible; even in eternity we will not see exhaustively, for all discovery only provokes renewed seeking. *"Ut inventus quaeratur immensus est"*, Augustine said — God is "beyond measure so that even when discovered he may be further sought". So that we may eternally investigate the depths of deity, the Spirit of God who "searches the depths" will be placed in our hearts (1 Cor 2:10, 12). Yet because this Spirit is already placed in our hearts (Rom 5:5), together with Mary as our model, we can begin the research securely believing, though not understanding everything, that God always opens himself up, even on earth, to the one who contemplates.

The Rosary is a prayer that both preserves and actively ponders, a prayer in which we, asking Mary for her vision, can penetrate the inexhaustible mysteries of the self-revealing God.

33. "Worthless Servants"

If you have a servant working in the fields herding cattle all day, when he comes in from work you don't wait on him at table as if he were your lord. No, indeed, you insist that he first cook the meal and serve you: "Make my meal, get dressed, and serve me. After I have finished eating and drinking, you can sit down and eat and drink" (Lk 17:7-8). The servant serves with all of himself rather than serving for a few hours and then turning into a master with lordly expectations. And because his whole purpose is service, when he does what he is supposed to do, he does not have to be thanked specifically for what he has accomplished (17:9). He also has no basis for considering himself indispensable, for another servant could do what he is doing—perhaps even do it better. Nor can he, as in the Hegelian dialectic, transform his consciousness of being a servant into a secret sense of superiority based on the fact that he, not his master, is doing the really productive work. His proper attitude is the one Jesus describes as he concludes the parable: "You should say the same thing when you have finished the work assigned to you: 'We are worthless servants; we have only done what we were told to do'" (17:10). Worthless here means "of limited value", since the servants were unable to do more than what they had specifically been told to do.

This speaks to issues in the life of the Church. There are many in the Church who are singled out for service, and the point of their being singled out (we commonly say "honored") is nothing other than service. Jesus himself offers an illustration: "Which is greater—the one who sits at table or the one who waits on tables? The one who sits at the table, of course. But in your midst I am the one who waits on tables" (Lk 22:27). This is the paradox of the gospel that is continually hammered home in constantly changing ways. To be singled out is indeed an honor, something immediately apparent when we look at Jesus: "You call me Master and Lord, and rightly so, for that I am. If I then, your Lord and

Master, have washed your feet, then you must also" (Jn 13:13–14). If the master does a servant's work, things have reached their limit. For the "servant", even if he has been singled out, "is not greater than his master" (Jn 13:16).

No thought is expended here on a proper reward for the service given. If Jesus plays waiter and goes so far as to wash his guests' feet—the work of a slave, pure and simple—he does so without suggesting a reversal of roles. His self-effacement is neither an obligation that he places upon himself nor a disguise; rather, it is the natural portrayal of his attitude as "Lord and Master" and contrasts with the attitude of earthly "powers" who enjoy being called "benefactors" (Lk 22:25). Jesus proclaims a God who demonstrates the magnitude of his being in an utterly realistic descent and self-effacement. Jesus is the "ambassador" of the God who sends him (Jn 13:16), a God who does not remain withdrawn "above" but reveals his own mind in this mission.

When Jesus has the servant who has done his duty call himself "worthless", he intends that he himself, who has done the Father's will fully, should be reflected in this unworthy servant. In his service as a slave he is not motivated by questions of reward or usefulness; rather, he does what is useless as far as his essence is concerned. Love is always for nothing. Love has no purpose beyond itself and has no reward beyond itself. Thus one should not say that he was a servant up to his death on the Cross so that in the Resurrection he might be transformed into a master. The distinction between master and servant has no meaning either before or after the Resurrection.

If we now ask which of these positions—master and servant—Jesus takes up in the celebration of the Eucharist, we realize how much this is the wrong question to ask. At the Eucharist who sits at the table, and who serves? We are certainly still the guests, and he is still waiting on table at the great banquet prepared by God the Father for the wedding of the royal Son, the banquet at which the king appeared in order to take a look at the guests (Mt 22:11). The Son remains invisible in that parable—at most he is to be found on the table as food and drink, if we are to continue the eucharistic allusion. He remains invisible in other parables as well (as an "unworthy servant"), for his purpose in them is to symbolize the way the Father's care and concern descend to the prodigal son or the lost sheep found by the shepherd. The Son fades away into his serving; indeed, he makes himself unnecessary even as mediator between the Father and us: "At that day you shall ask in my name, and I will not tell you that I will pray the Father for you, for the Father himself loves you" (Jn 16:26). He has reached the goal of service done "for nothing", done gratuitously. "When you have done all you were told to do . . . " (Lk 17:10).

34. THE PARABLE OF THE FATHER

The central figure in the parable we know as that of the prodigal son is clearly the father: "A man had two sons." His having sons and the kind of sons he has become the means to characterize his fatherhood (Lk 15:11–32).

We are given all the details about the younger son's story. The event that sets all the rest in motion is his asking for his inheritance and the granting of his request. The way in which he wasted it and thereby found himself in trouble is of only secondary interest. What is most important is that the father acquiesces to his son's thirst for independence, raises no objections against it, and sends him off without admonition. God gives people complete control over what they demand as their proper inheritance, over what once lay hidden with God but which people insist they have coming to them. Nothing is said about whether God foresees the abuse of the freedom demanded, about whether the son has requested this freedom before the legal time for it had arrived. Indeed, the parable says nothing at all about justice or injustice, appropriate or inappropriate. Essentially the story characterizes the father as the one who gives away and places no emphasis on the point of the "giving", which is subsumed by the son's claiming "what he had coming to him".

Hunger compels the spendthrift to consider going home. We are told nothing about his state of mind as he makes up his mind and decides on the words he will use to greet his father. "How many of my father's hired men have plenty to eat while I starve to death here. I shall arise and go to my father and say to him, 'Father, I have sinned against heaven and before you; I am no longer worthy to be called your son—consider me as one of your hired hands.'" Is this cold calculation or heartfelt repentance? The text does not say; the context makes it difficult to exclude the motif of calculated self-interest. As far as the story is concerned, it makes no difference. To portray the actions of God the Father, it matters little how imperfect the sinner's repentance is as he makes his way home, having reached the end of his rope. The story's entire emphasis rests on the father, who is watching for the son, sees him coming from afar, runs toward him, hugs him, and kisses him. He listens to the culprit's memorized speech but does not take him up on it. Instead he immediately orders him outfitted in the finest clothes and announces a great feast to celebrate his return. We are surprised that the story wastes not a single word on the son's reaction to all this, especially after all the words devoted to describing his departure into the wide world. The son is simply draped with the cloak of fatherly love and disappears under it into the festivity, into "music and dancing" (15:25), into the contagious joy his father has commanded as an expression of his own exuberant rejoicing. There is nothing wrong with trying to imagine how this sort of reception must have moved the heart of the one who "was lost and is now found", but if one dwells on this theme, then it should be considered solely as an effect of the absolutely undeserved love of the father, a love that swallows up all kinds of calculating.

Although we cannot estimate how much "cold calculation" played a role in the younger son's thinking, it is very obvious in the older son: indeed, it dominates all his behavior. Already from a distance the sounds of the festive music arouse his suspicion, and he seeks out a servant to find out what is going on. Enraged by his father's apparent injustice, not only in not rewarding him for his steady service but also in showering kindness on someone who doesn't deserve it, his bitter reproach is the voice of unblinking justice. To him both sides of the equation seem equally unjust: that "that fellow" has been given the fattened calf while he, who "never disobeyed a single order", receives not so much as a young goat. The resentment has obviously been smoldering for a long time, but a spark—"Your brother was dead and is now alive"— kindles bright flames. The father's words can be understood only out of his love, not out of the oldest son's wrath: "You have always been here with me, and all I have is yours." The son who received no particular honor simply cannot accept this answer. For him justice is the greatest of all virtues; for the father, "mercy is completion of justice" (Thomas Aquinas, *Summa Theologiae*, I, qu. 21, art. 3, ad 2), and thus "compassion triumphs over judgment" (James 2:13). If the righteous brother had recognized the father's frame of mind, he would have realized that he was loved and favored even more than his younger brother because he shared not merely in some particular goods of the father but also in everything the father owns. God does not need to perform special feats for those who are faithful to him; the marvel is in the fact that we can be his children and that he withholds nothing that is his own from us. Miracles take place on the periphery, fetching back those who have run away, giving a hint to the alienated, celebrating those who have returned. The day-to-day life of faith needs no miracles, because sharing the Father's goods is marvelous enough. All we have to do is avoid distinguishing between mine and yours, for in the light of fatherly love both are one.

We are not told what impression the father's words made on the righteous son. Each of us must finish telling the tale.

35. "First He Sits Down"

Someone who wants to build a tower first sits down and calculates its cost to see if he can afford it. The king who wants to go to war with an army of ten thousand first sits down and considers whether his troops can adequately counter the foe who approaches with twenty thousand. Jesus draws the following conclusion from these examples: "Thus whoever of you does not renounce all he has cannot be my disciple" (Lk 14:28–33).

The capital that one needs to carry out the Christian construction project is the realization that one has no capital. In contrast, the king could win his war in a Christian manner, even against forces twice the strength of his own, if he follows Paul's instructions and fights with God's weapon against supernatural powers.

Thus the calculating we are required to carry out with all deliberate care has two aspects: negatively, considering whether we are prepared to renounce everything we have, and positively, considering whether we are ready to fight only with God's weapon, not with our own (which we must renounce). Both aspects involve a kind of courage that envelops one's whole existence—the courage to let everything go and thereby to trust "in the shelter of the Most High"; the courage to believe that one will be protected by God's faithfulness even if "a thousand fall at your side and ten thousand at your right hand" (Ps 91:1, 7).

Jesus' insistence that one must calmly consider all this seems strange. Can a person really calculate whether he is ready to renounce everything, whether he has courage enough to put all his hope in the shelter of the Most High? Yet, are not both of these already comprehended in simple baptismal faith, in the threefold "do you renounce . . . ?" Are you ready, when the chips are down, to put nothing ahead of faith, ahead of the obedience to God's will that is required of you?

Each believer can think that over for himself, and one need not seek in oneself the strength to withstand the hard test, for faith itself means trusting this power of God, and one can only do that if one is not holding on tightly to a piece of one's own power. What one must contribute from oneself is made easier by the days of "sitting down" and "reflecting" that we call "spiritual exercises". For the whole purpose of these is to gain practice in letting go of everything so that God can have charge of one's entire life. "Abandoning" does not mean letting go of everything externally and entering the desert or a Carthusian monastery; it simply means letting go, relaxing the fingers that are clenched around something so that it can be offered: "Take all my freedom, my memory, my understanding, my will" and give me in exchange "your grace and love—that is enough for me".

Whether undertaken by oneself or in a Spiritual Exercises retreat, this process has the precision of a real calculation, which requires leisure, inner peace, and distance from immediate concerns—a "sitting down". An approximation or a vague hope that everything will somehow find its own course will not do. Indeed, in this period of reflection one's entire existence, including the unforeseeable future, passes before one's eyes. It is necessary to include in the calculations what one cannot foresee, what one cannot survey. This is possible because it can be anticipated in faith, which unconditionally requires one's existence as a whole and thereby carries within it perfect trust in God's helping grace. *Pistis* (faith) means both "to hold to be true" and "to trust".

Therefore it makes no sense to try to imagine one's way into the most extreme situation and to ask oneself if one would then have the strength to endure. Indeed, Jesus expressly forbids this. In his discourse about the imminent tribulations of the Church, menacing assertions ("they will put you in prison; you will be betrayed by parents, brothers, and friends; they will kill many of you") constantly alternate with pledges of divine aid: "Do not be anxious about what you will say when on trial, for the words will be given to you, and no hair of your head shall be harmed" (Mt 10). When the worst comes, "lift up your heads, for your salvation approaches". If and when the ultimate test comes, then the ultimate help from God is assured (Lk 21:12–28).

Under these conditions established by God, the kind of calculating Jesus demands is possible and necessary to avoid being laughed at ("this man started to build but ran out of resources to finish" [Lk 14:30]). But, despite the impenetrability of the future, it presupposes the one thing that Jesus insisted on: "Whoever of you does not renounce all he has" and who is not determined to follow through with it "cannot be my disciple".

36. "The Peace of God That Surpasses All Understanding"

Peace was what the Lord left as his final gift to the disciples before his Passion and was the first gift he brought them in his Easter return from hell. In imitation of the Lord, Paul begins his letters by wishing the Christian communities peace, and in the letter to the Philippians he concludes by wishing them a peace that, because it belongs to God and is granted "in Christ Jesus", "surpasses all understanding", a peace that exceeds everything humanly thinkable and imaginable, a peace that exceeds everything attainable by human effort. Because of this, the peace that Paul desires for Christians cannot be measured psychologically, even though something of what belongs to God and is communicated by Christ from God rings out in Christian hearts. Still, it is an object of faith more than anything else. When Jesus wishes his disciples peace, their first reaction must be one of "incredulous" astonishment — after all, they abandoned him, even denied him during his Passion. They first have to accept in faith what he offers before it can turn into inner joy. The same is true of John's words that promise us "if our hearts judge us, God is greater than our hearts" (1 Jn 3:20) — it is not our uneasiness, not our bad conscience that offers the final standard for measuring peace or lack of peace; rather, peace is measured by God's "being greater".

Neither Paul nor John intends to tell us to live peacefully with our sins, because sin cannot be related in any way to God's peace. All of the Old and New Testaments would contradict such a dialectic or identity of peacelessness with God and peace from God. Instead Jesus and the apostles both promise and wish God's peace for us. God possesses peace, and he offers it to anyone who will accept it, even if such capacity to receive seems beyond comprehension. It is as if God offers unconditional peace terms to the man who has attacked him as an enemy — human acceptance of the terms would then seem to be a victory to human understanding and a fundamental defeat for God. Why does God make peace when we are still in a state of war? Because he is greater than my heart, because my rebellion against him does not extend to his peace just as the roiled-up surface waves cannot disturb the quiet depths of the ocean. Because all man's rebellious ingenuities cannot disturb God's plan to save. "Why do the nations rise up, and the peoples mutter vain things? He who is enthroned in the heavens laughs; the Lord has them in derision" (Ps 2:1–4) and responds by sending his Anointed One, to whom he "gives the nations as an inheritance" (Ps 2:8).

Making peace with the world costs God a lot, but he pays the price without letting it disturb his peace. His Son establishes God's peace in the world by killing hostility with his crucified body; he became "our peace" in that, by dying, he "tore down the wall of separation" erected against God (Eph 2:14–16). It is this work of peace that Jesus leaves behind for his Church, "my peace, . . . not as the world gives it" (Jn 13:27) and understands it. For his peace surpasses all understanding.

Thus Christians, if given the grace for it, can endure in imitation of Christ every sort of torture, even in the most extreme circumstances; indeed, following the example of the One abandoned by God on the Cross, they can enter into the night where no peace can be sensed at all in the soul because that peace is stored up with God for a time—it is, after all, in essence *his* peace. In God this peace is always complete and ultimate. "Not in the way that the world" understands treaties of peace: as temporary ceasefires, as a hot war transformed into a cold war, as inevitably a precarious wandering through an erupting, volcanic landscape, perhaps even as a "balance of terror".

Christian faith is never merely an assent to truth, to the truth that God has offered his peace. It is always essentially an acceptance and self-surrender that permits God's gift of peace to be true in our lives. It is out of this relationship of faith that Christians should demonstrate that they are "peacemakers" and thereby "children of God" in the world and for the world (Mt 5:9).

37. "No One Shall Snatch Them out Of My Hand"

Jesus says this about his sheep: "They hear my voice, I know them, and they follow me" (Jn 10:27). His assurance of eternal relationship is solemn and unconditional. Its inviolability rests on Jesus' mission: "It is the will of him who sent me that I should not permit one of those whom he has given me to perish" (Jn 6:9), a commission Jesus kept repeating to the end: "I have not lost one of those whom you gave me" (Jn 18:9). The entire Good Shepherd discourse, from which our text comes, is shaped by this certainty: the hired laborer may permit the sheep entrusted to him to perish, but the true shepherd willingly dies to save his flock. And this dying is an aspect of the inseparability of shepherd and flock. To prove this, Jesus refers everything back to the Father: "My Father, who gave me them, is greater than all, and no one can snatch them out of my Father's hand" (10:29). We encounter here the closed circuit of unassailable predestination: "All whom God foresaw he also predestined to be conformed to the image of his Son, and those whom he predestined he also called, and those whom he called he also justified, and those whom he justified he also glorified [in eternal life]" (Rom 8:29–30).

Thus we face the fearful problem of predestination. "My sheep"— but who belongs among his sheep? Certainly not simply the visible Church, which, according to Augustine, contains many sinners. And Jesus speaks of "other sheep" who belong to him even though they are not in his sheepfold. Yet the true sheep, wherever they may be, together constitute the community, the "real" Church that Augustine calls the "Dove", the "Immaculate" (Eph 5:27), the Church that is certainly predestined to belong to Paul's closed circuit, indeed, that is identical with that circle. Two facts make it clear that the "Dove" cannot simply be identified with the visible Church yet also has an inner relationship to her:

on the one hand, the life-giving sacraments can be misused and neglected, yet, on the other hand, someone who desires to participate in true life can receive the sacraments *in voto* (by desiring them) and thus can belong to the invisible Church of Christ.

Can an individual know with certainty that he belongs to the predestined "Dove"? Not if "certainty" is understood as a guarantee given to an individual. For Paul this is demonstrated by the central story of the Old Testament: "Our fathers were all under the cloud, they all passed through the sea, . . . they all were baptized into Moses, they all ate the same spiritual food and enjoyed the same spiritual drink. . . . Nevertheless, God was not pleased with most of them, and they were overthrown in the wilderness" (1 Cor 10:1–5). The promise to the people was actually carried out only for this "remnant". "This was written as a warning to us" (1 Cor 10:11). The letter to the Hebrews takes this warning to the limit: "If someone participated in the word of the Holy Spirit and tasted the goodness of God's word, yet fell away" (Heb 6:5–6), how can such a one be brought to repentance? Do we know whether we have so tasted of the grace of perseverance, the most crucial grace of all, that we have really grasped it?

Where a guaranteed certainty is denied, God offers something better: perseverance in trusting hope. If we had guaranteed certainty, we could not clutch onto trusting, saving hope. Indeed, God denies us the first so that we will choose the better. Trusting hope is precisely the thing that keeps us vigilant, and one has Christian hope only if one does not focus egotistically on one's own salvation but reaches out to include all brothers and sisters for whom the Good Shepherd died. And that is possible because we cannot draw any precise line between the Church of Jesus Christ and the "Dove". That is why the New Testament deliberately leaves open the possibility of being completely lost, which applies to me more than anyone else, while simultaneously holding wide open the possibility of hope for all. The two fit within a single thought: "Father, the hour has come. Glorify your Son, so that your Son can glorify you. You have given him power over all flesh so that he might give eternal life to all whom you have entrusted to him" (Jn 17:1–2).

38. The God of Patience

"May the God of patience and of comfort" grant to the Church these gifts, which "we already hope for through the patience and comfort of the Scriptures" (Rom 15:5, 4). Already in the Old Testament God granted a people who had waited for centuries something that belonged to himself. How patient he had to be with Israel! Often it seemed as if he could take no more and would have to lash out against them; but once Moses' offer of self-sacrifice shielded the people from God's wrath; on another occasion God seems to have remembered his own divineness as he abandoned the long-overdue judgment (Hos 11:9). The author of the book of Wisdom praises God's righteousness, glimpsing its summit in God's power to spare offenders: "Although you are sovereign in power, you judge with mercy and lead with great forbearance" (Wis 12:18). This takes place, as Paul knows, with a view toward the forgiveness accomplished by Christ: "This was to show God's righteousness, because in his divine forbearance he had passed over former sins; it was to prove at the present time that he himself is righteous" (Rom 3:25-26). This "passing over" is a "keeping to oneself" when anger would have been justified. It is an almost inappropriate patience, the same patience of which Paul spoke to the Gentiles in Athens, since "God has overlooked the times of ignorance" (Acts 17:30) because his view was fixed upon the coming Savior.

We must also mention the "patience of Christ" (2 Th 3:5), which was occasionally stretched to the utmost by human stupidity (Lk 9:41). Jesus' entire life, despite his longing for the final "baptism", was a perseverance in the transient—precluding nothing, wishing to know nothing in advance. He continues God's patience while taking up the human patience that must persist in mundane things within time. As an example we are given the farmer who has to let his seed grow without being able to accomplish anything (Mk 4:26ff.). "Be patient, brethren, . . . behold, the farmer waits for the precious fruit of the earth; he persists in patience until the crop receives the early and the late rains. So too you must persevere patiently" (James 5:7–8). Likewise, in one's heart, one can only "bear fruit in patience" (Lk 8:15). Christ's patience leads directly to that of his disciples. Both observe the same law: patience grows only when challenged by opposition. "Suffering produces endurance" (Rom 5:3), but this takes place by means of "keeping to oneself": "Self-control produces patience" (2 Pet 1:6). Thus patience is not simply the result of an inactive waiting but grows out of an active, dynamic perseverance. In the light of Jesus, "who endured from sinners such hostility against him", "we should run with patience the race set before us" (Heb 12:3, 1). The struggle is unavoidable: "Persevere, if you are disciplined" (Heb 12:7), "what you need is patience, so that you might do the will of God and win what is promised" (Heb 10:36). One might also speak of "steadfastness", so long as the word is understood to mean not "standing still" but steadiness in the dynamics of life.

Patience therefore frequently appears together with faith and hope (James 1:3; 1 Th 1:3; 2 Tim 3:10; Titus 2:2), making clear that this is no purely human power or accomplishment; rather, it is given by God. For it is by God "that you are equipped for all patience" (Col 1:14) and inspired to patience by Christ's example (1 Pet 2:20–21). God's patience can have many other names: it is closely related to his mercy and constant love. In this way our fundamental attitude as Christians, this enduring patience (of which Revelation speaks with particular pointedness: "Patience and toil" [2:2]; "patience and faith of the saints" [13:20; cf. 14:12]) leads directly to its divine model, and only in regard to that divine model can it be taken as a characteristic Christian attitude.

Thus it is not too much to ask of the Christian that he tuck a bit of patience with God into his faith and hope, since, for the time being, God does not reveal what we believe or give what we hope for. It is not too much to ask in view of how much patience God the Father has with us, in view of the lamblike patience of the Lamb of God. "By your endurance," he calls to us, "you will save your souls" (Lk 21:19).

39. "Not an Iota or a Dot of the Law Shall Perish"

Christ came not "to abolish the law or the prophets" but to "fulfill" them to the limit (Mt 5:17–18). Yet, if God's will is limitless in its purposefulness, does not the Old Testament law limit it in many ways, and does not Christ shatter precisely this limitedness when he reduces "the whole law and the prophets" to a love of God and neighbor (Mt 22:40) that transcends all boundaries? And does he not contradict himself when he follows up his words about completely fulfilling the law—down to the last crossed *t* and dotted *i,* as the Pharisees tried to do—by insisting: "Unless your righteousness exceeds by far that of the scribes and Pharisees, you shall not enter the Kingdom of heaven" (Mt 5:20)?

The Old and New Covenants contain a covenantal order established by God that permits people to become partners with God. Because people remain in their limitedness in their relationship to a limitless God, God's guidelines that make people "fit for the Covenant" must be limited insofar as they relate to people, even though, in regard to God, they are appropriate to his limitlessness. The structure of righteousness (laws) that is essential to the Covenant and is defined from the perspective of God's righteousness (*rectitudo*) cannot and dare not be eliminated in the New Covenant. It can only be "far surpassed" (Rom 8:37) if the Son fulfills it in the Spirit of God, who is limitless, and inserts this Spirit, this divine limitlessness, into human hearts. This transcending was not yet present in the Old Covenant but was promised with utter clarity: "I shall put my law within them and shall write it in their hearts. Then they will no longer need to instruct each other but will all know how to know me" (Jer 31:33–34). Thereby the slaves become, through Christ, free men, sons, and friends of God.

Still, those who have this Spirit of sonship calling, "Abba, Father", in their hearts remain limited creatures. The freedom they receive has to ripen into its full measure through "guidelines" that are fitted to them. Kant was certainly right to say, "One cannot mature into freedom if one has not first been set free" (*Religion within the Limits of Mere Reason,* IV, par. 4). But they can mature only if they have something toward which to mature—an order given by God. Outwardly this order remains the same, down to the individual "iota", but inwardly it has undergone a complete transformation through the Incarnation of the Son who fulfills the Father's will on earth. The divine order is now so thoroughly interpenetrated by limitless love that the Son, the perfect Mediator, the very essence of the Covenant order, is the structured, active relation between God and men through which the liberated man can mature into complete covenantal freedom. One could put it in another way: by keeping the entire law and the prophets and thus making the limitless divine love transparent, Jesus has transformed the laws into forms of the Holy Spirit through which the Spirit as both "form" and "institution", as "order" and "legal standard", inwardly trains and shapes the freedom of the children of God into trinitarian love.

People set free by the grace of justification can have only one ideal of freedom before them: the absolute, divine freedom. Yet this divine freedom can offer participation in its "rightly ordered-ness" only through a covenantal order. Thus a call to freedom can never mean a license to indulge in human libertinism (Gal 5:13); rather, it places one in the free "obedience that leads to righteousness" (Rom 6:16), in the "law of the Spirit and of life in Christ Jesus" (Rom 8:2). This law—even as order, law, and institution—is a "gift of God, as eternal life in Christ Jesus our Lord" (Rom 6:23).

To bring about this inward transformation of the law, it was necessary that Jesus our High Priest endure the full, unyielding, divine absoluteness of the law for a people alienated from God. It was this inexorable pitilessness of the law that had doomed the sinner, because he despaired in the face of the apparent impossibility of fulfilling the law and gave himself over to sin all the more, until "everything was consigned to sin" (Gal 3:22). Jesus' task was to endure all of mankind's opposition to the law in order to bring a lost world to the point of encounter with God through his obedience to what was apparently impossible to fulfill ("to drink this cup"). In complete freedom Jesus did this apparently impossible servant-work for God and man. When Jesus lets us participate in his freedom, the law may appear to us to be tedious to the point of impossibility, even though it has been transformed in all its details into the pathways of love. What are now in themselves channels of love may still appear to us as expressions of "you must" rather than "you may". Although their entire meaning aims at freedom, they still seem like fetters to us. Although it is a great gift to be invited to the Lord's table, our obligatory weekly churchgoing seems burdensome to us. And so it is with all that the law contains, for its essence must be fulfilled up to the most minute detail.

40. The Cleansing of the Temple

It may surprise us that Jesus, meek and mild at heart, here with whip in hand drives out "the sellers of cattle, sheep, and doves" from the courtyard of the temple and "dumps out the money-changers' coins and overturns their tables" (Jn 2:14–15). "Don't make my Father's house into a marketplace." Was not all of the commerce necessary if the customary temple worship with its prescribed animal sacrifices and the temple tax paid in proper coinage was to run its course? When he was asked where he got his authority, Jesus replied by pointing to his body, the true temple that would be torn down and rebuilt in three days. In other words, he replied with a hint of what the future would bring, with something no one could have understood at the time.

The whip sweeps clean all the way to the foundation upon which so many doubtful and ambiguous things have been constructed. How many features built into the simple Covenant with Abraham and with Israel were not in the blueprints, but were wrested from God as concessions? The prophets knew full well that there had been no talk of sacrifices in the beginning: "Did you bring me offerings and sacrifices during the forty years in the wilderness? I hate and I despise your feasts; they nauseate me; I cannot stand to look at your fattened sacrificial beasts" (Amos 5:21ff.). "They love to sacrifice—when they can 'eat' of it" (Hos 8:13). "What do I care about your countless sacrifices? I have had my fill of the fat of fatted calves; the blood of bulls and rams makes me sick. . . . Your new moons and festivals have become a burden to me; I am tired of putting up with them" (Is 1:11, 14). The "priestly document" portion of the Pentateuch anachronistically inserted the entire system of sacrifices into the story of the wanderings in the wilderness one thousand years earlier. The great penitential Psalm makes this obvious: "If I were to offer you burnt offerings, you would not accept them"; what you desire is the sacrifice of a broken and contrite heart (Ps 51:18–19 [16–17]). But then someone who knew better comes along and adds the concluding verse, which makes God once more pleased to find sacrificial animals on the altar (vv. 20–21 [18–19]).

Was even a temple in the original plan, or did the longing for one develop out of a desire to keep pace with the Egyptians, Babylonians, and Canaanites? In Nathan's prophecy God rejects David's plans to build a temple: God himself will build the king a house, for the Messiah will originate from among his descendants (2 Sam 7). But here again someone who knew better has added verse 13, which lets us know that David's son Solomon will build this house as a temple.

One must even raise questions about the entire Davidic kingdom with all the promises made to it. In 1 Samuel, chapter eight, we find the story of the people's struggle with God over its establishment—God laments that the desired kingdom would displace him as the true king of Israel (8:7); when God gives in to the people's pressure, he does so with a scornfully superior preview of all the evils that will follow from the monarchy (8:10–18).

Finally, Jesus himself relentlessly portrays the degree to which the garden God planted has become overgrown with the weeds of "traditions" contrary to the Covenant: "How exquisitely you set aside the commandment of God to make room for your 'tradition' to hold sway" (Mk 7:9).

How much of the Judaism that Jesus encountered is ideological superstructure that must be carted away if the original "house of my Father" is to be excavated from the rubble that covers it? The prophets made great efforts in this regard, but instead of paying heed to them, the people murdered them, either in mind or body (Mt 21:33ff.), and Jesus understood that the same thing would happen to him. He can assert that no stone of the temple will remain on top of another with a calmness that implies it has already taken place (Lk 21:6); the event that decisively concerns him is the destruction of the true temple, his body (Jn 2:21). First, however, this "cleansing of the temple" must take place in order to create the situation in which "true worshipers will worship the Father in spirit and in truth" (Jn 4:23). For Jesus that hour has already arrived.

Then all the ambiguous overpainting of God's Covenant will

be dissolved away, and the image originally intended by the Father will shine forth again. Then the temple clergy will make way for the single "High Priest in eternity", the kingdom Israel coerced God into granting will make way for the true "King of the Jews": "Yes, I am a king", but "my Kingdom is not of this world" (Jn 18:37, 36). And then the true law, as God intended it and promulgated it, will have been fulfilled to the last iota, filled to overflowing. If the one swinging the whip is "consumed" by "zeal for your house [the Father's house]" (Jn 2:17), this refers only superficially to the Herodian temple and much more profoundly to the "temple of Jesus' body", the true dwelling place of the Father and the Holy Spirit. Therefore, it also refers in a profound way to that body of Christ that, on the basis of his Eucharist, is the Church, for the Church also requires the lash of constant reformation (*Ecclesia semper reformanda*).

41. "To Eat This Passover Meal with You"

Jesus' "great yearning" (Lk 22:15) is directed toward the common meal that differs from all earlier common meals because he offers himself in flesh and blood. But the accent clearly lies less on this unheard-of innovation and more on the "with you". The uniqueness that distinguishes this meal from all others includes within it the "with". It was already incorporated when he ate "with tax collectors and sinners". Table fellowship characterized him from the beginning (Mt 11:19: "A glutton and a drunkard, a friend of tax collectors and sinners"). Yet in the multiplication of the loaves, which represents a foretaste of his Eucharist, the "with" is missing. We hear only of the distribution of the bread; its reception is not emphasized.

Here at the Last Supper the taking receives as much emphasis as the prayer, although no relationship between the two is apparent. On the one side we have an extravagant, seemingly "wasteful" self-sacrifice; on the other, a receiving totally out of proportion with what is received. Yet the meal has no meaning for Jesus apart from such contrasts. In being eaten and drunk he somehow receives an equal gift from them. To him communicating himself means commonality with him. It is as if his reverent prayer of thanks goes out not only to the Father, who permits him such an exorbitant self-sacrifice, but also to those who receive him, who open their doors to him and invite him in to dinner. What odd words of humility are found in the book of Revelation: "Behold, I stand at the door and knock; if anyone hears my voice and opens the door, I shall come in to him and dine with him and he with me" (Rev 3:20). "I shall dine with him" initially means, "I sit down at the table he has prepared"—only then does the guest reveal himself as the real host.

This is confirmed by the meals that took place after the

Resurrection. The disciples heading for Emmaus invite the unknown traveler in to share their table fellowship, and only at the blessing of the bread do they recognize in the stranger their incomparable host. He asks the eleven to offer him a bit of their food ("Do you have anything to eat on hand?") in order thereby to give them the Easter joy of his presence. He directs the same question to the seven men in Peter's boat: "Children, have you anything to eat?" Only then does he give them something—a miraculous catch of fish, and, even after they drag the bulging net to shore and catch sight of the breakfast that is ready to eat, he still will not play the host's role alone but asks them to give again: "Bring some of the fish you just caught over here" (Jn 21:10).

The Eucharist can be celebrated in only one way: "I with you and you with me". As astonishing as it may sound, the one who imparts endlessly more than anyone can take up ("twelve baskets" of uneaten food were left over) receives a gift from those who receive him. As they receive him, he receives them. He receives them not merely as additional members in his "mystical body" but also as those who participate in the innermost mystery of his being. "To all those who received him, to them he gave the power to become children of God." These children no longer have a physical origin as separate individuals born of an earthly conception but are now, together with him, "born of God the Father" (Jn 1:13). Even the words *brother* and *sister* are pale metaphors drawn from earthly relationships that fall far short of describing this ineffable "with". One realizes this because he "pours out" his own spirit of Sonship into our hearts or "breathes into us" the Spirit who in us cries out his (and now our) "Abba, Father".

42. "SATAN HAS DEMANDED YOU, THAT HE MIGHT SIFT YOU"

Jesus' words to Simon Peter reveal to him and all the disciples present Peter's perilous situation (the word *you* is in the plural in the Greek text of Lk 22:31). "You" who wish to follow me, you who thereby will find yourselves exposed to as much danger as I am. These words were spoken on the eve of his Passion. But if Jesus is exposed in the fullest sense in his suffering, the emerging Church is sustained by him: "I have prayed for you, that your faith may not falter" (Lk 22:32). He prays for the Church and for Peter, responsible for her at her head: "And you [singular], when you have turned again, strengthen your brethren" (22:32).

The Church's enduring life, suspended between Satan's demand and Christ's prayer, the Church in her entirety—in her institutionality as well as her existence—is not unassailable. Satan insists on sifting her institutionally and in all other ways. In the book of Job Satan received permission to toss Job in his sieve until all the chaff was blown away to see whether any real wheat remained. Likewise in the present instance, Satan's demand is not rejected out of hand. In the first place, sifting is the same activity as that undertaken by the Messiah: "He has his winnowing fork in his hand and sweeps out his threshing floor; he will gather his grain into his granary but will burn up the chaff in unquenchable fire" (Mt 3:12). Statements to the effect that Jesus has come to test and discern all the way to the bone's marrow abound. One might say that his appearing on the scene "to baptize with the Spirit and with fire" (Mt 3:11) made hell hungry again for its own portion. Yet against the aspect of judgment that is essential in his appearance, he throws all the counterweight of his prayer into the "breach" (see Ps 106:23): "I consecrate, sanctify, sacrifice myself for them" (Jn 17:19). Satan's desire to sift cannot simply be brushed off, for it is too closely connected to Jesus' own messianic mission. But Jesus undercuts Satan's claim with the intercessory character of his Passion, with which he sweeps away in advance the chaff of Peter's self-confidence ("I'll follow you in prison and in death"). He gives Peter a glimpse of his denial of his Lord, a denial already buried in his overweening certainty. Peter is permitted to know that a bit of wheat will remain after the sieve has stopped shaking, but it will survive only as the pure gift of his praying Lord and as a simple responsibility: to strengthen his brethren.

Ecclesial office must never lay claim to any other certainty than that which is revealed by this dramatic turn of events, and ecclesial office must never separate the event from the context in which it occurred. The disciples must never exercise the Easter authority the Lord gave them to bind and loose without recalling that he suffered for it while they failed him in their fearful cowardice. Peter dare never forget that his infallibility rests on the Lord's Gethsemane prayer, a prayer prayed while Peter slept, only to deny Jesus later with curses. Peter has the promise, together with the Church, and he is forbidden to doubt it. The swaying rope bridge over which he must lead the Church across the abyss of the centuries will not come crashing down. But what keeps it intact is not something tangible in this world but is rather the intangible, seemingly fragile, prayer of a Lord who consecrates himself to this work.

The authority to govern that Peter and his brethren receive cannot be compared with the world's power because it rests on the absolute powerlessness of the One who in his total dedication cannot be anything but a winnowing, separating judgment on the world. When Peter advises him to avoid the suffering headed his way, he is shown to be a Satan and abruptly dismissed (Mt 16:23), for it is only through fully enduring his suffering separation from his Father that the satanic winnowing perpetrated by evil on the Church can be undercut and fended off. But the Church must do her part: "Strengthen your brethren."

43. "As I Hear, I Judge"

These words (Jn 5:30) lead directly to the heart of Jesus' being—which is incomprehensible to us. The discourse in which these words are found seems to contain an obvious contradiction. On the one hand, he insists he can do nothing on his own but only that which he sees the Father doing—only because the Father reveals all things to him can he, the Son, do anything (5:19–20). On the other hand, he emphasizes that the Father has turned over to him all judgment so that everyone will honor him no less than the Father. Moreover, this handing over is no mere temporary loan; rather, it is his own possession: "As the Father has life in himself, so he has granted the Son also to have life in himself" and thereby also "authority to execute judgment" (5:26–27).

The decisive point lies in the phrase "granted . . . to have in himself". Is this "to have in himself" a real transferral in which the thing given is separated from the giver, or is the thing given so bound up with the "givenness" that the "in himself" remains dependent on the act of giving? The second possibility appears to fit closely all the utterances of Jesus that are equivalent to the first: I can judge only as the Father grants me to judge. "He testifies to what he has seen and heard [while with the Father]" (3:32). "I declare to the world what I have heard from him" (8:26). "I do nothing on my own; rather, I speak what the Father taught me" (8:28). "I have said nothing on my own [authority]; rather, the Father who sent me has commanded what I should say and proclaim. . . . What I say, therefore, I say as the Father said it to me" (12:49–50). Pure dependence, it would seem. What has happened to the "on my own"? It is there. "Even if I do testify to myself, my testimony is true, for I know whence I have come and whither I am going" (8:14) sheds a little light: the "about myself" involves a "from somewhere" and a "to somewhere". In the lines that follow it becomes clear that this knowledge about his origin and destination has two aspects. One is that he is sent from the

Father, that the sender really lets the sent one go. The other is the Father's own assertion, in the sending itself, of the credibility of the one sent and of his mission: "I testify for myself, and the Father, who sent me, testifies for me" (8:18).

It is thus impossible to play off the Son's dependence on the Father against his independence, since the "self-identity" of the Son consists precisely in his being the Word of the Father, yet a Word that, as he himself says, has life as completely as does the Father (5:26). It becomes clear that Jesus is speaking these words just as much from his divine as from his human awareness. His divine independence extends so far that he can say, "As the Father raises the dead, . . . so the Son gives life to whom he will" (5:21). He can announce his own will to his Father: "Father, I desire that those you have given me may be where I am" (17:24). But then why must he listen to the Father precisely when carrying out the judgment handed over to him by the Father? Because he received all of his divine freedom from the Father. A relinquishing is contained in the Father's handing over: "The Father judges no one but has given all judgment to the Son" (5:22). The Father's relinquishing is a central part of his sending of the Son, "for God has sent his Son into the world not to judge the world but that the world might be saved through him" (3:17). But does the Son really judge if the Father judges not? He seems to be contradicting himself. "I judge no one, but even if I judge, my judgment is true." Why? "For I am not alone; rather, the Father who has sent me is with me" (8:16). Now if the Son is concerned not about judgment but about saving (12:47), who does the judging? It is the unaccepted word of salvation, it is the man who remains in darkness by refusing to let the light shine in him, who judges (3:19–20). Those who receive the word of grace come forth to the resurrection of life; those who have refused it, "come forth to the resurrection of judgment" (5:29). The love of God can be merciful but cannot be unjust.

The mystery of the Son and his continually received independence owed to the Father is the model for the mystery of the graced creature who has been given the liberty of the children of God with no strings attached, yet whose liberty is full of giftedness, of having been given. When the child of God obeys the breathing of the Holy Spirit in his heart, he does not thereby become dependent but rather becomes freer than he would have been if left to himself. For what he catches hold of in his obedient listening is eternal freedom.

44. THE GLORY THAT COMES FROM THE ONLY GOD

How thin the line between true and false, belief and unbelief, Christ and Antichrist! Jesus comes in the name of the Father, and his sole concern is the Father's glory (Jn 5:43–44). He does not speak on his own authority, for "he who speaks on his own authority seeks his own glory" (7:18). Yet does not a man who speaks of God—a prophet, for example—necessarily speak from his innermost, existential self as he puts his whole self on the line? Is that seeking one's own glory? What if he feels inspired to speak in the name of God? Jeremiah clearly distinguishes between "dream" (which all ancient peoples understood as a divine inspiration) and "word". Yet the prophets who "tell their dreams to each other think to make my people forget my name. . . . Let the prophet who has a dream tell the dream, but let him who has my word speak my word faithfully" (Jer 23:28). How can the two be distinguished? God continues: "What does straw have in common with wheat? Does not my word burn like fire, and is it not like a hammer that crushes rocks?" (23:28–29).

Thus there are two kinds of fire. The one flashes forth from the midst of the proclaimer and captivates the hearer: "Glory" (*doxa*) or "honor" streams from the center of his person. He hammers away forcefully but is also hammered by the word he proclaims. Isaiah is one of those crushed by its blows, but so is Moses, and so also Abraham. Finally, so is Jesus, who has come in his Father's name and is consumed by zeal for God's house (Ps 69:9 = Jn 2:17)—the Psalm continues: "The insults of those who insult you have fallen on me." Thus the testimony of the Baptist proves worthy of belief (Jn 5:32) in the same way that the witness of Moses (5:45–46) and the prophets sent from God proves authentic (Mt 23:37). Jesus adds himself to their number (Lk 13:33).

"How can you have faith if you accept glory from each other?"

(Jn 5:44). That people do this is so natural that no one would consider it a fault. One judges another according to the import of his person (*kabod, doxa,* glory originally meant "weight"). For this reason no prophet is honored as such "in his hometown, by his relatives, and in his own household" (Mk 6:4) — because his weight, his import, was evaluated there from the start. If he claims to have received a different import from God, he is "scorned" (6:4) and dismissed angrily (Lk 4:28). Throughout the Gospels we find people trying to reduce Jesus' claim to be merely the Father's messenger to an authority measurable by human means. Jesus calls this reductionism "unbelief" (Jn 5:44) and prescribes a single antidote: "Whoever does the will of him who sent me will know intimately whether my teaching comes from God or whether I speak on my own authority" (Jn 7:17). One must place oneself, together with the other mouthpieces for God, under the hammer that shatters rocks, that ultimately shatters the rock of my resistance to the sole glory of God. "Whoever seeks the gravity [*doxa*] of the one who sent him, he is true, and there is nothing false in him" (7:18). He does not radiate the glory of his own center; rather, he has made this core transparent so that it can radiate a more profound glory. Taking this to heart leads one further into the attitude of faith. But it demands a renunciation of the general human criteria for what is valid or invalid, what is interesting and important or uninteresting and superficial. This renunciation must be an active doing — entrusting oneself in faith to God's challenging criterion as it shines through the witness.

Whoever refuses to do that can only aim at one thing: to rid the world of the prophet and his challenge, a challenge the human spirit finds so insufferable. That is why Jesus could add, for no apparent reason, to his statement about true transparency for the glory of God, "Why do you seek to kill me?" (Jn 7:19). One cannot say that he himself swings the crushing hammer of God — since he lets the word of the Father shine through him, he can call himself "gentle and lowly of heart" (Mt 11:29). But because the full force of the Father's love does not reach those who ought to honor it, it comes down hard on the proclaimer himself and smashes him. Outwardly it is the Jews who seek to take his life, and they succeed in killing him, but inwardly it is the Father who permits the crushing of his Son in the place of the hard-hearted.

45. "He Did Not Speak to Them except in Parables"

That Jesus spoke exclusively in parables (Mk 4:34) indicates that he wanted the one focal point of the parable to stimulate his listeners to seek a second focal point lying infinitely beyond the parable. Unlike hyperbole, the second focus cannot be estimated from the first; rather, seeking it requires one to take off into the incomprehensible. Discourse in parables invites one to take this flight. It is not an audacious invitation, because the focal point of origin fuels the confidence of someone willing to take a risk. This seems to be the Gospel writer's point when he justifies Jesus' parables with a word from the prophet: "I will open my mouth in parables; I will utter what has been hidden since the foundation of the world" (Mt 13:35). Of course, if the listeners lack trusting courage, if they can respond only with a blank stare to the proffered glimpse without longing to see the full vision on which it is modeled, then the parable's window on insight has been opened in vain, and the parable has been presented in vain—eyes that should have seen remain closed; ears that should have heard are hard of hearing (Mt 13:14–15).

Now the disciples, of course, begged Jesus to explain his parables to them, and the Gospels give occasional examples of his expositions. But what do they offer? Do they hold out the second, infinite focus? Or do they merely illuminate thoroughly the first point so that the takeoff into the second one can be attempted more courageously? The second point is, as Jesus says, the "Kingdom of God", and he can well say of it that it has "come nigh", that it "stands on the threshold", indeed, that it has crossed the threshold and is truly present in the room, that it has "come" (Mt 12:28), even if having come it stands "unknown among you" (Jn 1:26). Yet at the same time he warns, "If anyone says to you, 'Behold, it is there, look here!' don't go" (Lk 17:23). "Many will come in my name and say, 'I am he!' and, 'The time is at hand!' but do not run after them." For the Kingdom to which I continually am pointing, the Kingdom which I call on you to seek, cannot be reached through worldly means, cannot be grasped "definitively" (Lk 21:8; 17:20). It much more resembles Paul's imagery: launched out into an orbit toward infinity, he runs after the goal, knowing that he has not reached it but has been reached by it (Phil 2:12–13).

The crucial characteristic of Jesus' parables is that they take off from the most common, most mundane, most thoroughly familiar points imaginable rather than from something mysterious that must be mastered like a crossword puzzle. No such puzzles confront us at all; instead, a coin or a sheep has been lost, or one wonders from whence come weeds that one never planted, or one simply has to wait until the seed ripens over the summer into harvest, or one is offered an image of a plain loaf of bread made from flour and yeast. Every gardener knows that the size of the seed does not measure up to the bush that grows from it.

And so Jesus begins, "To what can we compare the Kingdom of God?" (Mk 4:30). It is as if he is searching for a suitable image that points effectively enough to the hidden truth that really matters to him. When he chooses to use something mundane and familiar for that purpose, why should it inspire a comparison? Because the familiar itself carries something unfamiliar and marvelous within it, perhaps scattered around like the treasure in the field. Is not the piece of bread that we are able to produce and that keeps us alive something of a hidden marvel? What about grain's growth, a process we cannot actually see but that goes on whether we are awake or asleep? And what of the recovery of something that was lost, which reminds me that I need this estranged thing in order to be fulfilled and happy? One must discover, must uncover, the hidden wonder of existence itself, something that simply cannot be taken for granted, in order to move from this wonderment to the Wonder of it all. All of the natural and taken-for-granted things on which Jesus draws are far more marvelous than the total of all humanly produced technical marvels. The lilies of the field are more marvelous than all of Solomon's splendor.

Among these wonders is human language, which can communicate profound ideas in audible sounds. All language is itself parable.

All of God's discourse in human sounds must be nothing other than parable in which God communicates the incomprehensible and divine by means of comprehensible concepts. At the end of his life the disciples say to Jesus, "Behold, now you are talking plain talk [*en parrhesia*] instead of parables" (Jn 16:29). They are taking hold of Jesus' prediction: "These things I said in parables to you; the time will come when I shall no longer speak in parables but shall tell you plainly of the Father" (Jn 16:25). But they are in too great a hurry. Immediately after they say this, Jesus tells them that they will flee from him during his Passion. Yet, after the Resurrection, when the Church has received the Holy Spirit, she is granted a secret, wordless knowledge of the parables' infinite focus beyond all earthly language: "You have the anointing of the Holy One and all of you know. I have not written to you because you do not know the truth but rather because you know it" (1 Jn 2:20–21). "We have received the Spirit that is from God so that we may thereby realize what has been given to us from God" (1 Cor 2:12), even if "still by faith, not by sight" (2 Cor 5:7).

46. "My Soul Magnifies the Lord"

That Mary begins her song of thanks to the Lord (Lk 1:46–55) with four verses that speak of herself and of God's relationship to her shows that she is not just any young woman among her people, but that she is the original chosen and unique one. God's "look of favor upon the lowliness of his servant" is not merely a search that eventually leads him to choose one among many; rather, it is an eternal gaze that precedes all her historical predecessors, something to which we shall return. Although at the end of her song "Abraham and his seed" are mentioned, an original gospel precedes even the election of the chosen people. This primordial good news is found in God's words to the serpent announcing the enmity between the serpent and the woman that would last through all time, despite the fact that shortly thereafter Eve is sentenced to be a lowly servant of her man ("your desire shall be for your husband; he shall rule over you" [Gen 3:15–16]). Yet God sees not this lowliness resulting from the fall but rather the lowliness of the creature who, as a creature, owes him awe and worship. To the creature, God's gaze always means mercy (Lk 1:50). The one who receives God's grace at the Annunciation has now become the woman promised at the beginning, which is why she exults to God in her uniqueness, fully aware in her humility of her incomparability: "All generations will call me blessed." As a servant girl (*Magd*) she has the courage to serve by standing vulnerably and alone before all generations as God introduces her as the uniquely chosen one. A sinner's humility prefers to keep itself hidden; Mary's humility beyond sin permits her to place herself on the lamp stand so that she might illuminate everyone in the house. She permits all generations to call her blessed because all that can be seen of her is the "great thing" that the "Mighty One" "has done" to her. "His name is holy", she says, and she gives not the slightest thought to the fact that this holiness of God could shine on her. She does not adorn or embellish herself—when the "heavenly Jerusalem descends from heaven", it is "adorned" by God alone (Rev 21:2). It does not come from itself but "from God"; it "possesses" not its own glory but "the glory of God" (Rev 21:10–11).

Mary has no thought of confining within her person this great thing that the Mighty One has done in her, for that would limit its divine proportions. Instead, she permits this great thing, which is essentially God's "mercy", to flow from "generation to generation", as far as it finds acceptance among those who fear God (Lk 1:50). She draws no line of demarcation between her uniqueness and the numberless generations. By not doing so she enters into communion with all these generations within the encompassing mercy of God, enters into an inward communion of destiny. It is a calamitous destiny, one from which she does not hold herself aloof.

Precisely because she is the only one who knows no confining egoism, she is able to enter into solidarity with all. The authentic faith of many of Abraham's children finds its place not beside but inside her faith, but so too does the dark side of Israel's story—her maternal soul has a place for Israel's alienation and aggravating aversion from God. She is the maid, and Israel is the hired hand; "God has taken notice of Israel, his servant", with the same "mercy" with which he looked upon his lowly maid. Even less can or does she want to distinguish between the two sides since she knows that she carries "God, her Savior", within her, the One who will be the true Servant of God adequate for all. She senses that in this One "the mighty will be put down from their thrones, and those of low degree will be exalted"—it is almost as if she heard in advance Jesus' words, "He who exalts himself will be brought low; he who humbles himself will be exalted" (Mt 23:12). God sends the rich away empty, like the wealthy grain farmer who loses everything overnight and the spiritually wealthy Pharisee who returns home from the temple devoid of grace. The hungry, however, will be filled with goods, as the multiplication of loaves in the wilderness would show. All of this is both past ("as he has spoken to our fathers") and future at the same time. For Mary, who carries the Lord within her, both are brought together in the present, in a present that encompasses all time within it and thereby transcends all time, a present that never passes away: *in aeternum* (Lk 1:55).

Earthly future—in which the haughty remain mighty and the God-fearing remain humble—is also caught up in the eternity that she carries within her and out of which her spirit rejoices to God her Savior. The future is already past, and the rule of God and of the Child she has in common with God is already established even in mankind.

47. "HE WAS OBEDIENT TO THEM"

We are told that Jesus was obedient to his parents (Lk 2:51) immediately after the story of his apparent disobedience when he stayed behind in the temple without their knowledge. Yet even that is explained as an act of obedience: "I *must* be in my Father's house" (2:49). How do these two seemingly irreconcilable forms of obedience relate to each other? Briefly put, one might note that the law, which contains the Fourth Commandment, is a law given by God. Thus the child who obeys his parents thereby obeys God. Situations can arise in which the urgency of obeying God directly supersedes the obedience mediated by the law: one must obey God more than men (see Acts 4:19), or, as Joan of Arc put it, *Dieu premier servi* ("serve God first"). God is the Lord of all the commandments on the second table of the Mosaic law, and he can suspend these restrictions—which he himself established—when he desires such a suspension for the sake of service to himself. Wherever that does not happen, the natural and Divine Covenant of law envisions that the obedience owed to God can and must be fulfilled through the intermediate institutions that represent him: the family, the state, consecrated religious life. Jesus himself submitted to this law of an apparent dual obedience—in such instances and for as long as the Father envisioned it. The course and outcome of this incident from his life as a twelve-year-old indicate the legitimacy of both direct and indirect obedience.

In Jesus' case there is a unique aspect to this general interrelationship. His relationship to his Father was from the beginning without parallel. One cannot, as one grows up, suddenly discover that one is the eternal Son of the Father, that one is, in fact, God. An implicit awareness of his Sonship was present and continually expressing itself more profoundly in his humanness as he grew older—as he "grew in age", he also "grew in wisdom and grace (*charis*)" (Lk 2:40, 52). *Wisdom* here indicates the wisdom of God, while *grace* indicates the inner presence of the Father's incomparable loving good pleasure toward him. Participating in the divine wisdom, he begins to understand from within and from above all the external divine guidelines that Israel encountered. Specifically, this meant that he, the eternal and now incarnate Son, was the destination toward which all these rules aimed and the destination in whom they were inwardly and personally to be fulfilled. As a child, when he learned the commandments of the law and the prayers of the Psalms, he learned them not as outer material to be encountered and mastered but as the expression, the outflowing into language, of the unique, immense, and gracious will of God that had always rested on him and in him, the will of God he had always known within himself as the wisdom and grace of the Father.

These two aspects are equally and inseparably true: the wise command of God rested in original fulfillment in him—the Son of God—already before it was expounded in the "Ten Words", yet in becoming man as one Israelite among many he saw the will of God as something facing him and requiring implementation. He really learned what he already knew in a deeper yet veiled way, and in his learning what lay within him already fulfilled unfolded itself, revealing the summit of divine wisdom that indeed surpasses all the individual commandments. He himself is this summit—he and no one else. Even Mary does not yet comprehend the words of her twelve-year-old.

Yet the individual does not disappear into the whole. The Fourth Commandment is still present and must be kept. For that reason "he was obedient". For that reason he required the same of those who followed him—that they obey the entire law down to the last dotted *i* and crossed *t* but that they obey in an attitude that far surpasses the Covenant faithfulness of the scribes and Pharisees (Mt 5:17–20). When a disciple then advances from the attitude of a servant to that of a child and friend, the entire external variety of the law most fittingly resolves itself into a single attitude: "Whoever loves has fulfilled the law" (Rom 13:8). Yet whoever loves also remains "obliged to love", and the growing child Jesus is increasingly and concretely aware that he will owe this obligation to the uttermost extreme. This awareness is inseparable from the "wisdom" and "grace" that the Father manifests to him, the wisdom and grace that enclose this unique law-transcending obligation.

It is not so important, however, that this man maturing in his mission should recognize in advance exactly what he must pay to satisfy his obligation of love. He does not want to know in advance, and he sets out no personal plans—the Father takes care of all of that. Like a man he permits the Father's will to advance toward him from the future. Meanwhile he obeys Mary and Joseph and is apprenticed in an ordinary trade. He is an Israelite, and it is part of his maturation process that the fate of Israel occupies first place in his heart—to assemble the straying flock, to lead the lost sheep back to the center of the Covenant. Yet from the very beginning he knows in the far reaches of his consciousness that Israel does not exist for herself but rather for all of mankind—ever since Abraham, and, with special clarity, since the Servant of God arrived. Thus he forecloses nothing; rather, he permits the dimensions of his mission to expand into boundlessness. The Father will see to it that what is necessarily fenced in by human limits receives the breadth found in his eternal wisdom and grace.

48. The First Provocation

Mark tells the story (Mk 6:1–6); Luke adds some details later (4:14–30). Jesus is teaching in the synagogue in his hometown. Both Gospel writers describe the shift from marveling to astonishment to rejection. Initially the approving applause is spontaneous. Then, hard on its heels, comes a moment of reflection: "Where does he get that?" We know him, we know his parents, his relatives live among us, he is one of us, and thus we can put our finger on the contours of his intellectual equipment—which he has clearly surpassed in this talk. He undermines long years of proven experience; he dismantles the categories he has occupied for decades.

Luke heightens the paradox by having Jesus open the Scriptures to a messianic passage from Isaiah and read it, applying it to his own person: "Today this Scripture is fulfilled." Even this application gains him applause, obviously on the basis of the "words of grace" of a speech undeniably inspired by God and marking him as prophetically endowed. The people cannot help but be astounded, yet at the same time they are alienated. So they insist on a proof that would make the incomprehensible easier to accept: Isaiah spoke of miraculous healings, and rumors have been making the rounds that you did something of that sort in Capernaum—therefore, why don't you show us what you can do (Lk 4:23)?

At this point both Gospel writers employ the same phrase: "Nowhere does a prophet enjoy less respect than in his home city, among his kin, in his own house." Familiar assessments are too well entrenched, and obvious signs of a divine calling are missing. How many called to the priesthood and to the religious life must experience this same thing, even if the wounds eventually heal after a time of rupture and rejection. Yet the examples Jesus offers—of Gentiles healed in foreign lands through prophets from Israel—indicate that sometimes the wounds never heal.

One might ask why Jesus has to begin with such an undiplomatic provocation. The answer is that genuine calls from God permit no gradual transition. He himself announced this when people who wanted to follow him tried to construct such transition stages: let me at least say good-bye to the folks at home, especially since my father has just died. Jesus' reaction to this request is harsher than anything else in the Scriptures, for it not only contradicts all custom but also runs in the face of what is specifically required in the law. He says, "Let the dead bury their dead" (Mt 8:22). The words ring out from one graced with divine authority, echoing from an incomparable summit towering over all the law's contents.

When life-changing vocations are involved, any mitigating mediation invariably disappears. Yet Jesus uses words of the same level of intensity to reply to his relatives and his Mother when they came to fetch him home. Put in Paul's words, at stake here are a dying and a rising as a new man—something that has no transitional stages. Neither is any gradation to be found in the parable of the grain of wheat that falls into the ground and dies in order to rise again like Christ as ripe grain. In this light the image of daily cross-bearing carries a christological rather than an ethical meaning. Likewise his insistence that one must hate one's "father and mother, wife and child, brother and sister, and oneself" for the sake of following him (Lk 14:26) and his words about losing one's life for the sake of Christ in order to gain it (Mt 10:39). None of these permit any temporizing.

All of the Gospel's provocations, beginning with the first one in Jesus' hometown, stem from the absoluteness of his eternal and temporal mission. Measured against that absoluteness, all creaturely things and their interconnections are secondary. If all these things exist from him and toward him (Col 1:16), then they must all be ordered in relation to his primacy. He himself is the First, the One who orders all things in his train according to the Father's command. All the relentless words of John's Gospel, spoken against the Jews, give evidence of that. He permits the sword of division, which his Incarnation was meant to bring to earth (Mt 10:34ff.), to be wielded against himself. Someone was always trying to kill him, and even the first provocation in Nazareth ends with his enraged fellow townspeople trying to lynch him.

49. "Although He Was a Son, He Learned Obedience through Suffering"

Here the Letter to the Hebrews speaks with deliberate paradox ("although") of *learning* obedience—viewing it from the perspective of the eternal Son of the Father, whose essence it is to be infinitely ready to submit fully to the Father's will (Heb 5:7–9). Suffering, which as God he knows not, forces him into a new experience, to learn anew within time something self-evident in eternity. His obedience must stand the fiery test of death; he must be willing in advance to experience the destruction of the obedient One ("If the grain of wheat does not die"). And, even though obeying the Father is life itself for the Son ("my food is to do the will of the Father" [Jn 4:34]), nonetheless this same obedience requires him to "hate" (Jn 12:25) his eternally beloved and to love his self-destruction. It is a requirement utterly unknown and unimagined, a demand that "convulses" his whole being to its core, like an earthquake. It shakes the foundation upon which the eternal relationship between Father and Son rests. This explains his indecision: "What shall I say? Father, save me from this hour" (12:27), and in even stronger terms, "Anything is possible for you; take this cup from me" (Mk 14:36). "His sweat was like drops of blood" (Lk 22:44). The author of Hebrews intensifies the picture: "He offered up prayers and supplications, with loud cries and tears to him who was able to save him from the power of death" (Heb 5:7).

The issue here is not simply the physical death that takes place thousands of times a day on earth. Rather, it is the death of the One who said of himself, "I am the life" (Jn 14:6; 1:4; 11:25). What he meant by this expression of his being was not merely a transitory earthly life but life itself, eternal life, life in its purest essence. The One who is learning obedience does not simply have life like others around him—he is Life itself. Now one can begin to grasp what was demanded of him. For Life itself death cannot simply be something to be endured as every limited and transitory creature endures it as part of its nature; rather, it must be a perishing proportional to Life uniquely itself. Paul put it this way: God "has made him who knew no sin to be sin" (2 Cor 5:21), to be that which is the eternal contradiction of eternal life. He must die his way into the opposite of the living God. That could not be learned within his eternal blessedness but rather only "in the days of his flesh" (Heb 5:7).

Should one perhaps modify the text to say, "His pleas went unheard, although he was the Son of God"? Or should one leave it as it is: "His pleas were heard because of his godly fear, and he learned . . . obedience, although he was the Son of God"? In the latter instance, the "loud cries" and "tears" would be precisely the means through which he learned this new and final obedience; his pleas were then heard on the basis of the obedience he learned by means of them. The Gospels tell us the result of his wrestling with the fear of death: "Yet not what I will, but what you will." He simply cannot will the ungodly thing into which he is to be plunged, but the Father can ordain it for reasons that are inaccessible right now. Thus precisely because of his resistance to that which is ungodly yet with which he is supposed to identify, precisely because of this "fear of God", his prayer is heard. And that permits the further statement: "And perfected, he became the source of eternal salvation to all who obey him" (5:9). His obedience cannot be imitated because he alone is eternal life and eternal salvation. Yet in his grace he can ordain that those who obey him, those who live out even in a faint imitation his contradiction, may partake of the salvation that flows from his "being made sin".

At the moment Jesus receives the sign that the hour of his "glorification" has come, he proclaims both his and his followers' destiny without making any distinction: "In all truth I say to you: unless the grain of wheat falls to the ground and dies, it remains alone; but if it dies, it brings forth much fruit. He who loves his life will lose it, but he who hates his life in this world will save it for eternal life" (Jn 12:24–25). Of course there is a love of one's own passing existence, even in the purely creaturely realm: "No one hates his own flesh; rather, one cares for it and preserves it" (Eph 5:29). Yet in our distant discipleship the Lord requires of us that we "hate" ourselves, meaning that we must prefer death and decay in the dark soil of earth, despite all our human protest against such waste; we must endure the crushing anxiety of the contradiction between what we love and the obedience discipleship demands. True obedience never takes place on its own. Even the One who thinks he "can do" it must "learn" it in the hour of decision.

50. New Wine in Old Wineskins

In both images—sewing a new patch on an old garment and pouring new wine into old wineskins (Lk 5:36–39)—Jesus deals with the true character of the tradition that finds its fulfillment in him. Each image contains two temptations: fitting pieces of one's new insight into the old and familiar or, with a slight shift of focus, salvaging pieces of the old within the new. Both attempts fail.

If you try to patch an old garment with a piece of a new one, you have to cut a hole in the new cloth, thus ruining it. And the new patch on the old cloth stands out so sharply that you can't wear the old garment either. This means that old as well as new are complete wholes and that one cannot cut pieces out of them to patch up something else. Even though the Old Covenant is directed toward and open to the New, it still has a shape that is deformed by chipping off pieces and pasting on new elements.

The second metaphor makes the same point more sharply. Old and fully fermented wine can be contained in old wineskins that have stretched to their limits with the wine itself. But if one were to pour new wine that is still fermenting into these same skins, they would burst: "New wine needs new wineskins." Content and container, meaning and form, constitute an indestructible whole. (Every theory of art recognizes this: a Caryatid cannot be separated from the ledge that it supports; a sonnet turned into prose is useless.)

Yet Jesus' statement carries unexpected consequences for understanding the relationship between "Old Covenant" and "New Covenant". We usually view aspects of the old as organically fulfilled and integrated into the new, especially when the earlier aspect already points to the new and more complete. Do not Jeremiah and Ezekiel already proclaim the coming "New and eternal Covenant"? Does not the image of the shepherd used for Yahweh and the Davidic Messiah find fulfillment in Jesus' own statement: "I am the Good Shepherd" (Jn 10:11)? Many similar examples could be listed.

Yet Jesus demands a total reconstruction in the transition from old to new, a "new birth", a relearning from the bottom up. For he himself is an indivisible unity, and he is anything but the sum total of a preceding column of figures to which a few more entries have been added. All that came before and pointed to him was temporary and, despite a certain unity in Jewish religion, was "God's speaking in many and various ways" (Heb 1:1). In the concluding Word each individual truth melts away into a single Truth. Everything that Jesus says, does, suffers, and inaugurates contains him in his entirety—he is his gospel; he is his work of saving the world; he is even his Church insofar as she is his mystical body brought to life by the Eucharist.

At the time of Paul and in the "circles around James" there existed a Jewish traditionalism that could not glimpse this newness and wanted to stitch a lot of old patches on the "seamless robe"; today similar efforts are made by groups of Jewish converts for whom the Church is too Gentile in character.

Both metaphors become intensely relevant in ecumenical affairs, where theologians and even simple laymen prance around in regular clown costumes. Catholics sew on a colorful assortment of Protestant patches that have to do with sacraments, ecclesiology, the Magisterium, the veneration of saints, and so forth. Protestants try to clothe themselves in individual Catholic rags, often in a most touching way, without realizing that it makes no sense to adopt Catholic confession of sin without discussing the Catholic understanding of office and of divine power of absolution or the possible recognition of some sort of Petrine office and without at the same time considering the role of Mary and the saints in the Catholic fellowship. Ecumenism consists almost entirely in a mis-understanding of these two parables. If the similarities seem to have surpassed the 50 percent level, the remaining differences play no more role, or one can at least postpone dealing with them until later. Yet Jesus' "robe", the metaphor for himself and his work, has no seams. All that remains between imagined unity and genuine unity is a leap.

Otherwise we are better off to hang onto the unusual conclusion:

"No one who has drunk old wine wants new wine, for he says the old is mellow" (Lk 5:39). Any connoisseur of wine will agree, as will many representatives of Eastern Orthodoxy, the original Protestantism, or Anglicanism. But then one can only ask whether the *Catholica* does not offer the oldest and most authentic.

51. "Dare One Do Good
on the Sabbath?"

Jesus' question contains two barbs: Is it permissible to do anything on the Sabbath (since the scribes had expounded the law
so as to limit activity to the barest minimum)? Furthermore,
is it legitimate to do good? Mark clarified this even more: "Is
it permitted to do good on the Sabbath or to do evil?" that
is, "to save a life or to let it die"? (In this regard an entire
system of casuistry had been developed: one was permitted to try
to heal a mortally ill person, or, "if one possessed only one sheep
and it fell into a hole, one might legally take hold of it and pull it
out" [Mt 12:11]—yet even this was expressly forbidden in the
Essene Damascus book [Dam A 13]. The rabbinical exegetes permitted one to save a human life on the Sabbath. Thus the system
was not consistent in its details.)

For Jesus the second point is the one that was of prime importance. To do *good* would include the first point within itself—
to *do* good. And in the name of doing good, which was not
merely one command among many for him but constituted the
very core of his mission and his person, he ordered the man
with the withered hand to stretch out his arm, thereby healing
it. The interpreters of the Sabbath law had come to be primarily concerned about negatives, about not doing. In the process
they had forgotten about the original positive significance of
the Sabbath: this day was holy to God because it was a day
on which Israel remembered God's saving act setting them free
from Egyptian slavery. "Therefore Yahweh your God commands
you to celebrate the Sabbath" (Dt 5:15). Cessation of external
activity was ultimately ordained for this reason, and only de-
rivatively was it connected to God's rest on the seventh day
of creation (Ex 20:11).

Jesus refuses to interpret the metaphor of God's rest as an image of God's inactivity and thus refuses to imitate God's supposed inactivity: "My Father is working still, and I too am working" (Jn 5:17), precisely on the Sabbath, the day on which men are not supposed to do their own work but to take time to pay attention to God's work—which for the Jews meant paying attention to the foundational act of salvation, namely, redemption from Egypt.

In this sense Jesus says that "the Sabbath is made for man and not man for the Sabbath" (Mk 2:27). It is intended to make the one at rest aware of God's saving activity. To do that he must elevate his authority above that of the rigid and vacuous Tradition: "Therefore [because he has authority to make this determination] the Son of Man is also Lord of the Sabbath" (Mk 2:28).

All of this becomes fully comprehensible only if one moves from the external rest of the Old Testament (including rest for the purpose of reflection) to the New Testament's contemplative rest, an active repose in the Holy Spirit that gazes on the constantly active Father and Son. It is a quietness that does not merely look at the inward, eternal vitality of God but that is indeed drawn into that activity through the Spirit. That is the only way to understand how genuine Christian contemplation can be so active and fruitful. To explain his work on the Sabbath, Jesus says that the Father loves the Son and reveals to him all that he does (Jn 5:20), and this not merely standing side by side but in an incomprehensible intermingling: "The Father who dwells in me completes his works" (Jn 14:10). That they seem to be the Son's works is no deception, for the Son is not celebrating Sabbath while the Father works in the place the Son has vacated; rather, what Jesus does is to permit the Father to work in him and to be absorbed into that working. In permitting the Father to work he is a contemplative; in being absorbed into that work he is active; both are inseparably intertwined.

It is in this two-in-oneness that the Holy Spirit is given to the believer. In our possession of the Holy Spirit we can no longer distinguish between what God does in his Spirit in us and what we do in his Spirit for him. To put that in Gospel terms: it is always simultaneously Sabbath and weekday for us, regardless of whether active contemplation or activity in a spirit of contemplation dominates. In other words, regardless of whether it is more a matter of our acting under the leading of the Spirit or more a matter of the Spirit's action that we permit, Sabbath and working day coincide.

52. "And Your Neighbor as Yourself"

The great commandment can be developed in such a way that love of God and neighbor appear as two distinct yet conjoined commandments, with the second one subordinate to the first. "You shall love your God with your whole heart . . . that is the first and greatest commandment. The second is like it: you shall love your neighbor as yourself. On these two commandments depend all the law and the prophets" (Mt 22:37–40). Or both commandments may be found in the same order but still more tightly joined together: "There is no greater commandment than this one" (Mk 12:31). In the parable of the Samaritan there is no talk of two commandments at all: "You shall love the Lord your God . . . and your neighbor as yourself" (Lk 10:27).

Yet each of these formulations, regardless of its precise wording, contains a double duality: between the loving person and God and between oneself and one's neighbor. Although the loving person and his God always remain distinct as creature and Creator, something of the Old Testament remains in this duality. This is clear if one considers the distance between the neighbor and oneself. It jumps out at one if the "Golden Rule" is taken as a point of departure (which, to be sure, has non-biblical parallels): "All that you expect from another, that do to him as well. Therein lie the law and the prophets" (Mt 7:12). The same concluding phrase is attached after listing the "two commandments" in Matthew 22:40; it can even be applied to the second command alone: "The entire law is fulfilled in a single word: you shall love your neighbor as yourself" (Gal 5:14).

As a foundation for human ethics, the Golden Rule is ambiguous. Why should I do to another what I expect from him? Because I want to give him the kindness that I experience or because I want to gain that kindness for myself? In the second instance the phrase "do not the Gentiles do the same?" would apply (Mt 5:47). Such ambiguity in basic norms for human behavior (taken in themselves) is unavoidable, since the unity that is unambiguous only in God becomes polarized in the creature — human unity lies not only in the indivisibility of the person but equally in the solidarity of humanness as a category of creature. For that reason, in ethics the pastoral pole (everyone loves himself [see Eph 5:29a]) can be taken as the norm for love of neighbor.

This basic ambiguity is blurred, though perhaps not totally eliminated, if one takes up the primary relationship — man-God (in the Old Testament sense) — and uses it to clarify the relationship between men. To be sure, love of God "with one's whole heart" cannot be measured in terms of natural self-love, and this unbounded love of God is Israel's answer to having been chosen in an incomprehensible manner by God, but in this love's total orientation toward God it also keeps in view God's special concern for Israel. In the command to love one's neighbor Israel's glance back toward itself does not entirely disappear. For that reason the parable that the Lord uses to clarify the double commandment makes the Samaritan — not the priest and Levite who hurry by — into the model for one's neighbor.

Both relationships — the vertical and the horizontal — shift in the New Testament. For, if God reveals himself as the Three-in-One in Christ, then "self-love" and "love of neighbor" coincide absolutely in him. God loves himself in precisely the same degree each of the Divine Persons loves the other in God. For there is no polarity between the Person and category, since each Person is itself only in loving relation to the other. When Jesus presents this to us as the model for a point of departure for Christian ethics — not merely as an anthropologically polarized schematization — then we must orient our love according to the christological (and trinitarian) norm. This becomes crystal clear when we see our whole behavior toward our neighbor interpreted literally as behavior toward Jesus: "Inasmuch as you have done this to the least of my brothers, you have done it to me" (Mt 25:40). This holds true because "the body [of Christ] is one and has many members; all members of the body, however, despite their variety, form *one* body", the body of Christ (I Cor 12:12). This is concretely expressed, for example, in giving preference to the poor (James 2:1–16; I Jn 3:17). But enough of that. Since Christ has "given us an example", "so that you too might do as I have done to you", and since Christ has thereby forbidden us to play the anthropological approach off against the trinitarian model ("the servant is not greater than his master" [Jn 13:15–16]), he provides for us in himself the divine norm, which in turn must be our norm. Self-love now can only be expressed as self-giving: "There is no greater love than to give one's life for one's friends" (Jn 15:13). "By this we know love, that he gave his life for us. So must we also give our life for the brethren" (1 Jn 3:16). Reflecting back upon oneself as a norm disappears in the absolute relativity of the Divine Self: "Whoever does not count his life as nothing cannot be my disciple" (Lk 14:26).

53. "LIKE A ROARING LION"

"Be sober, be vigilant. For your adversary, the devil, roams around like a roaring lion, seeking whom he may devour" (1 Pet 5:8). Evil and its seductive power are not confined to an unchanging perimeter that one could effortlessly patrol; rather, it is an aggressive force that no earthly limits can contain. It can hide in ambush nearby, ready to spring into attack, or it can betray itself by its roaring bluster. No one is overpowered by evil without first having caught a glimpse of it—at least, that is, if one remains "sober" and "vigilant", refusing to be robbed of one's senses by intemperance. "So then, let us not sleep as others do, but let us keep watch and be sober. For those who sleep sleep at night, and those who get drunk are drunk at night. But since we belong to the day, let us be sober" (1 Th 5:6–7). "Resist the devil, and he will flee from you" (James 4:7).

Although evil in itself presents overwhelming power, the peculiar thing about the Christian's encounter with the devil is that Christians are given weaponry adequate to conquer evil. Peter puts it concisely: "Resist him, firm in faith" (1 Pet 5:9). Paul speaks of the "armor of light" (Rom 13:12) and lists specific weapons: in addition to faith, the sword of the spirit, that is, the word of God, prayer, truth, righteousness, readiness to proclaim the gospel of peace. All of this equipment constitutes the "armor of God" because the superior power of the "rulers of this dark world" can be countered only with these, not with purely human weapons. The evil one shoots "fiery darts", which can be repelled only by the "shield of faith" (Eph 6:11–18).

If evil can be conquered only by God—by the God-Man and those who employ his weapons—then it would make sense for those outside this sphere to equate evil with the tragedy of existence itself. Anyone who does not simply deny the existence of evil, as a consistent Buddhist does, will succumb to evil. Almost nothing illustrates better than art the shifting boundary between a

Christian triumph over evil, an honest struggle with temptation, and a tragic, guiltless surrender to the overwhelming power of the devil. Romanesque portals and gothic devils constrained to servitude as gargoyles on cathedrals show the victory of the Christian God over seduction, inviting the viewer to imitation. The spiritual child praised by Christ wanders untouched through all earthly hells—from Percival to Oliver Twist and Goethe's novellas. The saint with a childlike soul endures the most terrifying and the most seductive onslaughts (Claudel's Violaine). Yet in the various portrayals of the "temptations of Saint Antony" one must note how much effort the artist devotes to the tempter's power—whether in Grünewald's or Breughel's or Bosch's versions or, finally, in Flaubert, for whom the endless variations of evil become the central theme. Even if the path from an inescapably evil existence leads to some kind of salvation (as in Strindberg), one must be able to distinguish how much of this is buddhistic and how much might possibly be Christian. The latter often remains hidden—a hero who struggles to free himself from guilt, who perhaps greets death as propitiation, may think he accomplishes this by his own strength and has thereby unconsciously grasped the hand of grace. (How much importance should be allotted to the Catholic themes in Schiller's *Maria Stuart*?) One also finds "pure fools", as, for example, are frequently encountered in the work of Wilder. These characters take up an impure means to a good end in a childish, playful mode—they avoid engaging the "lion" in direct combat (for example, Mozart's *Don Giovanni* or *Cosi fan Tutte*). But one can also simply render evil innocuous (as in the transition from Faust I to Faust II) and even make use of unauthorized borrowing from Christian teaching to mock the devil as a bumbler.

The images of the book of Revelation cannot help illustrating both at once: the way the trinity of beasts opposing God dominates the men who worship them and the victory over the powers of hell won by the martyrs, by the ones who have endured to the end.

54. "Speck and Beam"

"Why do you see the speck in your brother's eye but do not notice the beam that is in your own eye?" (Mt 7:3). And why does it never occur to you that the speck in his eye results from his having seen the beam in yours? You did not know anything about it, you say? Of course not, for an eye can see only another, not itself. But Jesus' parable will not tolerate that kind of an excuse. To call oneself sharp-eyed because one can see something huge in someone else he calls Pharisaism. Granted that "your brother has something against you"—then hold off on your prayers and "go and be reconciled with your brother" (Mt 5:23–24). It may be that his complaint against you is partially or completely justified. Even if it were true that you recognize with complete clarity that he has sinned, then "rebuke him and, when he corrects himself, forgive him" (Lk 17:3). The Lord does not forbid that we admonish others, but this requires from the outset a willingness to forgive, a willingness that must be apparent to the sinner so that he will in turn be willing to repent. This spirit of forgiveness must also be strong enough to outlast repeated sins and offenses: "If he sins against you seven times in a day and turns to you seven times saying 'I want to repent', then you must forgive him" (Lk 17:4). The example seems utopian, but it is visible precisely in the Heavenly Father's behavior and thus in Jesus' own heart.

Thus the saying about the speck and the beam does not set aside the validity of Christian responsibility for mutual discipline; rather, it makes fraternal correction into a necessary work of love in the Church. But the saying's warning remains equally valid: first look to your own faults. How often do we consider something worthy of criticism in another that we permit ourselves without question! That would be to pound away with one's own beam of self-authority on the other person's tiny speck. Elsewhere Jesus said of the Pharisees: "They make speeches, but they do not practice what they preach. They lash together heavy burdens and place them on people's shoulders [in the name of Christ: take up daily your heavy cross!] but won't lift a finger to help carry the load" (Mt 23:3–4).

People who have the cross of other people's authority on their shoulders should bear that cross and not try to escape it by groveling humility toward those who lead and train them. But the teaching about the speck and beam then applies with special intensity to those who are placed in authority. The authority they must exercise in the obedience of Christ is not the beam, even though others may consider it to be such and call it that. At most it is a crossbeam that cannot be set aside. But the person burdened with that authority must take care that no one can accuse him of what Jesus rebuked in the Pharisees. And if it seems hard to combine an unshirking exercise of the authority one has been given with a spirit of humility that is always ready to examine oneself, to correct oneself, to admit one's injustices, then look to the Lord's example: he joins without tension the majesty of the authority he has from his Father to a humility that permits him to be a Servant of all. His lofty claims were interpreted as arrogance: "You are only a man, and you make yourself God" (Jn 10:33). His response could only be that he "was sanctified by the Father and sent into the world" to embody as the "Son of God" (10:36) the Father's authority—in a pure service of love to God and men. As the "Lord and Master" he washes his disciples' feet so that they might do what he has done for them—carry out a servant's work while bearing his authority (Jn 13:14–16).

This task can be hard for sinful people—to be obliged to correct others ("let me remove the speck from your eye" [Mt 7:4]) yet to know how much one ought to correct oneself. If the one giving the orders knows this and makes an obvious effort to do it, then it will be apparent to the pupil or the person under his authority, providing he is not spiteful or obstinate. Together then they can shoulder the "light burden" of the gospel (Mt 11:30).

55. "I Too Must Obey, and I Have Soldiers under Me"

These are the words of the centurion who asked Jesus to heal his servant with a simple word (Mt 8:9), the words of a Gentile of whom Jesus says, "Such a faith I have not found in Israel" (8:10). He says the same thing—dismissively—about the Syro-Phoenician woman. But she counters him: "You are right, Lord! But even the dogs get a bit of the bread the children [that is, Israel] eat" (Mk 7:28). How is it that these Gentiles have greater faith than that found in Israel? Both of them know something that Israel has largely forgotten: that Israel's faith does not belong to Israel alone but is supposed to be a representative faith for the nations. Both of these Gentiles have acquired a degree of humility, which is focused sharply by their human situation. The centurion's statement is particularly significant: he knows that he must obey orders and that even his giving of orders occurs within the context of military obedience ("If I say to someone, 'Go!' he goes, and if I say to another, 'Come!' he comes; if I say to my servant, 'Do that!' he does it" (Mt 8:9). As a properly constituted commander he himself is accountable to a superior. The woman also recognizes the Lord's legitimacy—he has been sent for the chosen "sheep of Israel" who are placed ahead of her. The "children" sit at the table; she is under the table. The centurion cared enough about Israel's importance to have "built them a synagogue" (Lk 7:5).

Both of them take for granted the human context and view themselves as subordinates within it. The human context provides a model for understanding the cosmic order that seems to them to be adequate—subordination under a sovereign power subject to no one and with authority to say, "Go", and, "Come", and, "Do that". Both of them are granted the grace to perceive this highest power active in Jesus—in his bodily presence before the Cross and Resurrection; afterward it will be a spiritual presence pervading the world.

If men are not overcome by sin (lust and pride), they can observe from their own human condition that no one in the world gives commands without also having to obey. This is true in the political and physical orders; living things "are subject all their lives to the servitude of fear of death" (Heb 2:15). In this context Paul speaks of the conscience when he addresses a man's awareness of being subject to a superior law (Rom 2:15). The conscience tells him that the ultimate power of command cannot be subject to a still higher law. That is why this highest power "does not permit himself to be served by human hands as if he needed something" (Acts 17:25) but instead possesses the very sovereignty that the centurion glimpsed in Jesus.

If the Gentiles are to gain faith, both are necessary: an undistorted insight into the human condition, wherever one may be situated, plus light from above that shines on this situation and truly exposes it. Sin obscures the human condition; it comes into clear view where a person has the humility to let the truth about it be revealed.

Most people who have not encountered this light do not know that it shines upon all mankind. But since Christian Faith teaches that the Son of God bore the guilt of all, his light must reach everyone at least to the degree that the truth about one's existence and the humility which that truth urges on one are recognizable. But no man is authorized to try to decide where this light has been received and where it has been rejected.

Dogs under the table, men who say or act out the words, "Lord, I am not worthy", can be found in a temple to Shiva or in front of a Kuan-yin (Avalokitesvara) statue. But where is the Mediator who "turned around and said to the people following, 'Not even in Israel have I found such faith'" (Lk 7:9)? All people seek God (Acts 17:27), but one kind of searching seeks what has not yet been found, and another kind begins when one encounters, when one finds: "Seek heavenly things, . . . for you have died, and your life is hidden with Christ" (Col. 3:2–3). "*Ut inventus quaeratur immensus est* [he is beyond measure so that even when discovered he may be further sought]" (Augustine).

56. "Are You the One Who Is to Come?"

The question that a captive John the Baptist sends to Jesus by way of two of his disciples (Mt 11:3) is the all-encompassing question of the Old Covenant directed at the New. Drawing together all of Israel's longing, John had expected the eschatological Judge who would also be Israel's Savior. He spent only a short time in Jesus' company (Jn 4:1–2)—his arrest caused Jesus to return to Galilee (Mk 1:14) and made it impossible for John to keep track of Jesus' activity. But what he learned of Jesus' doings from his prison did not correspond to Israel's end-times expectations. The arrival of the messianic Kingdom seemed to require a fundamental rearrangement of this world's structures and relationships. Whether the last days could begin in the middle of history itself, without a total upheaval of that history, was the question that all of Israel asked Jesus: "Where is the promise of his coming? . . . Everything has remained as it was since the beginning of creation" (2 Pet 3:4).

Jesus' reply employed words borrowed from the Old Covenant itself: "the blind see, the lame walk, lepers are cleansed, the deaf hear, the dead are raised, the good news is preached to the poor" (Is 35:5; 26:19; 61:1). What Isaiah perhaps intended as a series of joyous images for the dawn of salvation now become literal reality in Jesus' work. He not only had healed the deaf, blind, lame, and lepers but also, just before John's question arrived, had raised the boy from Naim from the dead (Lk 7:11–17). The metaphorical and eschatological had come to pass in history, including even the eschatological resurrection of the dead, which now was occurring within time. All of this seemed so modest, so powerless to overturn the world's structures. Yet the phrase "the good news is proclaimed to the poor" was also an Old Testament phrase (Is 61:1), and it is precisely the poor whom Jesus lists first among those who are blessed—yet they are blessed precisely *as* the poor, not, as the Old Covenant normally assumed, as having been snatched out of their poverty ("he raises the weak from the dust, and the poor from the ash heap" [Ps 113:7]). The great transformation of which the Magnificat also sings does not take place sociologically—the "lowly maid" is not changed into a reigning queen.

The Old Covenant simply must bring its own expectation into line with the decree of God that was revealed clearly enough in Isaiah 61:1–2: the Spirit of the Lord has sent the Messiah "to proclaim good tidings to the poor, to heal the brokenhearted, ... to proclaim the year of the Lord's favor". And if "liberty" is promised "to the captives" and "redemption to those in shackles", this apparently means something beyond the sort of political development hoped for by the Baptist suffering in his prison. Social and political developments may well follow from the true eschatological event that Jesus constituted, but the order he established dare not be reversed. Had not Yahweh throughout the course of history repeatedly disappointed, indeed, deliberately crushed, his people's earthly expectations and longings?

When Jesus concludes with the warning "happy is he who takes no offense at me" (Mt 11:6), he addresses the entire Old Covenant in his direct answer to an imprisoned John the Baptist, who needs to tear down some of his "ideological superstructures" in order to uncover the simple meaning of the divine promises. What a withdrawal process Israel has already begun: the ark of the Covenant taken captive only to be destroyed by fire later along with the entire temple; not even one stone of the rebuilt temple is left standing upon another; the entire holy city lying in rubble. Should not Christians reflect on this object lesson and ask themselves whether the Crusades, the forcible conversion of the Saxons under Charlemagne, the cathedrals, and the Basilica of St. Peter can be a basis for, even a mere symbol of, "proclaiming the good news to the captives"?

57. "Many Sins Are Forgiven Her, for She Has Loved Much"

We are familiar with the scene in which the woman of ill repute disturbs the banquet hosted by the Pharisee by anointing and kissing Jesus' feet, weeping, drying her tears with her hair; the host's consternation; Jesus' parable about the two unequal debts being forgiven (one of five hundred, the other of five denarii). Finally, Jesus points to the sinner: "Do you see this woman?" (Lk 7:36–50). You gave me little, whereas she has "not ceased" to demonstrate her love to me in every way. Then comes the crucial conclusion: "Therefore I say to you: her sins, which are many, are forgiven, for she has loved so much; but he who is forgiven little, loves little." Only then does he say to the woman, "Your sins are forgiven."

Thus we have first Jesus' affirmation, "Many sins are forgiven her", together with an explanation—her great love. Only then comes the second explicit statement: "Your sins are forgiven." The first is an objective observation; the "other guests" learn from the second that forgiveness of sins takes place through Jesus himself. The first, descriptive statement of forgiveness is a conclusion drawn from the short parable—the larger debt (five hundred denarii) produces greater love and gratitude when it is forgiven. Yet the parable is told by Jesus and cannot be separated from his person. It is only from him that the guilt-laden one learns that she has been forgiven, and she knows this not because of the parable but because of what she already knew about his person—otherwise she would never have dared to carry out such a brazen performance in the house of a respectable host. She throws herself down before him and exposes before him her entire existence; in profound repentance she makes a complete confession. In such circumstances it makes little difference that others already know that she is a public sinner.

What we have here is a paradigm for the sacrament of confession. The sinner who is willing to hide nothing and to sorrow for everything out of love toward the forgiving God encountered in Jesus has already had her sins forgiven. Yet the willingness to lay everything out in the open—which takes on heroic proportions in this story—is contained in her contrition, so that the word of absolution found in the sacrament is in the end what wipes out the sins. It would be impossible for Jesus to have intended with his parable and its conclusion some sort of process between God and man independent of him. God has given to Jesus alone the power to judge the world and, taking its sin upon himself, to save the world. The consternation that arises here is the same that will attach itself to the power of absolution in Christ's Church. That here, before the Cross, he already has the power to forgive sins should not surprise us any more than the fact that he distributes his sacrificed body and shed blood to his Church even before his Passion.

Although Jesus compares his Pharisee host to someone who has been forgiven a much smaller sum of fifty denarii, the context makes clear that he owes no less to God, since Jesus astonishingly says: "He who has been forgiven little, loves little." Applied to the sacrament this implies the following: divine forgiveness can penetrate only superficially the heart of one who approaches with little love and contrition, and he thus takes away a tiny bit of love from the absolution he receives.

Jesus' words offer a precise commentary on the whole matter: "Those who are healthy have no need of a physician [meaning those who think they are well], but those who are sick. I came to call not the righteous but sinners to repentance" (Mt 9:12–13; Lk 5:31–32).

58. "Consider the Lilies of the Field"

Jesus' call to marvel at the Father's glorious way of dressing up the flowers along the path, even though they blossom one day and are burned up the next (Mt 6:28-29), sounds a new theme in the Bible. One finds, to be sure, a wonderful hymn to God's goodness manifest in all of nature—in the stars, in mountains and valleys, in the animal world (Ps 104)—but there man remains the climax of the created world, having been given from the beginning dominance "over the fish of the sea, over the birds, over the cattle and over all wild animals, and over all creeping things that crawl on the face of the earth" (Gen 1:26). Despite man's seeming inconsequence in light of the powerful works of God, the Psalmist praises God for "having placed him a little lower than the heavens" and "crowned him with glory and honor", placing all of nature "under his feet": "All sheep and oxen, the beasts of the fields, the birds in the sky and the fish in the sea". For all of that God's name is praised (Ps 8). The image of man remains that of the ruler, the user and governor, even though, driven out of paradise, he must feed himself "in toil from the earth" and in the sweat of his face until in the end he returns to the soil (Gen 3:17-18). Thus he thanks God for all the beneficial things of creation: "You make the grass to sprout up for the cattle and plants for human agriculture so that he might obtain bread from the earth and the wine that makes the heart glad and the oil that makes his face shine" (Ps 104:14-15).

Jesus takes a new view of nature. He is familiar with all the basic occupations people ply to earn a living. But when he observes the sower, it is not the bread expected from the seed that attracts his interest but rather the wonder of growing grain and the even greater mystery of the seed's dying within the earth. Man can do nothing to add to the gift of the grain that falls on good or bad ground, yet the dying seed springs to new life as the full ear. Moreover, he notes the simple existence of the most insignificant animals whose dying the Creator's compassion nonetheless knows and cares for (Mt 10:29). The same Creator concerns himself with the nests of birds and the dens of the foxes (Mt 8:20) and sees to it that these marvelous lilies bloom gratuitously and are gone in a day even though all of Solomon's costly splendor cannot compare to them. Jesus is not interested in the harvest yield or the usefulness of nature; rather, he considers the inner fruitfulness of a living being. A fig tree in his Father's garden has to bear fruit; in the servants left behind to manage the vineyard by its lord who went off on a journey he sees something like the trees whose purpose is to bear fruit. The old Adam who fills the role of lord over the earth has a fundamentally servile mind-set oriented toward power; the new Adam is the Son who rejoices childishly like the "Little Prince" in his Father's marvels, who takes it for granted that he receives "his Father's food" freely. As the "sole heir" he has no worry about being "poor", for he has everything and nothing all at once, a thought that Francis of Assisi and John of the Cross would have understood very well. He is not bothered by the fact that women serve him by placing their goods at his disposal (Lk 8:2–3) any more than he is concerned about having to pay the temple tax—which he does by taking the money out of a fish's mouth (Mt 17:27), for "the sons are free" (Mt 17:26). One must avoid calculating, as Judas calculated the cost of the wasted perfume (Jn 12:5). All of Jesus' miracles from Cana to the multiplication of loaves and the great royal banquet reveal the same spirit—the most wasteful one of all is the poor widow with her two pennies, who gave more than all the others (Mk 12:43–44). She demonstrates that only the poor in spirit really know how to squander.

Jesus knows human hardship and need, and he cares for the misery he encounters. He judges his own followers on the basis of their degree of concern (Mt 25:31ff.). But there can be no doubt that he does this by raising them to his level of childlike carefreeness. "Don't worry about tomorrow, for each day has enough troubles of its own"; the Father knows what you need (Mt 6:31–34). On the level of servility where one wrestles for control, the sequence of blow and counterstroke is inexorable (*sansāra*). The only way to escape is to offer the other cheek in a childlike spirit and permit the lust for power to dissipate (Mt 5:39). That leads to the Cross, to be sure, but precisely from the grain of wheat that falls to the ground arises the full ear. "Consider the lilies of the field."

The Church of Christ has to work, as the story of Peter's fishing boat at the end of John's Gospel demonstrates. But the seven disciples in that boat are doing a son's work, not a servant's— in catching nothing they haul in a wasteful abundance; they are beyond earthly poverty and earthly wealth. They are beyond calculations because they have received both Nothing and Everything.

59. "Power Went Forth from Him"

When Jesus turns around in the middle of a crowd pressing against him from all sides and asks, "Who touched me?" (Mk 5:31), "Someone touched me because I sensed that power has gone forth from me" (Lk 8:46), it indicates that an unusual sort of touch is involved here. This is obvious from what follows: the woman suffering from an abnormal flow of blood, whom no physician can help, touches the hem of his robe in faith, and Jesus sends her on her way with the words, "Daughter, your faith has healed you; go in peace" (Mk 5:34). When Jesus speaks of faith, he always does so in a theological sense—faith in God's power (the Bible knows nothing of any faith in the magic powers of a man), and this faith is the container into which the power of God that rests in Jesus can flow.

Yet the fact that Jesus talks about power going forth from him makes it clear that it did not simply pass through his humanness, that it is rather the power of his incarnate divineness, and that he experiences its departure as a loss, as weakness. The question he asks shows that he did not release the force himself but rather that the woman's faith drew it out of him, that her faith exercised some kind of power over him of which she was unaware. This certainly does not mean that men can seize something from him against his will but rather that there is within him a deeper will to put his entire incarnate divineness at the disposal of men. Such sacrificial openness is clear in the passage in which "an immense crowd of people assembled to hear him and to be healed of their illnesses. All the peoples sought to touch him, for power came forth from him" (Lk 6:17–19).

It would not be misguided to link this flow of power from Jesus to his Cross and his Eucharist. In them his loss leads to a self-surrender to death and to a complete transformation of his entire being into food and drink for believers. From the moment of his Incarnation he never lived among people closed in upon himself, for the Incarnation itself is the result of his self-emptying (as Paul says in Phil 2:7), and the Incarnation itself simply transforms his eternal and divine giving of himself to the Father into human existence. This too had to keep flowing all the way "to death on the Cross" (Phil 2:8) in order to carry the intra-trinitarian self-overflowing to its ultimate incarnational form. It is this incarnational form that demonstrates that his humanness is more than a mere channel for divine powers and rather that his humanness has to be incorporated into the outflow itself. It is this form of existence that constitutes the unbridgeable end, the condition beyond which one cannot penetrate. As an outpouring throughout all time and all space, the Eucharist permits Jesus' humanness to become the perfect medium for the intra-trinitarian self-outpouring, and—as required by the clear specificity of the Person of the Son within the Trinity—it does so without jeopardizing the personal reality of the God-Man Mediator.

Just as Jesus while on earth was at the disposal of the woman's faith, so his power is at the disposal of believers in the Eucharist. In the process a mysterious conversion takes place. For faith means, after all, that a man stands at God's disposal. If the power of Christ pours into a person who genuinely believes, by "losing power" Christ wins that person for himself as a member of his ecclesial body. In giving him the power to lose his life, the Father also gives him the power to win back—by losing—his power from the believer who receives it (Jn 10:18). Something similar happens in the "marvelous exchange" of the sacrament of confession: it is the confession of human sin, offered in faith, that Jesus takes into himself in order to destroy it in the weakness of death on the Cross, replacing it with the gift of the grace of his divine "weakness of life": "Go and sin no more" (Jn 8:11).

60. "Pay Attention to How You Hear"

Jesus' admonition (Lk 8:18) presupposes that the same thing can be heard in different ways. Not how I want to hear something but what it wants to say makes all the difference in hearing rightly.

What it says, when we are dealing with Jesus' gospel, is not something private but something that affects the entire world, not something particular but something universal and catholic. Jesus' words necessarily are particular, definite words, but their import is the totality, not the particular. If he truly is the incarnate Word of God, then that Word always contains a divine, unbounded meaning, a world-encompassing scope, in contrast to other limited human words. This belongs to his being and therefore also to his intent: in him "there is nothing hidden that will not someday be made manifest, nothing secret that shall not be known and come to light" (8:17). This dynamic tendency within the word establishes the right way to hear.

There is a perverse inclination to hear it as a word directed to me personally and applying to no one else, thinking that I have heard it in an especially intense and existential way. In fact, one thereby turns the "basket" of one's private existence upside down over the word, acting as if one were the "individual" intended by the word apart from the mass of people who would misunderstand it anyway. Practically speaking this privatization leads to two results: having placed the lamp "under the bed" (8:16), one falls asleep while the flame treated in such a manner burns out for lack of oxygen.

The word is heard properly when its light "is placed on a lamp stand so that whoever enters can see it". Those who enter my life should catch sight neither of me nor of the way I have utilized the light; rather, they should see the light itself. My life then becomes the lamp stand underneath the light, a utensil that attracts no attention, a structure whose purpose is to make the light visible to all who approach.

Only when one places the light so that it can shine forth does one really "have" the light—for oneself and for others. It can then be said, "To whomever has it shall be given" (8:18). He has the light, to be sure, but he does not give it to himself; rather, it must be given away by him, which can happen only if he desires it not for himself alone but for all who will permit him to give it to them. To wish to receive it for oneself alone is an attitude that inwardly contradicts any receiving. Jesus' concluding words say this with complete clarity: "From him who has not shall be taken that which he thinks he has." Supposing oneself to have something for oneself is a subjective deception; sooner or later one becomes objectively dispossessed.

This series of sayings concisely reveals much about the universality of the incarnate Word of God. First, it shows how astonishingly confident Jesus was that the truly mysterious words that he spoke to his uncomprehending disciples in a remote corner of Galilee have the inner force to penetrate into all time and space. Furthermore, these same words have the power to burst the bounds of his hearers' hearts, turning them into preachers to the entire world. "What I say to you in obscurity you shall proclaim in broad daylight; what I whisper in your ear you shall preach from the rooftops" (Mt 10:27). This applies not only to those days in Galilee but also to every word whispered into the heart of a disciple in prayer, contemplation, and devotion—words that he must present openly through word or example as a witness for all genuine truth.

For here too hearing is what matters—not only what one hears but also how one hears it.

61. "I Believe; Help My Unbelief"

Descending from the mountain of the Transfiguration, Jesus encounters a scene in which his disciples have tried unsuccessfully to heal a child tormented by the demon of epilepsy. Annoyed, he cries out, "O faithless generation, how long must I remain with you? How long must I put up with you?" (Mk 9:19). At his command the boy is brought to him; he rolls about on the ground, foaming at the mouth. They tell Jesus that the boy has done this since he was a child. Then the father makes his appearance at the center of the action: "If you can, help us and have mercy on us" (22). He uses the plural—he and his child share the malady. Jesus repeats the man's words, which express both hope and doubt simultaneously: "If you can", and adds, "Anything is possible to him who believes." To this the man shouts, "I believe; help my unbelief" (23–24). Luke merely tells the story of the boy's healing (Lk 9:42). Matthew adds the teaching Jesus gave the disciples: "If you have faith as a grain of mustard seed, you can say to this mountain, 'Move from here to there', and it will move. Nothing will be impossible for you" (Mt 17:20). Only Mark gives us the father's dramatic cry.

How can one resolve the contradiction these words contain? He confesses his faith and lack of faith all at once. He knows that he believes, yet he knows that this belief is inadequate. His faith is not even as large as the mustard seed necessary to bring about a miracle of faith. But who among us can say that he believes, that he has adequate faith? That he has faith that absorbs his entire existence, the faith written above Israel's portal, the faith of Abraham, who "believed God who makes the dead come to life and calls into existence what does not exist", who "believed in hope against hope" (Rom 4:17–18)? Abraham, whose body, like that of his wife, was beyond life-giving fertility, was promised a son, and he believed. The very son of this promise was demanded back from him, as if God contradicted himself, yet Abraham

176

believed. He remains the unattainable model, and the disciples were not even close to catching up with him. Jesus scolds the one who dares to climb out of the boat but begins to sink after a few steps on the water and has to be hauled up by Jesus in response to his cry, "Lord, save me!" "O man of little faith, why did you doubt?" (Mt 14:30–31). The disciples ask why they could not drive the demon out of the boy. The answer is that "this kind can only be driven out by prayer" (Mk 9:29), in other words, not through something that people possess or might acquire through great effort but through transcending all that is one's own, through giving oneself over to God's almighty ability.

That means, then, that prayer is not a technique that is at human disposal, a technique by which one might extort something from God. Even the act of prayer itself, the strength to pray, can be given only by God. One does not work miracles like the one in this text simply because one yearns for a healing. They come about because God inspires someone to pray for a healing. It could even be that God thinks it more fruitful for the father to put up with his epileptic son for a while longer.

A different matter is addressed by Jesus' instructions to ask the Father for what one knows God will not withhold from his children yet what one also knows God wants to be asked for (Lk 11:10–13). For God is no impersonally radiant Goodness; rather, he is the God of the Covenant who wants to receive human requests so that his people might receive divine gifts. In this perspective everything rests on the mutuality that itself is the underlying and encompassing goodness that assures the petitioner that he has already received from God what he is asking (Mk 11:24). In this regard one must be praying for an ever more unconditional faith, a faith that can overcome the suspicion that one's own faith is inadequate to receive genuinely what God offers. "A man with two souls", a doubter, who is "like the ocean billows tossed and blown about by the wind" (James 1:6–8), lacks the childlike trust that extends a hand and expects "only good gifts" from the Father (Lk 11:13).

Thus the believer who prays to God is more powerful when he asks God for a spiritual gift—which makes his prayer infallible— than when he merely pleads for a physical miracle. Humanly speaking, one cannot know whether a physical miracle is the better good from God's perspective. As God's Child Jesus prayed to the Father and knew that he was always heard (Jn 11:42). Thus it is that he can assure his disciples: "If you ask the Father for something in my name, he will give it to you" (Jn 16:23).

62. "I Saw Satan Fall
like Lightning from Heaven"

In the book of Job, Satan is an angel in heaven who makes an appearance as the accuser of men and is permitted to tempt them. In the book of Revelation, however, a battle rages in heaven after the rapture of the Child into heaven, that is, after the Messiah's Ascension. Michael and his angels fight against Satan and his hosts, and "they lost their place in heaven, . . . the dragon was thrown to earth, and his angels were thrown down together with him. . . . His wrath is great, because he knows that he has only a short time remaining" (Rev 12:7–9, 12). In the book of Revelation, the devil reveals his power on earth only after Christ's advent.

If, then, Jesus saw Satan fall like lightning from heaven (Lk 10:18), this means two things for men and especially for the Church. It fundamentally promises a final victory but likewise carries the reminder that the final struggle—Church history—will be bitter beyond human capacity. Jesus speaks these words to the disciples, who are returning from their preaching tour with happy reports: "Lord, even the demons obey us when we pronounce your name." Jesus confirms this superiority derived from the power he has given the Church: "I have given you the authority to tread on snakes and scorpions and to overcome all the power of the enemy." Yet they should not permit the excitement of victory to overpower them. Instead, they should be overcome with joy "because your names are written in heaven" (10:19–20)—that is, written where Michael and his angels have overpowered "the great dragon, the old serpent" (Rev 12:9, 14). Only in heaven has the battle already been won; on earth it drags on.

Jesus uses the most drastic imagery for that earthly struggle. "Behold, I send you as sheep among wolves" (Mt 10:16)—humanly speaking this is irresponsible behavior. Nor are the sheep promised a fairy-tale invulnerability. Jesus' commissioning speech in

Matthew (10:16ff.) alternates between ice-cold baths of threats and soothingly warm baths of consolation: Beware of men; they will haul you before the courts and scourge you, but don't worry. Brother will deliver up brother to death, a father will hand over his child, children will rise against parents, and everyone will hate you for my sake. But he who endures to the end will be saved. You will not have it better than I, your Master; therefore, have no fear of them. They can kill you, but they cannot harm your souls. Therefore, have no fear of them and do not think I have come to bring peace to the earth—no, I have come to bring a sword. Thus the final saying: "He who wants to find life must lose it, but whoever loses his life for my sake will gain it."

Church history after Christ has to face these paradoxes without flinching. There can be no talk of a naïve rejoicing over the devil's defeat or of lighthearted trampling of snakes and scorpions. Instead, we should be talking about a fight to the death in our consciousness, a struggle undertaken in order to gain life, but not the life one wants to gain—which must be lost—rather, that which I think lost is what I will gain. Throughout the New Testament we find physical death trivialized as an unimportant part of the final struggle. "Do not be afraid of those who can kill the body but who cannot kill the soul" (Mt 10:28). Paul is unconcerned that the "body is dead" because of sin; what is important to him is that the spirit is alive because of the righteousness transmitted by Christ (Rom 8:10). For Paul someone baptized into the death of Christ has put the fact of physical death behind him and has resurrection with Christ ahead of him (Rom 6:4–5). Christ's Passion was, in the manner of fruit squeezed to the very last drop, a promise of his life throughout the expanse of the entire world. Why should his Church, which is his body, be spared this destiny, this grace, throughout her history?

The book of Revelation portrays this paradoxical contemporaneity of destruction and victory in images: in the drastic colors that sketch the fate of the two prophets (Rev 11:3–13), once more in the victory and destruction of the great whore of Babylon (chap. 17–18), and finally in the Word of God riding forth from heaven to the final battle. Yet although the lines of combatants already face each other ready for battle (19:19), there is no combat.

Instead the enemy army is suddenly conquered. The same thing appears in another portrait, in which the devil receives one final opportunity to seduce the people in the four corners of the earth and with his hosts already surround "the holy city" (20:8–9). Suddenly fire falls from heaven and consumes the foe forever. God destroys evil instantly, not by wrestling with it. "*Now* is the judgment; now the prince of this world is overthrown" (Jn 12:31). Always like the lightning that Jesus saw.

63. "The Son Alone Knows the Father"

In the Holy Spirit Jesus exults that his Father, the Lord of heaven and earth, has "revealed to babes all that was hidden from the wise and intelligent". Nor does the revelation to babes occur directly, for "all has been delivered to me by my Father: no one knows the Son except the Father, and no one knows the Father except the Son and those to whom the Son reveals him" (Lk 10:21–22). Corresponding to the Father's will, the Son's will is directed not to the wise and intelligent but to the poor in spirit.

In the Old Testament Wisdom literature, divine wisdom was spread out over the entire creation and is accessible to all, yet the king had to pray humbly for it in order to obtain it. "Who would have known your will had you not given wisdom and sent your Holy Spirit from on high?" (Wis 9:17). Although her counsel was already active in the creation, she seeks a resting place on earth, settling upon Zion (Sir 24:10). Here all the wisdom disseminated among the nations assembles, and from here she spreads out anew her branches and fruits (Sir 24:16–17). And now she has once more concentrated and concretized herself in Jesus, the epitome of the wisdom of the Father, the wisdom poured out upon creation, the wisdom dwelling in Israel. Jesus possesses from eternity the Spirit Solomon asked for in order to know wisdom. In the Spirit is played out the relationship between the "Father, the Lord of heaven and earth", and his divine wisdom sent into the world, his Word active from the beginning in the world's creation and now the center and destination of creation. This Word now communicates in perfect freedom all the wisdom that goes forth from and returns to the Father. He reveals the Father, whom he alone knows; himself, who is the explication of the Father; and the Spirit, whom he has and can radiate forth and who alone transmits understanding of this revelation.

The reduction of cosmic wisdom to the wisdom of Israel and from there to the wisdom of Jesus—a reduction that Jesus rejoices in as the climax of the Father's purpose—is nothing more or less than a scandal to a world conscious of its own wisdom and intelligence. To the world this christological concentration seems to be an immensely arrogant claim that denies the world all its greatness. It seems so all the more because it portrays as fools precisely those who themselves strive for wisdom and understanding. What they seek has been "hidden" from them, while it falls gratuitously into the lap of the simple folk who make no pretension to wisdom. For "the Jews this is a maddening scandal, for the Gentiles it is foolishness, ... but God's foolishness is wiser than man's" (1 Cor 1:23, 25).

One could scarcely be surprised, then, that the peoples who carried out all manner of pious quests for divine wisdom would abandon that quest when wisdom became concentrated in Christ—for his claim was not hidden. The "voice" of his messengers "was heard throughout the whole world, and their word penetrated to the ends of the earth" (Ps 19:5 [4] = Rom 10:18). Abandoning the quest for wisdom, the nations then contented themselves with this-worldly science and technology. Christ's exultant shout is the hour of birth for atheism, whether of a Marxist or a positivistic stripe. Sects may proliferate alongside it, but the remnants of the great world religions are fading fast.

Yet the "babes" to whom the Father revealed wisdom still remain. "Consider then your call, brethren! Not many of you were wise according to this world's standards, not many were powerful, not many were from elite society, but God has chosen what is foolish in the world in order to put the wise to shame" (1 Cor 1:27), assuming that they have any shame left. The more technicized the world becomes, the more "garbage" is produced by the machine age: proletariat, "displaced persons", unwanted of all sorts, beatniks, millions of refugees and marginalized people. This sinful world mass-produces wards and orphans unable to care for themselves. These are not necessarily the ones Jesus called blessed, yet within their numberless ranks can be found again those who discover the One, the epitome of wisdom. Atheism and positivist secularism work like manure to make Christian seed sprout. Christians will never again triumph—and it is better that they do not—but they will resist. "He who endures to the end shall be saved" (Mk 13:13).

64. "God Said One Thing; I Have Heard These Two Things"

It is amazing that the Psalmist hears a single word of God dissected into two: "That the power is God's and yours, Lord, is kindness" (Ps 62:12–13 [11–12]). At the end he attempts in prayer to bring the two together again under the idea of "righteousness". In the Old Covenant righteousness means God's faithfulness to his Covenant. The entire Psalm is oriented toward this faithfulness of God. "For God alone my soul waits in silence, for my hope comes from him" (62:6 [5]). There can be no trust in the importance and power of human truth: "In the scales they rise up; their word is a lie; their power is robbery." God alone "is our refuge" (62:10, 8 [9, 7]).

What is united in God and in God alone is united — power and kindness — diverges in the world, for the most part, and can come together again only in a praying gaze toward God. Not only does a great gap open up in the human world between the desire for and exercise of power on the one hand and a will to kindness on the other, but also the world's way of picturing God as Creator and as Lord of the Covenant seems to split God up. People perceive a lot about God's power, both in their fragile existence and in the way God corrals his recalcitrant people. Although in the Psalms God's kindness and mercy are praised with exuberant song, yet this is always done with the anxiety that God's goodness may find its limits under the intervention of his power. This accounts for the many complaints and accusations against God that seem to "talk out of both sides of the mouth" about "what occasionally and coincidentally come together in human experience, asserting, namely, that God is both good and powerful, indeed, that both belong to his essence. Were he only one of these two, then these complaints would make no sense at all" (Robert Spaemann). If, however, such a complaint assumes the unity of power and love in God, it runs the risk of demanding (or at least humbly begging) that God's power change whatever we are unable to reconcile with his love. Are we indeed certain that these things are irreconcilable? Are we sure that the difficult, painful, insufferable, absolutely unendurable thing might not be precisely the way in which God's love wants to lead us—into a depth and refinement that we could never have reached without suffering?

It is true that things diverge here that we assume to be united in God if we are going to speak meaningfully of God at all. The ultimate reason for this is not so much the affairs of the world and human limitations as it is God's willingness to grant human freedom. Human behavior and destiny seem to contradict God's goodness so much that one begins to doubt God's power. Job's friends' arguments shatter against his passionate question—they build bridges where the last bridge has collapsed; they search for humanly insightful reasons for a reality that makes a mockery of any overarching theory. Yet God vindicates Job—not by rebuilding the bridge between power and kindness but by arguing with his might alone, which is able even to create monsters, and by demolishing every question and complaint.

The road from Job leads directly to the Cross, where the same "Why" rings forth, a "Why" that remains unanswered in suffering itself. Here and here alone, yet valid for all the other occasions, the answer resounds in the Resurrection to eternal life, proving that exactly this ultimate suffering was the ultimate love of God. Thus at Easter the exuberant power of God (which Paul calls "the violence of the power of his strength" [Eph 1:19]) coincides exactly with the exuberant love with which he loved the whole world in Christ. On this narrow point of the Lord's death and Resurrection the entire structure of Christianity stands. "If Christ is not risen, we are misrepresenting God and are the most miserable of men" (1 Cor 15:14-15, 19).

This does not mean that genuine petitionary prayer is powerless against the troubles arising from the evils of human freedom. It does not mean that God dumps into new evil those who cling to him in love. Christ himself prays for us and points us to a passionate kind of pleading—as in the parable of the widow and the unjust judge. But in the end this pleading must relax into a childlike surrender into God's hands, as the motionless ocean rests beneath the stormy surface waves. The Psalm with which we began itself begins with the words "for God alone my soul waits in silence; from him alone my salvation comes." After the lament we hear again, "For God alone my soul waits in silence, for my hope is from him" (see Ps 62:1, 5).

65. "He Who Does Not Gather with Me Scatters"

Christ presents himself as the One who gathers (Mt 12:30). He gathers in a superior sense that does not reduce what he collects to a uniform and faceless mass, since the unity within which he gathers is lofty enough and rich enough to permit each unit its own shape. Paul's metaphor of an organism in which the various members complement each other clarifies this admirably.

The image of gathering is a favorite one for expressing God's promises in the Old Covenant. The salvation that is on its way is above all a gathering together of the scattered children of Israel. Gripping metaphors portray the Israelites' return on broad and level roads or carried on shoulders or in litters. Their destination is the land that belongs to God, a land in which he desires to rule as his people's Lord and Shepherd and King once more.

Jesus also came to gather once again the "lost sheep of Israel" (Mt 15:24). Yet his task is larger than that—he will die in order "to gather into one the children of God who are scattered abroad" (Jn 11:52) beyond the borders of Israel. How will these be collected? In a manner precisely opposite to the direction of Israel's salvation— through the scattering of his disciples into the whole world, going to all peoples not to bring them into geographical unity but to tell them of the higher unity of the salvation of the Cross and Resurrection, of the Church and life in the gospel, which spans the whole world. Christ scatters in order to gather more universally. Christ scatters, and whoever lets himself be scattered by him in his mission will gather with Christ.

A universal outreach in mission that permits those who are reached—"all nations"—to retain their characteristics remains an outreach of a single, concrete center: Christ. Thus the universality of this outreach is completely different from an internationalism that has no fixed center to guarantee its unity. One can say the same thing about Christ's Kingdom that medieval philosophers said about God when they compared God to a circle whose centerpoint is everywhere. The centerpoint of the Church is wherever the Lord's Eucharist is celebrated. Focusing on the centerpoint does not run counter to expansiveness in the same way that the homecoming of Israel counters Israel's exile among the nations. One must not try to argue that Rome is the centerpoint toward which all must return in the same way that Jerusalem was. Rome is merely the guarantor that the universal shape of the Church does not dissolve into a vague multiplicity that no longer maintains the integrity of the true centerpoint: faith in a Christ who gathers. Rome's responsibility is to ensure that Christ's concluding scattering does not deteriorate into a purely earthly type of scattering that no longer assembles around Christ.

Here is where the most difficult ecumenical problems lie. It is so easy for the "collecting dispersal" to flip over into a "dispersing collecting" that, despite well-intentioned zeal, many fail to notice a shift has taken place. Although no human creed or statement of belief can ever fully express the depths of the Christian mystery, one can distinguish between creedal statements that, on the one hand, place no barriers to the fullness of the mystery (even if they do not claim to be identical with the content they express) and those, on the other hand, that claim to create space for the fullness of the mystery by boundary-setting, negation, and protest. Such boundaries, however, can at best prevent abuses. They deserve respect when they do so, but they would contradict themselves if they claimed to open up larger dimensions for the mystery of Christ. To collect too quickly, as if differences no longer mattered, would mean no longer to be collecting with Christ and toward Christ but rather to be trying to set the focal point oneself. Unions of ultimately heterogeneous Christianities have always proved to be sterile because they reach out on their own instead of under Christ's commission.

In contrast, even the humblest believer gathers with Christ if he keeps up his contact "with him" in the most mundane daily activity. It is a contact with him who is the incarnate Love of God toward God's creation. The "worker" simply tries to help him bring in the harvest.

66. The Circle of Love

John draws us into the circuit of love that sets up such a pulsing flow between love for God and love for neighbor that each of these loves lives, is effective, and derives validity from the other. In the process he frees us from our doubts about our love. Do I love my neighbor? Yes, if I love God. Do I love God? Yes, if I love my neighbor. Yet the energy powering this circuit comes from the unity of both poles in Jesus Christ, who lived out the love of the Father toward mankind at the same time he lived out human love for the Father. Only if one shares in Christ through immersion in his birth from the Father and in Christ's world mission, rather than through some purely theoretical faith, will our faith close the circuit together with Christ, permitting the power to flow. All of this is said clearly in 1 John 5:1–6.

"Everyone who believes that Jesus is the Christ is born of God, and everyone who loves the parent loves the One born [together] of him" (5:1). Here from the start faith in Christ is understood as faith in the One born of the Father, born in such a comprehensive way that everyone knows: God's Son became man solely in order to draw us into a shared birth from the Father. "To all who received him he gave the power to become children of God, . . . who [like him] are born from God" (Jn 1:12–13). Thus I am never alone in my faith as a child of the Father; rather, I become that which I truly am, yet I do so in community with others, who are also children born of eternal love and thus endlessly lovable. Here we have Christian love of neighbor anchored definitively in faith in the trinitarian origin of the incarnate Son of God.

"By this we know: we love [in each instance] the children of God when we love God and keep his commandments" (1 Jn 5:2). It is presupposed here that a child loves the father to whom he owes his existence, especially since the thought is given a christological foundation. But that the child who loves God also keeps God's commandments must be understood in a Johannine sense:

the command Christ received from the Father is that he love us as the creatures of God and draw us into his own Sonship. Because the Son loves the Father, he also loves his mission, which consists of loving and transmitting that love to us. All of this is a single reality for Christ; for us, who are to be drawn into it, it *ought* to be a single reality, since it *is* a unity in Christ.

"And this commandment we have from him, that he who loves God *should* love his brother also" (4:21). Love is an *ought* that follows from the truth of faith, where it simply *is*. What at heart is naturally the right thing to do becomes for us, since we are inclined to selfishness, something of an assignment, a task. Yet as a natural thing it is not an impossible task, as is apparent in the following lines:

"For this is the love of God, that we keep his commandments" (5:3). Love and obedience are not immediately one and the same for us as they are for Christ. We first have to admit the fact of their unity and practice them until they become one for us. Yet because they are factually (theoretically) one and because of the fact that we are already drawn into this unity (practically) in Christ, carrying out this unity is "not hard". It may seem hard to us if our neighbor is either alienated from God or humanly repugnant. But viewed with eyes of faith he is already (actually or potentially) a fellow child of God (5:1) and thus worthy of more profound love than a physical sibling. This may involve a struggle, but its outcome is already basically achieved.

"For whoever is born of God overcomes the world, and this is the victory that overcomes the world: our faith" (5:4). Our faith is not based somehow on our ability to fight but on the victory Christ has already won over a world alienated from God (Jn 16:33). Since we ourselves are "born of God", we already have this victory. If we earnestly believe, we thus fight as those who have already won. This is expressed all the more clearly by the following lines, because they point to the trinitarian basis for Christ's triumph: "Who is it that overcomes the world? No one but he who believes that Jesus is the Son of God" (5:5).

The proof of all this is laid out in the scope of God's act of love in Christ's Incarnation and Cross. "This is the one who has come by water and by blood, Jesus Christ, not in water alone but in water and in blood. And the Spirit bears witness to it, for the Spirit is the truth" (5:6–7). Water is the baptism, but blood is a laying down of one's life on the Cross—which makes baptism effective as birth from God. Both of these have divine power only through the Spirit of God active in Jesus' life and death. He gave up all three on the Cross, as John testifies with great solemnity (Jn 19:35–37): blood and water poured from the wound in his side, and he breathed out his spirit with his head bowed to earth. Risen from the dead, he builds the believing Church from all three.

And thus the circuit of love between God and man is completed in Christ.

67. "To Hurl Fire upon the Earth"

Three phrases that follow each other, seemingly without inter-connection, all seem to point to the turmoil visited by Jesus' very existence on a world preoccupied with itself. "I have come to hurl fire upon the earth, and how I wish it was already burning. I have a baptism to be baptized with, and how it weighs upon me until it is accomplished. Do you think that I am come to bring peace to the earth? No, I tell you, but rather dissension" (Lk 12:49–51). Whether Jesus himself piled these lines one on top of the other or whether the Gospel writer did so makes little difference. They all demonstrate a clear awareness of the scope of Christ's mission. From an earthly perspective it lacks any measure and speaks of destruction, yet at the very heart it refers to his own destruction. Ultimate courage, almost unbearable responsibility, yet in the midst of these a fear—not anxiety about courage but anxiety about something that gives him the courage to kindle the confla-gration and cosmic conflict in the first place.

Such words speak of having felt the immense weight of his mission, a sense of burden that not even the early Christians could have invented for him and placed in his mouth. The flame he lights in this corner of the world is an incendiary act—something he fully realizes—that unleashes a blaze that can never be put out as long as world history lasts. "The gospel must first be preached to all nations" (Mk 13:10). Jeremiah frequently spoke of a fire of God that no one would be able to extinguish (4:4, 17:4, etc.), which was also the fire of the word of God in the prophet's mouth (5:14). But here we have Jesus, the complete Word of God, the unquenchable fire. Not only will Israel's temple go up in flames but so will the temples of all religions. What sects might build on top of the ashes will be mere hovels. "Does not my [incarnate] Word burn like fire and like a hammer that breaks the rocks?" (Jer 23:29).

Yet the hammer smashes the Word himself so that the fire can flash forth from him. The Passion must strike down the Word into ultimate weakness and abandonment by God; it must cover him with a bottomless abyss of fear so that fullness might pour forth from emptiness, boldness might radiate from this death anxiety, and the flames of God's love might flash from his suffocation to set everything on fire. The "axiom of the Cross" (1 Cor 1:18), the "scandal of the Cross" (Gal 5:11), must never be diluted in even the slightest degree. Unless the hammer smashes the Word into its very atoms, the Eucharist that keeps the fires burning all over the world is impossible.

The most painful aspect of it all is that the One who brings unity must splinter everything in order to rebuild from the bottom up what had been brought together in the wrong way. "Brother will deliver up brother, and father will hand his child over to death. Children will rise up against parents and kill them. You will be hated by all for my name's sake" (Mk 13:12–13). "Consider the word that I spoke to you: the servant is not greater than his master. If they have persecuted me, so they shall also persecute you." But me they "hate without a cause" (Jn 15:20, 25). The divisions spread through every house: "Three against two and two against three" (Lk 12:52). Once more the hammer that shatters rocks. And only out of a shattered Christian, out of a shattered Church, can the bright flame that yearns to see Jesus be kindled.

A sword must pierce through the heart of the Church so that the true attitude of people becomes visible for all who come into the world. So that this attitude may once more rise to the surface, the One baptized into the "fall and rising of many" must first be immersed in his baptism. Because his Church must carry on his work through time, she must eternally be the troublemaker for human projects of satisfaction and self-liberation. She must be both hammer and anvil at the same time. By illustrating the peace that is possible, she thereby stimulates dissatisfaction. She preaches the humility of the Cross yet is accused of acting with arrogance. She points to love as the path to freedom and thereby goads people to hate-filled struggle for that freedom. The tumult will become so chaotic that one can no longer even distinguish the flames of Christ's fire from the contrary flames of hell. Only a few flaming martyrs' stakes, like that of Joan of Arc, tower above the battle, shining with the pure fire of sanctity as lighthouses for sailors in distress.

68. "If Salt Goes Flat"

One cannot restore taste to salt that has gone flat (Mt 5:13). Salt produced naturally by evaporation, for example, like that extracted from the Dead Sea, can become stale and is good for nothing at all, neither for seasoning food nor for fertilizing soil; in other words, it is not even fit for the compost heap (Lk 14:35). In Jesus' day people tossed it out into the street where "people trample on it".

The saying's context is a call to follow Jesus: "You are the salt of the earth." Anything purely human, lacking Christian salt, tastes flat, even if it tries to make itself tasty by adding all sorts of other spices. As the "salt of the earth" the disciple's contribution is to preserve his mission. He may be more or less perfect, may fall into sin and then repent of it—none of that counts in this context; rather, only his faithfulness to the assignment his Lord gave him is important. He must preserve that assignment within a commitment underlying everything else, a commitment to place his life at his Lord's service, yet while waiting to be chosen by his Lord rather than seeking that service for himself. He must permit his Lord the freedom to reassign him even after he has begun a task. In other words, he must simply be at his Lord's disposal. This is the fundamental and ever vital attitude that he needs to preserve the saltiness of his mission.

This carries the gravest implications of any aspect of the Christian life. Even serious sins, including those of a servant of Christ, can be forgiven if one repents, but there is no remedy for having rejected or wasted one's calling. It is like a pot that cannot be glued together again once it is broken.

This danger is not limited to the person who has accepted a mission and later abandons it. Rather, the danger is present right at the moment of calling, wherever a clear call of God to a specific task in the Church (for example, to the life of the evangelical counsels or as a priest) is deliberately rejected out of human reasons. The history of a call can be very complex and normally requires spiritual guidance. Often a supposed call fails to become clear despite honest candor in prayer—to follow an uncertain call would be dangerous. What I think is the better path to take, that is, an objective choice, should never decide the matter but rather only that to which I know I am called as a subject, as an actor. Only if one closes off such a call by shoveling it full of personal objections does one enter upon the sort of detour that will be paid for with a harsh fate unrelieved by a fruitful substitute calling. The paths of life may run in outwardly diverging directions, but the scar of a false choice will always remain more or less visible. Bitterness, listlessness, disaffection with the Church, even cynicism often indicate what has happened.

Of course Christians are not dispensed from a responsibility to accompany those who walk this path with genuine ecclesial love, to the degree that such love is not spurned. It is not the Christians who are commanded to trample the salt that has lost its saltiness. They must, however, be careful not to deal with people who choose to occupy bitterly the periphery of the Church as if they stood in the center. The epistle of Jude offers a graduated series of guidelines for dealing with Christians who have slipped into various degrees of alienation from the Church's center: admonition if it will do any good; "snatching them from the fire" if it is still possible; avoiding external contact if it is no longer possible to rescue them (Jude 22–23).

69. How to Make Friends

Jesus' parable about the "clever steward" (Lk 16:1–9) presents problems. In discounting the debts owed to his wealthy master, the manager obviously seems to be defrauding him. Yet Jesus praises him—for Jesus is "the Lord" in verse eight.

The primary point of comparison between the parable and Christian practice lies not in the manager's machinations but in his thoughts: What shall I do if I am soon to be fired (16:4)? I see no future for me except to find shelter among good friends. This is exactly the question that Christians should pose: What will happen to me if one day I am released from the servitude of this earthly existence? In both instances the deadline is fast approaching.

The manager who has to acquire friends in a hurry resorts to questionable means, to the sort of practices that characterize the "clever" commerce of the "children of this world, who think they are smarter than the children of the light", as Jesus tells us at the end of the parable. The steward simply lowers the amount owed by each debtor: he makes one hundred barrels of oil into fifty, a hundred sacks of grain into eighty. In other words, he does exactly what he has been accused of—he wastes his lord's goods (16:1). He who perhaps had been falsely accused now stands justly accused. Yet now we find him called a "dishonest manager" (16:8), and the disciples are told, "Make friends for yourselves with the help of unrighteous riches [*mammon*] so that when it fails you may be taken into eternal lodgings" (16:9).

Thus it could be that the unrighteous wealth the man was supposed to manage is best utilized by making friends through writing off debts. That is what the disciples are supposed to do: "Make friends with the help of unrighteous wealth" must surely mean that such riches are to be used as alms for the poor. But is that what the parable means? One cannot determine this with certainty, for it seems to be operating at two levels simultaneously. On the one level, trustworthiness is valued precisely in money matters. The saying appended to the parable insists on this: "He who is faithful in the smallest matters is faithful in the largest. If you are not trustworthy in dealing with unrighteous wealth, who would ever entrust true riches to you?" (16:10–11). Yet it would be surprising if Jesus' intention was to give instructions for the administration of earthly goods, since he is the one who tells us not to worry about tomorrow and who refuses to arbitrate a quarrel over an inheritance (12:14). Thus his admonition to the disciples must refer more to a spiritual trustworthiness, even in earthly things. The point to be drawn from the parable would then be that God's instructions and the Holy Spirit's suggestions are to be followed precisely. The Covenant relationship between God and man is to be characterized not by guesswork but by the very precision that Jesus models perfectly.

Yet on another level it seems that a childlike carefreeness characterizes Jesus' attitude toward earthly things, as illustrated by the wasteful manager. If we try to push a bit deeper, we may discover that Jesus himself is the one who discounts our debts toward God, doing so on his own authority and ultimately at his own expense—by placing the portion written off, indeed far more than that, on his own account. Is that not his paradoxical way of dealing with the goods of others—namely, our sins—his way of making them his own? If so, then it is Jesus who lies behind the saying added by the Gospel writer: "If you are not trustworthy in handling that which belongs to someone else, who will ever give you that which is your own?" (16:12).

Thus, in the end, wastefulness and preciseness come together in Jesus; the Heavenly Father is the one who wastes love, and the Son portrays with precision this wastefulness on earth. To the degree that Christians learn to unite these two in imitation of Jesus in the world, they make friends in heaven, where both of these coincide eternally.

70. "When the Son of Man Comes, Will He Find Faith on the Earth?"

Sometimes Jesus' words are like bolts of lightning to which nothing horizontal can be attached but instead travel straight down from on high. He has told a parable that admonishes us to pray incessantly: God is not deaf; he will "soon" hear us. But then comes a sudden flash illuminating all world history yet to come: Will anyone be found praying, believing, at the end (Lk 18:8)? Or will it be as he had described it only shortly before: "As it was in the days of Noah, so it will be in the days of the Son of Man: people ate and drank, married, and were given in marriage right up to the day on which Noah entered the ark. Then the flood came and destroyed everything. It was no different in the days when Lot left Sodom: fire fell from heaven and destroyed everything. So it will be on the day when the Son of Man is revealed" (Lk 17:26–30).

What kind of a preview of the Omega-day is that? Will God's last word echo unheard through history like an ever more ancient story that someday simply "ceases to be true" (Hegel)? Or will the path of Jesus' story so resemble his earthly path that it leads to a crucifixion, to abandonment by God, to a shout that turns to death? Or will Christ's return also be the day of his mystical body's resurrection into the other world? Will one finally dare to hold one's head high "when the Son of Man comes on a cloud with power and glory" (Lk 21:27–28)? Such a vision is at least partly corroborated by the imagery of the book of Revelation.

The Lord makes no statements; he merely asks the question. We also can only ask questions when we view world history and the Church's experience within history. This is true of each situation, since we are unable to assess the eternal value of any particular set of events. The crests of the waves may simply be earthly arrogance piled high; the troughs of the waves may be special times of grace, although we can never be sure. We think we can observe that the Church flourishes during times of persecution and stagnates during times of prosperity. But one cannot conclude that it must be so, that a "law of history" operates here. After the forty days that Jesus spent visibly with his disciples, he says that precisely the one who believes without seeing will be blessed. There are shrines where a shaft from heaven shone once upon a time upon someone, and hundreds of thousands make pilgrimages to the site long after the clouds have once more closed over the place. Innumerable miracles may indeed have taken place over the centuries, but they have a strange sort of silence about them, as if their echoes have been muffled. Presumably most of them—most of the genuine miracles!—remained unnoticed as such by people. Someone relates a surprising conversion—well, such things do indeed occur, and a psychologist would have many tales to tell. . . .

Thomas wanted to see and touch in order to believe. Christians want to experience something in order to brighten up their weary faith. Christian culture has produced all sorts of architecture, sculpture, painting, music, and literature in an effort to make the deeply obscure mystery visible and has certainly done much to the glory of God and edification of fellow believers. Yet we do not know what all of this adds up to in God's scale of values. It may be that all of this has to be taken away from us as one takes toys from children so that we can recall once again the opening words of the Sermon on the Mount: "Blessed are the poor in spirit."

Not that the Kingdom is not in our midst. "But it is not coming with signs that can be observed. One cannot say, 'Lo, here it is,' or, 'There it is.' And if one says of the Son of Man, 'There he is; here he is', do not run along behind them" (Lk 17:20–23). Often something dawns in someone's heart, in the teaching of someone who has matured in faith, in the prayer of someone poor and oppressed, and it shines on us like the revolving beam of a lighthouse. When that happens we should be grateful but not try to cling to it. We have merely seen the flash of a tiny piece in a great mosaic that remains in a shadow. "The wind blows where it will; you hear its sound, but you know not whence it comes and whither it goes" (Jn 3:8). The metaphor fits perfectly: sometimes we feel the wind blowing on us, but we cannot catch hold of what is blowing; if it were capable of being grasped, it would no longer blow. Many have sensed a trace of such a breeze from a tabernacle where the eucharistic host is reserved, from the sanctuary lamp, from an encounter with another person, or during a solitary walk in nature—one must be satisfied with such traces. *Breath* and *Spirit* express in English a single word used in the conversation with Nicodemus; both are equally free. Jesus, "the Lord, is the Spirit, but where the Spirit of the Lord is, there is freedom" (2 Cor 3:17). May it blow freely through all the ruins of the world and the Church.

71. GLORY, TEARS, and the WHIP

The structure of Luke 19:28–45 is striking: while the Messiah enters the holy city accompanied by a jubilant crowd, he weeps over the city and foretells her destruction only to go immediately to the temple, where he forcibly cleanses what had become a "den of robbers". It is his disciples who turn his entry into the city into a triumphal procession on a donkey obtained specifically for the occasion (certainly intended to point to Zechariah 9:9–10, where the Messiah-King rides humbly on a donkey). They spread their clothes on the path and lead the jubilant singing that celebrates all the miracles they have experienced. They work into their song the very words sung by the angels at Christmas: "Peace in heaven and glory in the highest". Thus the final phase of messianic existence confirms its beginning and thus confirms its entirety.

It is almost incomprehensible that, during this festively staged procession, Jesus should break into tears at the sight of the city, blind and oblivious to the peace so loudly proclaimed: "You did not know the time [*kairos*] of your visitation." For the city and for him it is too late. He can see in advance her siege and destruction, and he undoubtedly also sees his own demise. According to John he knows precisely what awaits him; he had been warned not to show up anywhere near Jerusalem. Everything is intertwined into an inextricable knot: Incarnation and Cross, rejoicing over the King who comes in the name of God, and misunderstanding of his true mission. Jesus admits the inextricability of it all: "I tell you, if they [the disciples] were to be silent, the very stones would cry out" (Lk 19:40). He refers to the stones of the city, the same stones of which he says, "no stone" shall "be left on top of another" (Mt 24:2).

The whole procession leads to the temple, which Jesus immediately begins to sweep clean. The commerce carried on there is thievery, the opposite of prayer. But why this forcible clean-up if the whole thing is soon to be destroyed? John says, "He spoke of the temple of his body" (Jn 2:21). His own destruction and the destruction of the holy place of Israel are two sides of the same event; therefore, just as the temple that he himself is will go to its death in purity, so too this building of stones will disappear, but in a condition suited to the purpose for which it was built. It is in the temple that Jesus poses the final, most decisive alternatives (Lk 20): he is the Son whom the vineyard workers murder; he confronts his opponents with an unanswerable question to which he himself gives no solution; he is the rejected cornerstone that smashes everything in its path; he rejects a politicized Covenant theology and instead proclaims a Resurrection that transcends earthly conditions; he is the Lord of whom David spoke; finally, he praises an act symbolic of his own complete sacrifice: the widow's offering.

No part of this concluding song on the eve of suffering is insignificant for the Church, the "Israel of God". It bears repeating: Jesus' disciples are the ones who strike up the liturgical *Gloria* recalling his miracles and who invent all sorts of ceremonies (the clothes strewn in his path) in order to "shape" worship to their own taste. Yet that does not reveal the mixture of heavenly and earthly-political theology in their thinking or show how much they long to sacrifice for Christ's sake compared to how much they are preoccupied with their own power. No one can say how many tears Jesus shed and continues to shed over the new Jerusalem, which remains oblivious to that which really serves her peace. And thus no one can say when the Lord is cleansing the Church of her "robbers' dens" or permits her to be oppressed by others (as in the Old Covenant the Assyrians and Babylonians served Yahweh as mercenaries in order to bring Israel back into line) so that he might dwell in her as in his temple and might proclaim something of the "glory of the heavens" in credible solidarity with the world.

"For the time has come for judgment to begin with the house of God" (1 Pet 4:17).

72. WOLVES IN SHEEPSKINS

At the end of the Sermon on the Mount Jesus warned about false prophets (Mt 7:15–23), specifically about those who appear disguised as sheep in the midst of the Christian community and prophesy, cast out evil spirits, and work many miracles in Jesus' name (7:22). He not only warns about them but also gives instructions on how to distinguish them from true prophets.

That false prophets are always found where true prophecy is uttered can be seen already in the Old Testament, where Elijah, and even more fiercely Jeremiah, engage in a life-and-death struggle between genuine and simulated divine callings. The criterion for distinguishing was already given to Moses, who promised the messianic prophet: "Perhaps you say to yourself: How shall we know when the word does not come from Yahweh? If his word remains without effect and does not come true, then it was not spoken by Yahweh" (Dt 18:21–22). The Prophet promised by Moses has now spoken. If others speak and act in his name from now on, how shall they be distinguished? Jesus gives an answer basically the same as that found in the Old Covenant: "By their fruits you shall know them" (Mt 7:16)—if what they say becomes reality, they are true prophets. The prayers of the priests of Baal on Mount Carmel remained without effect just as the prophecies of the peace-priests of Jeremiah's time never came to pass.

Yet in the era of the Church things are more difficult, since the wolves in sheep's clothing seem to work wonders in Jesus' name. One needs only to reflect on the large number of false mystics throughout Church history, indeed, on their increasing numbers as the modern age unfolds, and on their ever-increasing following. If we look at the New Testament writings in overview, we find at least five focal points through which, in Paul's words, one may discern the spirits.

The first three are given by the Lord himself. His teaching is an act of God, not merely a theory. Thus not the one who merely says, "Lord, Lord", but the one who does "the will of my Father" is the one who walks Jesus' way (7:21). Jesus requires no works of supererogation that we think up for ourselves, like the Pharisee praying in the temple. All Jesus asks is that we keep the commandment of love that he himself kept and commanded us to keep. We must do to others what he has done to us (Jn 13:14); because he loved us to the point of dying for us, we must also lay down our lives for the brethren (1 Jn 3:16). To lay burdens upon others that we ourselves do not carry is Pharisaism (Mt 23:3-4).

The second point is that false prophets seek themselves in their religious activity. They want to be seen, respected, honored (Mt 23:5-7; 6:2-5); they want to become rich (Lk 16:14); they want to sell their miraculous powers like Simon (Acts 8:18-24) or make a profit from prophecy (Acts 16:16-18); or, at the very least, like the Jewish magician Bar-Jesus, they want to prevent the apostles from having success (Acts 13:6-12). The *Didache* also warns the early Christian churches about itinerant Christian preachers who request money or anything else while "speaking in the Spirit". "Not everyone who speaks in the Spirit is a prophet but rather only the one who lives as the Lord lived" (chap. 11).

In the third place, the Lord teaches that false prophets can be known by their fruits, offering as an example the fact that each tree has fruit proper to it (Mt 7:16-17). This is the specific New Testament application of the basic Old Testament criterion. For followers of Christ fruit-bearing presupposes that the grain of wheat will die. Put in another way, it presupposes that one remains a branch attached to the trunk of the grapevine. Bearing fruit in the sense Jesus intended can be the result of a powerful charism (as was true of the saintly founders), or it can be the quiet radiance of a humble pastor or unassuming housewife. False mystics may make a great sensation, but they bear no fruit. They disappear like will-o'-the-wisps. In this way the Christians at Ephesus "tested those who claim to be apostles when they are not and found them to be liars" (Rev 2:2).

Then we have a fourth point, evident in Paul's zeal against his opponents within the Church. They cast doubt on his gospel because it does not hold to the letter of the Jewish-Jerusalem Christian Tradition. He claims the authority of the Jerusalem

Council (Acts 15) and exposes the traditionalists armed with letters of reference as "apostles of lies" who, like Satan, present themselves as "angels of light" (2 Cor 11:14). This is the same imagery as "wolves in sheepskins". Against them the phrase "the letter kills, but the Spirit gives life" (2 Cor 3:6) is directed.

Finally we have the opposite point, hammered home by Paul and John alike. Whoever is not satisfied with the Incarnation of the Word, whoever claims to progress "beyond it", "he does not have God" (2 Jn 9). The Corinthian charismatics do the same, putting the Cross behind them and wanting already to be resurrected in the Spirit. They insist on the Spirit alone and fail to understand that the Spirit distributes his gifts only as "ministries" for the Church of the eucharistic Lord (1 Cor 12:5).

Recognizing the last two detours for what they are leads back to Jesus' criteria. The path he followed and pioneered for his followers is a dying to oneself in love. It is the only "activity" of truth (see Jn 3:21) that can be expected to bear fruit for the Kingdom of God.

73. "Lord, Depart from Me"

In Mark (1:14–20) and Matthew (4:18–22) the first four disciples, Simon Peter and Andrew, James and John, are called in a single event. In Luke the first calling involves only Peter (5:1–11), although the sons of Zebedee "leave everything" in response to his confession.

Simon had already hosted Jesus, and Jesus had healed his mother-in-law. After that Jesus seems to have preached primarily "in the synagogues of Galilee" (Lk 4:44) before taking up contact with Peter again. Peter was one among several fishermen along the shore when Jesus stepped into his boat and asked him to "put out a little way from shore" so that he could teach from the lake, avoiding the press of the crowd along the shore. Thus Peter's second encounter with Jesus took place as he sat behind him in the boat. To the outward observer, Peter has done Jesus a small favor, extending him, as it were, the little finger of his hand. Suddenly Jesus grabs his whole hand. A small cloud swells into a storm—a request for a small favor becomes an overpowering command: "Put out into the deep [by yourself] and let down your nets for a catch!" It is doubly overpowering because it contradicts what an experienced fisherman knows about catching fish: "We toiled the entire night and caught nothing." Yet this is immediately followed by pure obedience: "But at your word I will let down the nets." He dares to vault over his own horizon. Jesus' authority out-weighs all that one possesses, including one's own skilled knowledge. Everything follows naturally: the huge catch of fish that threatens to drown them all—"nearly swamping" not only Peter's boat but also a second one that came from shore to assist. As is often the case with Jesus' miracles, the divine largess seems foolish to human minds: the excess of excellent wine at Cana, the multiplication of loaves in the wilderness into a quantity that even thousands could not consume.

This is the same faith that causes Matthew to call Peter blessed and leads to Peter's being chosen as the Rock of the Church. It must also be the same faith that inclined John the Evangelist to tell the story of the renaming of Simon, son of Jonah (or John), as Peter "the Rock" already at his first encounter with Jesus.

Yet in the instance at hand, in Luke 5, the poor fellow is almost washed overboard by Jesus' miracle. He is terrified to his depths by being drawn into a divine act without being asked whether he is willing. His reaction is like Isaiah's "woe is me, for I am a man of unclean lips, and my eyes have seen the King, the Yahweh of Sabaoth" (Is 6:5). A fundamental distance stretches between a sinful man and the calling that he has unwittingly accepted. This happens as the result of an act of faith that seems to him to be no act at all. He simply surrenders himself naturally to the miracle at home and the preaching in his boat. He trembles like an animal in a cage but is not set free. Instead he is told, "Fear not; from now on you will catch men." What he is is taken from him and given back to him at a completely different level. He remains the same yet completely different.

All answers are superfluous in such a situation. "They pulled the nets up on the shore, left everything, and followed him." Simon will need a lot of time to make the transition from his old being to his new one. He will overreach himself; he will betray three times the Master he worships, the One he is willing to die for. The distance he felt in the beginning will become immeasurably greater at this higher level. But it will thereby create the vacuum that his office ultimately will occupy. In this he is the model for all whom the Lord calls. A perfect distance that makes it possible to follow all the way to the Cross, to a crucifixion head downward—so that even in the greatest similarity a distance is maintained and so that no one has reason to confuse the two.

74. "DID NOT OUR HEARTS BURN?"

On the way to Emmaus the Risen One becomes a Scripture exegete, expounding his own word and being. For from the beginning he is the Word whose meaning fully unfolds only here, at the end, from the perspective of the Resurrection. The talk here of "Moses, all the prophets, and the writings" (Lk 24:27), as well as in the following scene in Jerusalem, where Jesus explains to the eleven what is written about himself "in the law of Moses, in the prophets, and in the Psalms" (24:44), uses the conventional three-fold division of the Old Testament books to refer to the completeness of the word that is communicated. In neither scene do we need to assume that Jesus held some sort of seminar in exegesis—we can perfectly well imagine the Risen One's words as epitomes that gave the emerging Church a comprehensive intuition that only gradually brightened into its fullness under the influence of the Pentecost Spirit. It was a perspective, an overview, placed in the Church's heart, from which she has drawn through the centuries and will draw in the future.

Both passages refer not only to specific texts—for example, the passage from Isaiah about God's servant or the Psalms whose verses Jesus prayed on the Cross that speak of the distribution of his clothing—but also to the totality of the Old Testament revelation. According to Jesus' own words, this totality can be fully understood only when the final word of God, the death and Resurrection of the Messiah, has been spoken. According to John's account, already in his earthly life the Lord says that Moses wrote about him and that Moses cannot be understood without looking to Christ (5:46). The letter to the Hebrews portrays magnificently how all of Israel's faith proceeded in advance of its fulfillment and cannot be complete without that fulfillment (Heb 11:40). Moses chose the abuse Christ suffered over the treasures of Egypt (11:26). Abraham's exemplary faith referred entirely to "my day" for its real meaning (Jn 8:56). All of Israel's history—so full of unfulfilled promises, unsatisfied plaints and complaints against God, and destructions that leave only a remnant to survive and hold onto unrequited hopes—remains an unsolved puzzle until her final death and final resurrection to indissoluble unity works itself out in the Messiah's destiny. The most profound question from the abyss: "My God, why have you forsaken me?" and the utterly profound answer from the heights: "Therefore God has raised all things in him", are interwoven in the ultimate message about the Covenant between God and the world.

The Church's heart glows in the light of this revelation, which lays out a single meaning for all that has happened from the primordial beginning to its completion. For this exegesis is also an unveiling of God's flaming heart, an unveiling that can be legitimately undertaken only by God himself. We are dealing here not with a neutral knowledge but rather with the confession of a deeply wounded, bleeding love that can only be received by a glowing human heart. A cold heart cannot even hear the confession.

Thus the invitation: "Stay with us, for it is growing late" (Lk 24:29). After walking together like this, it is impossible to say good-bye. Outwardly they might have talked ever so matter-of-factly and soberly, but glowing hearts were beating a single rhythm. The scene concludes appropriately enough with the ultimate realization of this intertwining: the perfect, incarnate Word places himself in breaking of bread in the disciples' ardent hearts. And their hearts then contain the seal of that unity and totality of the word, the completion of the Covenant, God and man united, which he has expounded. Just as appropriately, the outward form of the Word disappears: it is no longer a visible form side by side and face to face; rather, it is a totality that has absorbed all dialogue into itself.

75. "If It Is My Will That He Abide"

The disciple Jesus loved is the bearer of ecclesial love. And it apparently is Jesus' will that this love last not merely for a period of time but "until my return" (Jn 21:22–23). We must explicitly refute the foolish notion that John would not die—Jesus said nothing of the sort. What is involved here is rather that the love embodied by John will abide and persist to the end of history. Since the question about love's perseverance is raised by Peter, who is given the office of administration, this implies by extension that this office must also exercise its task of feeding Jesus' sheep until he returns. Both love and administration continue parallel and interwoven with each other, since Peter received the office only upon answering the question "Do you love me more than these?" yet, seeing the disciple of love still standing next to him, could only ask in surprise, "Lord, what will become of him?" (21:21).

Peter has to be satisfied with his Lord's authoritative and evasive answer—which underscores the parallel yet intertwining relationship of the two. They are intertwined as love is integrated into office—thus John appropriately stepped aside to permit office (Peter) to enter the empty tomb first; yet they are also parallel as John, the recipient of direct insight into the presence and will of the Lord, communicates that insight to the office of Peter (21:7).

Situations can arise in the Church in which office forces love to cower in a corner, as is evident already in the second epistle of John, but since love has only to abide (one of John's favorite words), this corner can be the place where love is best cared for. In a corner, hidden from sight, love accomplishes what constitutes its essence: not only "abiding" itself and assuring its survival but also assuring the abiding and survival of the entire Church, including the Church's office. For "love is long-suffering"; that is, it knows no impatience and refuses to break off communication; "love will not permit itself to be irritated" and thus "does not hold a grudge";

by letting evil shatter against it, love shows its concern for the good of its opposite, from which it "bears everything", "endures everything", and perhaps foolishly "believes everything" and "hopes everything" even of something unfaithful and hateful (1 Cor 13:4–7). Thus love outlasts all gifts based on worldly, or even supernatural, insight—which are "piecemeal" in comparison to love. "When that which is perfect comes, they will pass away" (13:8–10).

Love's "abiding" is thus no mere guarantee that an aspect of the Church will survive (merely an aspect because "abiding" is neither an organizational nor a missionary activity). Rather, it is the promise that the entire Church will survive through love that endures and hopes all things, including trials within the Church. All that is visible in the Church thus survives through what is most unpretentious.

It is right that John, who first appears together with Peter at the beginning of the book of Acts, completely disappears after Paul makes his stage entrance. (Luke's vignettes at the beginning of Acts offer the best illustrations for the symbolic meaning of the great scene enacted between Peter and John at the end of the fourth Gospel.) Moreover, it is characteristic that the First Epistle of John seems to concentrate entirely on relationships within the community and to lack any missionary tendency. The letter is concerned exclusively with the genuineness, that is, the Christ-likeness, of the love practiced among the brethren. This love must exhibit all dimensions: from an inward likeness of the love of the Trinity to simple social community: "If anyone has goods of this world and sees his brother in need yet closes his heart against him, how can love for God abide in him? Little children, let us not love in word or speech but in deed and in truth" (1 Jn 3:17–18).

76. "The Power of Darkness"

"What could light and darkness have in common?" (2 Cor 6:14). One thing only: "The light can shine in darkness" (Jn 1:5), although this does not necessarily mean that the darkness wishes to receive the light—someone who dwells in darkness can refuse to enter the light that shines (Jn 3:20–21).

With that we find ourselves in the center of the mystery. From one perspective the dawning of light in darkness may seem natural and neutral: "The people who sit in darkness have seen a great light, and for those who sit in the land of death a light has dawned" (Mt 4:16). Yet mere "sitting" can also be described as a deliberate "walking": if we claim to be in the light "yet nonetheless walk in darkness, we lie" (1 Jn 1:6), for in fact we are preferring darkness to light (Jn 3:19) and are doing the "unfruitful works of darkness" (Eph 5:11). There are those who claim to be "a light to those who walk in darkness" but themselves dwell in darkness (Rom 2:19). When the "light shines in the darkness", something much more dramatic than a natural phenomenon is involved. Darkness can resist a penetrating light. Because it has this power, Jesus could tell his tormenters as he entered upon his Passion, "This is your hour and the power of darkness" (Lk 22:53); not merely a human but a satanic power directed against God is portrayed as "the powers, rulers of this dark world, evil spirits" (Eph 6:12). This darkness has not "comprehended" the light that appears in its midst because it has not been "grasped by it".

How will mankind, sitting in this realm of darkness and the shadow of death, receive the light that makes its appearance? One can speak of an excess of love that "snatches" people "from the power of darkness" (Col 1:13). It can also be expressed with less violence: God, "who calls you from darkness to his marvelous light" (1 Pet 2:9). Thus, on the one hand, an overpowering light, as in the parable of the stronger man who "ties up the strong man" in order to enter his house and rob him of his goods (Mt 12:29);

on the other hand, we find a degree of human willingness to enter into the light bringing one's inner darkness along, to become "a child of the light". "For everything that is brought into the light [even if it is darkness, sin] is light" (Eph 5:13–14). In this process the cooperation of someone who is already in the light is clearly expected. Christians are told to "hand over" (*elenchein*), to bring out into the open, to reveal the true nature of those who dwell and act in the secrecy of darkness. This is exactly what the Lord required of his apostle when he sent him to the Gentiles: "You shall open their eyes for them so that they might turn from darkness to light, from the power of Satan to God" (Acts 26:18).

But this ecclesial task of enlightening presupposes that the Christians who themselves once dwelt in darkness have been "torn from the power of darkness and transferred to the Kingdom of the Son of love" (Col 1:13). They are told, "Once you were darkness; now, however, you are light in the Lord" (Eph 5:8). They could be wrested free because the light of Christ not only lit up the darkness powerfully in all truth but also entered into the (overly) powerful darkness. Christ might have fought against this overpowering darkness and refused to drink the cup, but he did not. He let himself be delivered up by the Father to the power of darkness, giving his assent to the Father's plan. God's omnipotence gives to the opposing power the power to surrender life to death: "You would have no power over me," Jesus told Pilate, "if it were not given you from above" (Jn 19:11). In order for God's light truly to shine in the darkness, the darkness must, as it were, receive it into itself, wrap itself around it. Only in this way is darkness conquered from within. *Dux vitae mortuus regnat vivus* (the living leader of life, having died, reigns alive).

Delivered from darkness Christian life continues to the end under the command: "Walk as children of the light!" (Eph 5:8). The Johannine Christ puts it with great intensity: "I am the light of the world. . . . Yet for a little while the light is among you. As long as you have the light, walk in the light, lest darkness overtake you. He who walks in darkness knows not where he is going. Believe in the light as long as you have light so that you may become children of light" (Jn 8:12; 12:35–36).

77. "He Who Finds His Life Will Lose It"

With slight variations this statement recurs eight times in the Synoptic Gospels. *Find* may be replaced by *save, gain,* or *preserve,* but the point intended by the contrast is the same: the aim is to lose one's life or self (*psyche* can mean either one) for the sake of Christ (and "for the sake of the gospel") in order to find it, to save it. Gaining the whole world would not help if a person suffered damage to his soul in the process. The soul cannot be bought with anything (Mk 10:39; 16:25, 26; Mk 8:35, 36, 37; Lk 9:24; 17:33).

Seeking and finding oneself means not simply living an egotistical life but rather also refer to an obsession with grasping one's own self, to the pursuit of security through self-knowledge. This is to pursue what all of antiquity and all of Christian history considered to be wisdom: *"Gnōthi sauton"* (know thyself)—in the words of the inscription placed on the Delphic temple. Originally this exhortation may have pointed to the awesome distance between the human self and the divine sublimeness; later it pointed to the quasi-divine dignity of the human self itself; at times it has pointed paradoxically to both at once. But it has always been taken as the indispensible prerequisite for moving from the realm of appearances and illusions to the realm of valid understanding.

This contradicts Jesus' words, which equate not only the seeking but also the finding of this self with its loss (Mt 10:39), a loss that can be transformed into an authentic finding if one "loses oneself [or one's life] for my sake". The preceding verses emphasize that to prefer worldly goods to the Person of Christ is to be "unworthy of me", and one's own self is included among these goods (Lk 14:26). By losing oneself in oneself because one loses oneself in Jesus, one gains oneself but only in Jesus. If this is applied to self-knowledge it simply means: since it is impossible to see oneself (the eye can see everything but itself), one sees and knows oneself in Jesus, not merely as in a mirror (which simply reflects one's own image) but as in a conceptual realm that permits one to see everything at once—what one is in oneself, what one should be, what one truly is in God. If one still insists, despite these reservations, in describing Jesus as a mirror, then he is a most dramatic one, a mirror that reflects a very dynamic rather than static image: what I am but dare not be, what I am on the basis of Jesus' divine work yet not statically but rather on the basis of his work as a living challenge to me. Thus "finding" oneself in Jesus is also an encounter with a presence that will soon be past—because of Jesus yet also through me—an encounter with a future that is present for him yet will be also present through me. The simultaneity of being and ought-to-be expresses the reality that my true self lies in God but both as a gift and as a responsibility.

Because the truth of the self rests in God (and "has been bought with a price" [1 Cor 6:20]), it has a preciousness that cannot be assessed by any worldly value. "What could one give in return for one's self?" (Mt 16:26). But also because it rests in God, one cannot find it in oneself, and if one did find it in oneself, it would have no special value. Thus some religions believe there is no such thing as a self, that one therefore must sacrifice the self that is worthless in the world, the self that is a mere illusion, in order to find pure selflessness in God. This, however, would contradict Jesus' words, which guarantee a finding of one's self (or life) in God.

The difference is that this self found in God is arrived at through a completely different kind of selflessness than the religions envision. It is a selflessness that is self-giving rather than self-abandonment, the kind of self-giving that Jesus modeled for us in his existence for God and for the world, an existence that thereby gives us a glimpse of the inner life of God, where the selfhood of Father, Son, and Spirit exists in pure giving to each other, in losing oneself in oneself in order to find oneself in the other. If God shelters our self in himself, then we can find ourselves there only by becoming like him.

78. "Then the Scandal of the Cross Would Be Eliminated"

This would happen should Paul preach and insist on circumcision alongside the Cross of Christ (Gal 5:11). That dare not happen, for then circumcision would still be religiously valid—circumcision here represents the essence of the entire Old Testament law—and the Cross would have to share its power with that of the law, or, in Pauline terms, the effect of divine grace would be shared with the effect of human effort. To put it in yet another way: the work of Christ that brings grace would not be the fulfillment of all the promises that preceded it but only an imperfect aspect of what went before, an aspect that would reach completeness only through elements of the promises.

That the Crucified One fulfills and surpasses the law is the *skandalon,* the rock of offense, a cause for argument and anger, a stumbling block, a cause for sin. Can all our effort to satisfy God's requirements suddenly be considered useless, indeed, considered a pharisaical rebellion against God's grace? Considered as the sole source of God's grace, the Cross becomes an insult to man and all his religious energies. Precisely there lies the scandal. Is not the Covenant bilateral? Of course it is established by God and thus a work of his gracious favor, but it also requires some effort on the part of men if it is to be correctly called a covenant. Now all of a sudden we are asked to believe that the Covenant is unilateral, that God ultimately does it all himself. Paul bases himself on Abraham's faith—but if this was sufficient for his justification, then why did God also require circumcision of him (Rom 4)? Certainly not merely so that "sin might abound" (Rom 5:20)? How could the law be referred to as "holy, just, and good" (Rom 7:12)?

According to Paul this scandalousness cannot and should not be eliminated or set aside. It should, indeed, be constantly fresh and challenging, so much so that the Church must not merely proclaim it but should always keep it acutely present in the form she shows to the world and in her course of history. Paul's lifetime of persecution proves his point: "If I were to preach circumcision as well, why am I then persecuted?" (Gal 5:11). The scandalousness of the Cross is made present in his being persecuted. He extends this to the Church as a whole: the immediacy of the axiom that "the Cross of Christ dare not lose its power" is brought home to the Church: "The word of the Cross is foolishness to those who are perishing, but to us who are being saved, it is the power of God.... Consider your calling, brethren! ... What the world considers foolish, God has chosen in order to embarrass the wise, ... what the world considers lowly and despicable, God has chosen in order to destroy what seems worthwhile to the world" (1 Cor 1:17-18, 26-28). Thus the apostle and the Church are supposed to make the scandal a reality. But are they also supposed to eliminate the force of the Old Covenant's claims? Has the two-sided character of the Covenant established by God become one-sided on the Cross?

Does not the man Jesus Christ, the "Servant of God" and "Son of Man" himself, complete the bilateral Covenant through giving himself perfectly to God's covenantal will? Does not his perfect obedience in Incarnation, life, and Passion provide the opportunity for God's Covenant will—which was always pure grace—to triumph in the world? And is it not the unity of Christ with his Church, which is his "body", that constantly makes real the scandal of grace? Paul certainly does not boast of his keeping of the law; rather, he boasts "with joy in his weaknesses, so that the power of Christ may dwell in me. Therefore I am pleased with weaknesses, abuse, lack of necessities, persecutions and anxieties for Christ's sake: for when I am weak, then I am strong" (2 Cor 12:9-10). Only in this sense are the apostle and all Christians "cooperators with God": in the world-scandalizing paradox that they lose "their life" through complete self-surrender to the work of God and thereby "gain", in the paradox that they lose their desire to be themselves in order to find their personalities in God. This alone is the perfected two-sidedness of the "New and eternal Covenant".

79. "Praise the Lord, You Sea Monsters and All Deeps, Fire and Hail, Snow and Clouds"

Yahweh's congregation draws the cosmos and its dangerous and destructive forces into its cosmic song of praise (Ps 148:7–8). In the ancient religious myths the monsters of the ocean represent the threatening enemies of the deity that had to be overcome in a primordial struggle; here they are part of the divine creation that praises God in its totality. God parades the most monstrous creatures in the world before Job's eyes in order to demonstrate God's superiority over a fragile man: "Can you catch the leviathan with a hook; can you put a rope on his nose? Can you play with him as with a bird; can you put him on a leash for your daughter?" (Job 40:20ff. [41:1–5]). God himself created the monster in order to play with him (Ps 104:26).

Nature's wild creatures praise God as much as her tame ones: "The lions roar for prey and seek their food from God" (Ps 104:21). Surveying his work, the Creator considered even a world in which one eats and is eaten to be "very good" (Gen 1:31). The protological image, which returns eschatologically in the prophets, of a natural world in which only plants are eaten (Gen 1:29–30) and in which peace ultimately reigns among all animals (Is 11:6ff.) points to an ideal, to a wholeness that transcends this world: "The land will be full of the knowledge of the Lord, as the waters cover the sea" (Is 11:9).

All elements have their sphere of operation, even if they are destructive for people. "Fire and hail, snow and clouds" (Ps 148:7–8), are called upon to praise, together with "all rain and dew, all his storms, fire, and heat; winter cold and summer heat; ice and cold, dews and snow, darkness and light, clouds and lightning" (Dan 3:64–73 [Song of the Three Young Men, vv. 42–51]). None of these, no matter how fearsome to men, is excluded from praising

God and therefore from God's creative will. If the first account of creation seems to portray images of an evolutionary development in creation's coming into being, and if such a development is not imaginable without struggle among creatures and the extinction of the weaker ones, even so there can be no talk of blame in this process of formation. For "life and death praise the Lord" would fit equally well in the cosmic psalms.

When Paul refers to an indefinite and tense straining of all of nature (*apokaradokia* [Rom 8:19]), it means in the first place that nature unconsciously strives toward mankind. But when he subsequently talks about the subjection of creation to futility in solidarity with sinful mankind, with both of them "groaning and in labor" so that nature might attain her final goal together with mankind fallen into the "bondage of decay", the goal of "the freedom of the children of God" (Rom 8:20–22), the cosmos' unconscious expectation, is included in mankind's great hope: to attain the "Sonship" of God and to participate in the "firstfruits of the Spirit" that lie beyond mankind (8:23). None of this is now possessed fully; rather, it takes place in an immense dynamism that includes the entire cosmos, a dynamism that is still sustained by groaning together with the Divine Spirit. Ascending from the evolutionary drive of nature to the groaning hopes of mankind to the Spirit's pressing toward the revealed "glory" of the children of God is an indivisible movement that reveals its unity in a double solidarity: nature-heaven and mankind–Divine Spirit.

Thus already the Old Testament person could permit a natural world experienced with supreme realism to join in the song of praise to God, and the New Testament person not only comprehends the cosmos in himself but also, carried forward by the Divine Spirit and all his force of hope, transcends his nature to draw the cosmos into the glory of God.

80. The Temptation to Flee

A believer's situation among his own people, in his own surroundings, can seem so hopeless to him that he sees no purpose in sticking it out. To stay any longer seems life-threatening; thus Jeremiah's thoughts as he considers where he might spend the night if he were to flee: "If I only had a refuge in the wilderness as a pilgrim, I would leave my people; I would leave them far behind" (9:1). At home he encounters only deceit and distortion, lies and violence (9:3-4). Likewise the Psalmist thinks about flight: "If I only had wings like a dove, I would fly away and be at rest. Yea, I would flee far away; I would lodge in the wilderness, sheltering myself before the raging wind and tempest" (Ps 55:7-9 [6-8]). The decision to flee can be a well-intentioned one, growing out of the realization that the foundations of the nation, society, and the Covenant with God are so undermined that all resistance is in vain: "Fly like a bird to the mountain! See how the wicked bend the bow, fitting their arrow to the bowstring to shoot in the dark at the upright in heart. If the foundations are destroyed, what can the righteous do?" (Ps 11:1-3).

The one facing this challenge refuses to flee. As the Psalms so often express, he knows that he is safe in God. God is enough for him, for it is impossible that God will forget his Covenant and break it. Even if all the representatives of the Covenant law among the people of God—the kings, judges, even the prophets— are tottering and untrustworthy (see Ps 82), the throne of God with Israel as his footstool (Lam 2:1; Ezek 43:7)—a metaphor for the Covenant—is immovable. Because God is present in any earthly chaos, even in the Church's chaos, flight is unthinkable. One would, after all, be fleeing from God himself, and where would one find an oasis along the path of such a flight? Surely only in the wilderness.

The New Testament argues even more forcefully for "staying put". In the Old Covenant the chaos among his people could reach such a climax that Yahweh could do nothing except to drive them into exile, assuring them that a "remnant" would return home. In the New Covenant such an exile cannot be, for there is no foreign land that does not belong to Christ. At most the Christian may, together with his Lord, suffer "outside the camp" and share his abuse—indeed, the Christian may be explicitly told to do that (Heb 13:13), "for we have here no lasting city; rather, we are searching for the one that is to come" (vs. 14). As a "pilgrim and stranger" on earth (1 Pet 2:11) the Christian cannot experience ostracism, since his manner of life (*politeuma* [Phil 1:27]) is found in heaven, not on earth. We see this most clearly in the book of Revelation, where a Christian existence on earth becomes completely impossible (Rev 13:15ff.), where, indeed, Christians find no place of refuge at all. Even if they wanted to, they could not "drop out". But in the book of Revelation one can never be sure whether these scenes take place on earth or in heaven or in both places at once: on earth it is an existence as a witness for the Lamb; in heaven it is simultaneously a following of the Lamb "wherever he goes" (Rev 14:4). Christians are just as vulnerable to death as they are ultimately invulnerable; in this they resemble the Lamb himself, who stands both alive and sacrificed on God's throne.

Thus flight is even more impossible for Christians than it was for the Israelites. The wings of the dove of the Holy Spirit are at the Christian's disposal all the time, but not to flee into the wilderness, rather to fly to the heaven of the living God where one's true home is—even though the Church's existence during world history quite properly is called an exile in the wilderness, facing the dragon's frenzy (Rev 12:14ff.), yet preserved and fed by God in safety. The entire Church is in this wilderness, and it therefore makes little sense to seek a particularly protected wilderness within ecclesial existence (for example, a monastery or hermitage), unless God has personally directed one to such a place. Modern religious orders have discovered that one can lead a wilderness life for God more easily in an unbelieving metropolis than in the most secluded cell. Nowhere can one evade the "rage of the dragon against the woman" and his war "with the rest of her offspring", the Christians.

81. "He Who Can Receive This, Let Him Receive It"

These words were spoken in regard to celibacy for the sake of the Kingdom of heaven (Mt 19:12). They follow directly Jesus' explanation that God created mankind as man and woman, that the man should be attached to his wife, and that no one should break up the "one flesh" that results from the union of husband and wife. Thus the counsel given at the end of the passage depends on a very positive assessment of sexuality and contrasts with all earthly, gnostic, and other ascetic insistence on sexual abstinence.

The word translated here as "receive" literally means "have space for something". The stone water jars at Cana were said to "hold twenty or thirty gallons each" (Jn 2:6). Jesus says to the Jews: "You have no space for my word" (Jn 8:37). Thus celibacy for the sake of the Kingdom of heaven must find empty space in the souls set apart for it, a space not already occupied by the demands of sexuality. This does not mean that sexuality does not make claims on such a person, merely that such claims leave enough space for other, higher, claims. According to Jesus' words, the higher, more pressing claim is a person's insistence on the Kingdom of heaven.

Sexuality's claim is certainly primarily located in human nature, which is oriented toward survival and reproduction. It is a very strong drive, since it dynamically constricts the freedom of movement for both men and women, claiming the individual for the service of the race. And, as Jesus points out, it does this throughout man's life span, since, unlike animals, man is personally bound by his sexuality into a lasting commitment established by the Creator and indissoluble by human power. Since Jesus rejects the idea of a legal writ of divorce, his disciples become very uneasy as they consider this lifelong commitment: "If that is the way it is between husband and wife, then it is not good to marry" (or "it is better not to marry" [Mt 19:10]). Jesus does not contradict them on this point, but he also refrains from laying down any general law. Nor does he offer a psychological solution, suggesting that marriage is suitable for some and not for others. Instead he transfers discussion of the entire matter to a higher level: the "open space" for the Kingdom of heaven in a human soul is not granted according to one's wish but is obviously a matter of the Kingdom of heaven, of grace and vocation. Paul says the same when he states a preference for the celibacy he himself followed but immediately relativizes that preference by asserting that it "is better to marry than to burn" (that is, to give prime space in one's heart to sexual desire). God distributes his gifts individually, "one kind to one and another kind to another" (1 Cor 7:7).

Yet pointing thus to the free choice of God by no means suggests mere passivity on the part of men and women, as if they must stand by to see whether "open space" for celibacy emerges in themselves. Jesus expects an active attitude: "He who can grasp it, let him take hold of it." That can involve some effort; it certainly requires a free, responsible decision. The effort is primarily that of reflection on whether one has such an open space in the center of one's soul, making sure of it before God in prayer. If one reaches an affirmative answer, then one must place this open space at the disposal of the "Kingdom of heaven". Because most people do not undertake this two-part consideration, "there are few workers" in God's great harvest. Since the chosen one is both called and made aware of his calling by God's doing, Jesus continues, "Pray, therefore, the Lord of the harvest to send laborers into his harvest" (Mt 9:37–38).

Grace and the ability to receive intertwine themselves in a mysterious way that defies establishing overall rules in the matter. Yet there is a comprehensible guideline for how an individual can and should place himself under the rule God has for him: he must simply be ready and willing for every decision of God. If one summons up before God this sort of willingness, God will give enough light to decide which obligation or which cross he should freely take upon himself: the cross of marriage or the cross of celibacy for the sake of the Kingdom of heaven.

82. "Countless Tutors, but Not Many Fathers"

Paul says to the Corinthians: "Although you have countless tutors [pedagogues, trainers] in Christ, you do not have many fathers, for *I* have fathered you in Christ Jesus through the gospel" (1 Cor 4:15). He speaks as the founding apostle but also envisions a succession of unified leaders in the individual church, as becomes clear in the Letter to Titus: "This is why I left you in Crete, that you might set straight what was still lacking and appoint elders from town to town, as I directed you.... The bishop, as God's steward, must be blameless" (Titus 1:5, 7). To be sure, the title "father" does not continue in use, but the singular "steward" is important. It is a label that Paul claims for himself and for his "assistant bishops" (1 Cor 4:1–2), and Jesus himself uses it to describe the divinely established "administrator" of the congregation who "gives God's servants their portion of food at the proper time" (Lk 12:42).

This term *administrator,* or *superintendent,* (*episkopos*) seems to characterize not only the central task of the bishop but also the central task of his coworkers, the priests: the task of the person at the head of a congregation. Just as the pasturing of Christ's flock was assigned to one Peter (*one* pastor as bishop of a congregation is all that is needed to see to the unity of the entire Church), so *one* bishop assures the unity of a diocese, and *one* pastor assures the unity of a congregation. Having many coworkers at all three levels does not jeopardize the central task of unity; indeed, it advances that goal. As an example we have Paul sending Timothy, then Titus, to Corinth to establish healthy union with the congregation's now distant "father"—Paul.

The primary focus of unity in a congregation, as in a diocese, naturally is the Eucharist, over which the single leader rightfully presides, just as the power of absolution, which is oriented toward the Eucharist, should be undertaken by him alone. The "pastoral power" cannot be separated from these. As far as the official proclamation of the gospel's truth is concerned, the leader at least bears responsibility for it, even if he has assistants in that task. It is good for him to delegate many things so that he can be better concerned with the unity of the spirit.

Since Christ is both the head of the Church and has the Church for his body, it is from Christ that one can best perceive that the Church's "hierarchical" and "communal" forms are so interwoven into a single pattern that neither is conceivable without the other. Both of these ecclesial aspects are based on the dual vision of Christ as *Christus caput* (Christ the head) and *Christus totus* (Christ the whole).

When priests are in short supply, it can be difficult, if not impossible, to provide each congregation with a priest who would perfectly incorporate the principle of unity. In that instance, however, one should recall that the parish is simply an accessory structure within the diocese and that the diocese alone is the theologically indispensable principle of unity. Pastorally it is disadvantageous for a priest to be responsible for more than one parish, permitting himself to be represented by lay assistants in many matters, but theologically it is not wrong to do so, as long as these assistants do not usurp priestly functions and as long as the necessary distinction between the two remains apparent to the faithful. To look toward the unity of the diocese and its "steward" in such cases is not to make the best of a bad situation; rather, it is very much an open vision for what is essential.

As long as the task of assuring unity in the Church remains primarily a spiritual rather than an organizational task, the apostlic term *father* may be used in imitation of the apostle. The flock of Christ cannot be pastured apart from "laying down one's life" (Jn 10:5), and this "giving up of one's life" is primarily a spiritual fecundity, whether it is perceived outwardly or not. Thus there is no reason, if the above is respected, to be quicker to address a member of a religious order as "father" (or "mother") than to address a priest thus. (In French the two categories merge through the use of the term *Père*.) In the case of a bishop and above all in the case of the Pope this spiritual fatherhood can be recognized with less hesitation—which presupposes the corresponding spiritual fatherhood on their part. The texts for the consecration rites for bishops and priests make this clear enough. Official and ministerial priesthood should be an example to all believers of what all Christians ought to do: participate in their own existential priesthood.

83. "It's Not Me, Is It, Lord?"

The number of studies of Judas Iscariot increases steadily. Recent ones argue that much of what is said about him is legendary—the black sheep shoulders all the blame; Judas the betrayer helps to cover up Peter's denial—momentary confusion but quickly corrected by tears. Oddly enough, although the other disciples "ask each other which of them" might betray Jesus (Lk 22:23), Peter alone appears not to have asked himself this question. Instead, he is the one who insists, "I will give my life for you" (Jn 13:37). He alone then hears his threefold denial predicted, although it does not change his course of action. To the others Jesus merely spoke generally: "All of you will fall away because of me tonight" (Mk 14:27; Mt 26:31). And indeed, all of them abandoned him and fled (Mt 26:57), one of them even leaving behind his only robe.

Viewed from the perspective of this flight, this "being embarrassed" (Mk 14:27), the disciples' uncertainty when they heard Jesus predict his betrayal is understandable—it is not impossible that any one of them could be the traitor. For a believing Christian this uncertainty grows into certainty when faith says to him inwardly that Christ died for all sinners, that is, precisely for him and thus by him [= at his hands]. Augustine loved to express the unity of for and by with a metaphor: that of a patient drinking as healing medicine the blood of a physician whose murder he arranged. The image expresses what so many saints ceaselessly reflected on in a mixture of sorrow and gratitude. Jesus insists that we drink this healing cup without mentioning how it comes to be: "If you do not drink my blood, you do not have life in you" (Jn 6:53). This is the *felix culpa* (happy fault) of the Easter Vigil's *Exultet* proclamation.

We try to run away from the fatal linkage between guilt and propitiation. Yet the effort Peter made to do that by his denials only leads more obviously toward the connection. Deep in ourselves lie possibilities of which we are not aware, that we angrily hope to dismiss. It is impossible that I would curse and swear that "I don't know this man, don't know what you are talking about" (Mt 26:70–74). The Lord sees better than we do what we are or could be capable of doing, and he can hold that up to our self-assured bluster. Anxiety, confusion, perhaps torture can force remarkable things out of a person. Is there any defense against it? Again, Augustine: "You want to run from him? Run to him." Indeed, "I hide myself in your wounds." Mine in thine, even if I helped cause them. Your wounds are the only place where I can bury mine, hoping that this burying may, in an unknown and, to me, incalculable way, give me a share in your wounds, a share in "completing what I lack" in suffering (Col 1:24). Not like Thomas, who wanted to probe your wounds in order to draw near; no, completely uncertain, as you yourself gave yourself up as the uncertain Wounded One. And this not for a short time but forever, since you have taken your wounds with you into eternity, and you let your blood flow always new and fresh in all the chalices of the world, washing away the sins of the Church continually (as Catherine of Siena realized), permitting your servants to "wash their garments white in the blood of the Lamb" (Rev 7:14).

84. "Even If He Dies He Will Live"

It is nearly incomprehensible how lightly the New Testament deals with physical death. For Paul a Christian has died with Christ in baptism and gone on to a new hidden and resurrected life. In that light, to speak of physical death is hardly worth the effort. He bases himself on the Lord's statement that a grain of wheat must be buried in the earth if it is to multiply and produce living fruit (see I Cor 15:36–37).

Jesus' own words are even more paradoxical: "This is the bread that came down from heaven, not such as the fathers ate and [nevertheless] died; whoever eats this bread will live in eternity" (Jn 6:58). "Whoever believes in me, even if he dies, will live, and whoever lives and believes in me will not die in all eternity" (Jn 11:25–26). Here earthly death is mentioned in passing as meaningless in order to underscore the denial of death made in the concluding line. If eating is the most important condition for immortality in Jesus' discourse of promise (Jn 6), then in Jesus' words to Martha faith is central. Both are apparently only two sides of the same thing: only eating in faith makes sense in the context of the entire discourse of promise, since it is a question of receiving the Father's word in this form of bread and drink. And in his words to Martha, the Risen One—once more the incarnate Word—must be recognized as the foundation of eternal life: "Do you believe this?" is both a question and a command.

Yet one might well say that this sort of trivialization of death contrasts strangely with the emphasis on the death of Jesus in the Gospels and the weight that the Epistles as well as the book of Revelation place on existential dying with the Lord. A life shaped by death actually becomes the proof of authenticity for Christian existence, even if a gleam of eternal life shines through this dying: "For your sake we are killed all day long; we are regarded as sheep for the slaughter" (Rom 8:36). "While we live we are always being given up to death for Jesus' sake, so that Jesus' life may be manifested in our mortal flesh" (2 Cor 4:11).

Yet the last phrase indicates that Jesus' death is something different from daily human dying, and that something similar is intended by the sign of this death over the life of faith. For Jesus "bore our sins in his body on the wood of the Cross so that we might die to sins and live to faithfulness to the Covenant" (1 Pet 2:24). If sin gives birth to death (Rom 5:12; James 1:15) because it is the denial of genuine life, then Jesus' bearing of sin and dying because of sin are the death of death. The power of his will to love embraces life as well as death: "I have the power to lay down my life and to take it up again" (Jn 10:18); "I was dead, but behold, I shall live forever, and I have the keys of death and Hades" (Rev 1:18). The burden of sin that is carried into death gives dying its unique gravity but also contains the conquest of the unity of sin and death, just as John shows the unity of Jesus' death and Resurrection by employing the term *glory*.

Resurrection, with which Jesus identifies himself, is the existence of the entire person from birth through death and within deathless eternal life. What Jesus "died, he died to sin once and for all; what he lives, he lives [for] God. So should you also" (Rom 6:10–11). And precisely because of this "once for all" penetrating of the ultimate finality of death, the event of earthly dying can be reduced to insignificance: it is always absorbed by the single, genuine death that really counts. Earthly death, to be sure, remains a boundary that cannot be erased: "The body indeed is subject to death as a result of sin, but the spirit [*Pneuma*, the person led by God] lives because of faithfulness to the Covenant" (Rom 8:10). Paul calls the living and Risen Lord "Spirit" and "life-giving Spirit" (1 Cor 15:45). For that reason he can describe his entire earthly life as a "quasi" death that, because it participates in the death on the Cross, already rests under the sign of life: *quasi morientes, et ecce vivimus* (as dying, and yet behold we live) (2 Cor 6:9).

This is not at all an earthly rule for existence, a "die and become" that one must possess inwardly in order to be a proper guest on earth. Far more than that, it has to do with the rule of the God-Man, who communicates it as a head communicates to its members.

85. "The Flesh Is Useless"

Jesus says this directly after having said, "If you do not eat the flesh of the Son of Man and drink his blood, you do not have life in you" (Jn 6:53). How can these be reconciled? "It is the Spirit who gives life; the flesh is useless. The words that I have spoken to you are spirit and life" (6:63). Yet these words, after all, became flesh, flesh and blood. The entire discourse forms a crescendo: the word that the Father speaks to the world is the true food of mankind, "the bread from heaven" (6:50); as God's Word, Jesus is this bread, and he is the Word made flesh and blood. Hearing, believing, and eating are one and the same. The word that we hear in faith is also the incarnate Word; the bread that we eat is the Word heard in faith and received in hearing. This is "Spirit and is life"; therefore, the flesh is useless.

In our eating in faith we thus, as the prophets say, "learn from God" (Is 54:13; Jer 31:33–34). But we learn only through the medium of God's word, for God does not teach us except through his word—so that every one led by the Father is "drawn" (Jn 6:44). Both directness and indirectness, or mediation, exist simultaneously between God and man, for the Son, not the Father, became flesh. The word receives itself from the Father in a divine thanksgiving (Eucharist): it "bears witness to what it has seen and heard" (3:32); it receives itself in a "feeding that you know not", in food that consists in receiving and carrying out the Father's will—the Father's will is the Father himself (Jn 4:32–34). Thus the "bread from heaven" mediates to us his own Eucharist: "As I live through the Father, so will the one who eats me live through me" (6:57)—through direct participation in my Eucharist through me, the Mediator.

The Divine Eucharist "is spirit and is life" because the Holy Spirit is the living unity between the Father's self-speaking and the Word's self-receiving. The Word spoken by God to the world and incarnate for that purpose communicates this Eucharist, and he thus refers to himself as spirit and life. Flesh separated from the Word, from believing reception of the word, is useless.

It is of little import whether this "flesh" is understood as the human body as such or as the entire earthly, transient, world-oriented man (what Paul calls the "psychical", animate human body) (1 Cor 2:14; 15:44). It has far more to do with two orientations: below and above. "You are from below; I am from above" (Jn 8:23). "He who comes from above is above all; he who is over the earth is earthly and speaks of the earth" (3:31). He does this as long as he is not "born from above" (3:3)—then he is as intangible from below as is the "wind that blows where it wills" (3:8). "The spiritual man, however, judges everything, while he himself cannot be judged by anyone" (1 Cor 2:15).

This applies not only in an explicitly religious sphere but also in every aspect of human studies, whether in psychology or in interpersonal social and sociological relationships or a science that affects and determines a person's being. In all of these areas the "flesh" is useful only insofar as it is interpenetrated by "Spirit and life"—no matter how mysteriously. Earthly concerns certainly have their own principles, and dealing with them requires a method suited to them (Vatican I; DS 3019), but despite this admitted "autonomy, the creature becomes incomprehensible if God is forgotten" (*Gaudium et spes,* 36). To name only one example: the scientifically defined course of a relationship between a doctor and patient in psychoanalysis is "useless" in the final result if no breath of the intangible *Pneuma* has been felt.

Viewed from the widest possible perspective: the entire cosmic evolution with all its unimaginable dimensions is useless if it does not at least strive to meet the "One coming from above" and if its transience is not caught up, transformed, and rescued for permanence. The "power from above" (Lk 24:49) is powerful enough to penetrate down into the lowest of the lowly—not merely to raise mankind on high as the last offspring of creation but also to raise on high the entire cosmic prehistory that is inseparable from mankind.

86. "I Do Not Know This Man"

The spectrum of this ignorance is infinitely broad, reaching from a cowardly and deceitful denial to the simple lack of knowledge characteristic of the one who has never heard of Christ.

Let us leave open the matter of the man who found himself saying these words (Mt 26:74). He may have said them in fear and confusion, although in between his three denials he would have had time to think it over. Then there is the whole crowd of those who also have truly known yet ever more feverishly try to convince themselves that their knowledge never existed, that it was an error, a fact that must be forgotten and buried under a series of steadily new arguments for its falsehood. The rock pile, from which one can always pry loose a stone or two for stoning this knowledge, is indeed immense. What marvelous arguments are presented by that scientific exegesis that proves by impeccable reasoning how little we know of the "historical Jesus" and demonstrates how the early community of faith stuffed their own interpretations into the package—supplying even Jesus' own words, to say nothing of his miracles. Is there any verse whose authenticity cannot be doubted? For example, that verse in Luke: "Then the Lord turned and looked at Peter" (Lk 22:61), a verse that rates a thorough stoning.

Then there is the rock pile of Church history. Is it, in general and in detail, a repetition of the "man" who claimed that the Kingdom of heaven was at hand in his Person? Just the opposite of the Kingdom of heaven seems obvious: something demonic seems to have been turned loose upon history with his coming and the consequences of his having been here. All manner of stupidities, persecutions, and cruelties have been committed in the name of the One who said he was "meek and lowly of heart". There would be no point in recounting the mass of arguments with which Christianity has contradicted itself over the centuries. The only surprising thing is that each time it seems to be dead once and for all, it stirs again, making it impossible to put an end to the persecutions and mockery.

Still, there seems to be more hope today that the vermin has finally been eradicated: the chemical factories of positivism and "anthropological science" have almost eliminated the philosophy that once constituted a solid foundation for the Christian Church. Philosophy now seems like an alien being in a technicized world. How can one explain to children who sit in front of the television screen, watch home videos, and play with electronic toys the meaning of such terms as *Incarnation, salvation on the Cross,* and *sacraments?* They are meaningless to them. If there is such a thing as a religious drive in people, it is taken up with the totality of science, which initiates the curious into its many mysterious branches, into "secret sciences" unknown to the average person: the hidden powers of the cosmos, the mysterious capabilities of the human mind, secret knowledge about life before birth and after death, mysterious contacts with the dead or with inhabitants of other worlds. All of this is incredibly exciting compared to the tired old liturgies and sermons that bore one in church.

How many of these who "do not know this man" really have not been touched by him, and how many of them have deliberately turned their attention away from him? And how many ultimately seek him through the detours of surrogate religions and sects? How many of them construct an altar "to the unknown God" in a hidden corner of their hearts?

Discerning the spirits is most difficult with the clergy. For all of them have presumably at some point had a face-to-face encounter, and many of them have also zealously buried what they have experienced. The Gospel's demands seem so inhumane, and, after all, is not humaneness the first commandment both in private and social matters? Thus we end up with such slogans as "justice for the world" instead of discipleship of Christ. Where "propitiation" is required, we find it easier to be successful with talk of "reconciliation" among peoples and races. Ecumenical progress is much more easily achieved under such banners. Sticking with the Ancient-Eternal places one hopelessly behind the times. The Grand Inquisitor.

87. "I Will Show Him"

"I will show him how much he must suffer for my name" (Acts 9:16). These are the Lord's words during the conversion and calling of Paul. The words, indeed the entire process, carry with them an element of violence aimed at a man who was a fanatical persecutor of the Christians. "I will show him" refers not merely to the lightning bolt from heaven that knocks him to the ground but also to his entire existence. Paul never forgot it, and he used his "suffering for my name's sake" as his credentials and as his only claim to fame in his relations with the Christian churches. "Far be it from me to glory in anything other than the Cross of our Lord" (Gal 6:14); "I will gladly boast of my weaknesses . . . the insults, hardships, persecutions, and calamities for the sake of Christ, for when I am weak, then I am strong" (2 Cor 12:9–10). The "must" in Christ's promise is as stern and unyielding as iron.

"Saul, Saul, why do you persecute me?" The question "Who are you, Lord?" is hardly more than an editorial comment to complete the words of Christ that follow: "It hurts you to kick against the goad" (as if he were a donkey or a mule). "I am Jesus, whom you persecute" (Acts 26:14). In this instance the goad is stronger than the animal. The stronger one names his name as a commentary, for the events themselves must have made clear to the conquered one who it is that speaks to him from the light and what the light is. And surely the evidence itself, which seared into him like a branding iron, contained a direct glimpse of the entire mystery of glory: the Cross and the Resurrection. Paul's preaching of the Cross, which threads its way through all his letters, certainly has its origin here, yet it is inseparable from the preaching of the Resurrection. The Lord appears here in his glory, not in the veiled form he took during the forty days after his Resurrection. And he appears openly, not privately—for either Paul's companions heard the voice without seeing anyone (9:7), which means that Paul did see the Lord, or they saw the light but heard no voice (22:9), or they fell to the ground with Paul (26:14).

The impact of the light, or the form revealed in the light, is so violent that it strikes him blind. A man accustomed to commanding becomes as powerless as a child who can be given only simple instructions: "Get up and go into the city, and you will be told what you are to do" (9:6). He can get up but, since he can see nothing, must be led into the city, where he sits in the dark for three days without eating or drinking. Only with the laying on of hands and baptism (which the early Christians called "enlightenment") do the scales fall from his eyes as he receives the Holy Spirit. Paul learned the meaning of blind obedience in a most literal sense: to follow an order that throws everything into disorder and to do so without being able so much as to walk unassisted. The claim that "my word is like a hammer that shatters the rocks" (Jer 23:29) comes true for Paul.

Paul certainly is a man who knows his abilities and can employ them when necessary. But there is one thing he cannot do: claim even the slightest merit in his own conversion. He himself underscores this point: "If I were to proclaim the gospel of my own will, what would my reward be?" (1 Cor 9:17). At most he can repudiate earthly reward. When he points to his extensive labors, he must immediately add that not he but "the grace of God in me" led to success, since, as he puts it, "I am what I am" entirely "through the grace of God" (1 Cor 15:10).

This "must" that was laid upon him, which he recognizes and responds to as a branding by the love of Christ (Gal 2:20), becomes obvious in the way he is continually covered up with every sort of spiritual garbage. His efforts are rewarded by being treated like "the worst sort of dirt" and being put down "like a death-row inmate" (1 Cor 4:13, 9). "I shall show him"—he was shown plenty until the very end, since "no one took my part during my trial; everyone deserted me" (2 Tim 4:16), and since, the more he loved the Church, the less he was loved by her (2 Cor 12:15). To defend the authority of his calling he can gesticulate, strike himself, and curse his opponents (Gal 1:8–9), but in a deeper sense he cannot move a finger, for "with Christ I am crucified" (Gal 2:20). "Through him the world is crucified to me and I to the world" (Gal 6:14).

238

88. THE GOOD SHEPHERD

The intricately branching discourse about the Good Shepherd (Jn 10:1–30) weaves two themes together tightly. One is *theological* (that is, trinitarian), and the other is *economic* (that is, high priestly). They are knotted together in the Son's laying down of his life.

This sacrifice is primarily something that takes place within the Godhead and is thus necessarily a mutual self-giving between the Father and the Son. The words "therefore the Father loves me because I lay down my life" (Jn 10:17) may at first seem to allude to the Son's economic self-giving. But this is possible only because there is an intra-trinitarian dynamic originating in the Father's sacrificial gift of life. The perfect mutual self-giving between Father and Son is expressed in the word *knowledge,* taken in its Semitic sense. Its Greek form, *gignōsko,* thus means more than mere knowledge (*oida*)—it is a mutual embracing in love. All of the Son's economic self-giving has no other purpose than to draw the "sheep", the "followers", and the "believers" into this loving knowing. This is clear in John 15:9–10: "As the Father has loved me, so have I loved you"; as the Son abides in the Father's love, so the disciples are to remain in the Son's love. The famous "Johannine" saying in Matthew 11:27 and Luke 10:22 refers to the exclusivity of the knowing between Father and Son and to the free and gracious inclusion of mankind in this trinitarian loving knowing. If the sheep follow the shepherd of the Good Shepherd discourse because they "know my voice" (Jn 10:4) and thus "heed my voice" (10:16), this knowledge and obedience depend on the free communication of intra-trinitarian knowing that opens itself to the world; a hearing and heeding that exist in the mutual loving knowing of Father and Son. Because, in eternity, "life" and loving knowledge are identical, they are given to a person as a single gift: "As the living Father has sent me, and as I live through the Father, so he who eats me [who lets the incarnate Word enter into himself, who incorporates it into himself] will live through me" (6:57).

The free communication of knowledge of the Father that the Synoptic Gospels speak of is expressed in Johannine terms in the ability of the sheep to recognize the voice of the shepherd. The sheep follow the shepherd on the basis of this knowing—that is what following Christ means—and he leads them to a "pasture" where they "have life and have it in abundance" (10:9–10) in the trinitarian life.

Thus the Son's entire economic mission, in which his giving of his life to the Father through the Father and his task (10:18) of giving his life *for* (*hyper*) the sheep (10:11) are interwoven, becomes a single "way" (14:6) or "door" (10:9) that ushers the follower into the trinitarian life. In the language of the Letter to the Hebrews, Jesus' "high-priestly" function is an application of his intra-trinitarian self-giving, which transcends all earthly power—a self-giving that wastes itself on the world in his death. The love with which "the Good Shepherd lays down his life for his sheep" (10:11) is already part of the trinitarian love of the Father for the Son (10:17). And this pouring out of his life for his sheep, because it is trinitarian, is not only freely given ("I lay it down of my own accord" [10:18]) but also possesses trinitarian power (*exousia*) that is found far beyond the limits of earthly life and death. Thus Jesus can say, "I have the power to lay down my life, and I have the power to take it up again", meaning not that a dead body restores itself to life but that life and Resurrection are part of the same mission decreed by the Father and accepted by the Son as a single task. The concluding verse must thus be understood from the perspective of the unity of the Father's mission and the Son's acquiescence: "I and the Father are one" (10:30).

The world's inclusion in the triune life is universal, since the partial participation in trinitarian knowing that is given by the Son's sacrifice is expressly extended to the "other sheep" who "are not part of this fold. I must lead them too; they will heed my voice, and there will be one flock and one shepherd" (10:16). We find the same expansion at the end of the high-priestly prayer: "That they may all be one, even as you, Father, are in me and I in you, that they also may be one in us" (Jn 17:21). We glimpse how inexpressible is the unity attained in our entry through Christ into the trinitarian life when we consider words from the first epistle of John: "We are called children of God, and so we are. The world does not know us because it did not know him. Beloved, we are God's children now; it does not yet appear what we shall be, but we know that when he appears we shall be like him, for we shall see him as he is" (1 Jn 3:1–2).

89. "I Go and Shall Come to You"

In his farewell discourse Jesus refers repeatedly to his departure but in a way that seems ambiguous to our minds. Again and again his words of consoling promise overcome the pain of saying good-bye: "I go to prepare a place for you, and when I go and prepare a place I will come again and take you to myself so that you may be where I am" (Jn 14:3). He simply assumes that they know the way. When they insist they do not, he explains that he himself is the way. He will take them through himself to himself: if the path and the destination are identical, then it is absolutely certain that one will reach the destination. Another saying follows: "I am not leaving you behind as orphans; I will come to you" (14:18). Will he come himself, or will he send someone in his place? "I will ask the Father, and he will send you another counselor" (14:16), who will take what is mine and declare it to you, and that "will be better for you" (16:14–15, 7), for he will expound to you what you cannot yet understand about my words. But does this replacement prevent him from coming? "The world will see me no more, but you will see me, for I live and you shall live. . . . Whoever loves me will keep my word; my Father will love him, and we shall come and make our home with him" (14:19, 23). Earlier Jesus came in order to take us into his home; now he comes with the Father to take up residence in us. In other words, the Spirit will not represent an absent Person; rather, the Spirit will expound the One who is present.

Yet between going and coming (whether to fetch or to stay) lies that "little while" between "see me no more" and "see me again" that puzzles the disciples (16:18ff.). During this "short time", Jesus explains, there will be time for "weeping and wailing", which he nonetheless compares to the suffering of a woman in labor, a suffering forgotten once "a child is born into the world. So you have sorrow now, but I will see you again, and your hearts will rejoice, and no one will take your joy from you" (16:21–22).

All these statements lie side by side in contradiction as far as the disciples are concerned: Jesus will really depart (to prepare a later dwelling place for them), and during this absence they will "weep and wail", yet he will at the same time come to them—not alone but with the Father—and make his home with them, which will be an immediate cause for great joy for them because he is not returning alone but with the Father, who is "greater than he is" (14:28).

It seems as if the reason a single event can have different appearances results from two perspectives: from heaven to earth and from earth to heaven. Viewed from heaven to earth, the "short time that you see me no more"—the time up to the Resurrection as well as the time up to the Second Coming (*parousia*)—has no duration for the Lord. This is true not only because he is both the Resurrected One and the One returning in glory but also because the apparent distance between the two means no absence at all for him—he is constantly present in the Church in the form of the Eucharist, the Word, the other sacraments, mutual Christian love. "Behold, I am with you always, even to the end of the age" (Mt 28:20). From the perspective of heaven there is no temporal or spatial distinction. It is only from the perspective of the earth that Jesus speaks of a "short time".

Viewed from earth to heaven, there exists a distance between the living and seeing faith of which John speaks and the "vision of the Lord as he is" (1 Jn 3:2), a space within which "weeping and wailing" find room alongside joy in Jesus' presence. Seen from heaven, these earthly hardships are nothing more than the birth of a child whose existence has always been in sight. Thus for the believer the distance from earth to heaven is completely different from the heaven-to-earth distance glimpsed by the one who enjoys the beatific vision. In precisely the same way, the Father's absence from our desolate crucified Lord cannot be compared with the Father's presence with the crucified One. Any attempt to reconcile these two is in vain, because it would render impossible both salvation and the discipleship that Jesus portrays so insistently in his farewell (Jn 18:20–24).

Matters are no different with Paul. He continually speaks of our life "in Christ", referring not to someone absent but to the sphere of the living Person through whom and for whom we live even though we "groan in our present earthly tents, longing" for our "eternal house in heaven"; "walking" even now "in faith, not in sight" and becoming used to being unconcerned "whether we are under way or at home" (2 Cor 5:1–2, 6–7). Still, in this situation a Christian longing dominates, a longing "to leave this body and be at home with the Lord" (5:8)—in other words, to bridge the gap between death and Resurrection in the same way that it is already bridged from a heavenly perspective.

90. "He Has a Demon and Has Gone Mad"

Jesus tells us that he has come to bring a sword because his words and deeds sow discord (Mt 10:34). John's Gospel shows us again and again how he "splits" the crowd that followed him (Jn 7:43; 9:16; 10:19). His talk and behavior are so provocative that no one can remain neutral in response. On one occasion many would have liked to recognize him as the Messiah, but for that he would have needed to have come from Bethlehem, not from Galilee. In other words, those who are convinced by his words ("never has a man spoken like this man" [7:46]) are reminded that all the Scripture experts know he comes from the wrong place. In a second instance, his Sabbath-day healing of a man blind from birth, the miracle speaks in his favor but not having honored the Sabbath speaks against him. Despite all appearances questions are raised about the identity of the man, and his parents make themselves scarce. Alone of all of them, the blind man who now sees argues with those who doubt blindly despite their sight: "It astounds me that you can't see whence he comes—after all, he has opened my eyes. . . . Since the beginning of the world no one has ever heard that someone made a blind man see. If he were not from God, he could do nothing" (9:30–33). They proceed to expel the formerly blind one from the synagogue. In the third instance the contrasts reach a climax: the assertion that Jesus is demon-possessed and insane against the quiet insistence that "that is not the way someone possessed by a demon talks" (10:21), accompanied by a reference to his having healed a blind man.

The Gospels carry this divisive provocation through the millennia. One might think that its splintering impact might have weakened after such a long time. But the alternatives, either of God or of the devil (today we prefer to call it "mental illness"— how many have claimed to be the Messiah or the Son of God in such circumstances), have lost none of their virulence. And this despite countless efforts to reduce the two extremes ("from above" and "from below") to a harmless anthropological center: Jesus, who was certainly some sort of prophet, was transformed by his disciples into something he never wanted to be. People even think they can reconstruct scientifically the stages by which this process of alienation was carried out. But it will not work. It is too much to assume that zealous forgers produced the genius and cutting clarity of the words of Christ (the apocryphal writings seem incredibly "tedious" by contrast, as do many of the speeches placed in the mouth of the Buddha). It is equally unconvincing to explain Jesus' words and deeds by means of certain contemporary situations and movements (Essenes, Mandaeans, Zealots). The "division" of the crowd is as evident as ever, and a clear choice remains: psychiatry or revelation. The answer to the hypothesis "he is insane" is "these are not the words of a madman" (10:21).

Taken in their entirety and from that perspective examined individually, his words possess such lucid coherence that they reveal themselves as an indivisible unity in their opposing tendencies. They are so transparent that they must be either accepted or rejected as a whole. Accepting them requires a single and simple eye (*haplous*) that perceives the simple in its simplicity (Mt 6:22; Lk 11:34). Rejecting them can happen only through an ocular schizophrenia that refracts what it sees: because it *cannot* be unified, it *is* not unified. Jesus' unity is divisive in its impact: "For judgment I have come into the world, so that those who do not see may see and those who see may become blind" (Jn 9:39).

Proof of this judging-divisive effect is offered by the lasting and unabated animosity that faith in Christ encounters. When people nonchalantly turn aside, their easygoing appearance simply disguises a hidden hostility. Even though the majority may adopt such an attitude, a clear-eyed observer will not be fooled. Nor should one be taken in by the fact that constantly new and rapidly changing objections to the Gospel's provocation are brought forward. Nothing could have been expected with more certainty. "Do not be led astray by them" (Lk 21:8), Jesus said with equanimity, for he had no illusions of the mass success of the Gospel—he did not even expect a majority to believe. "Nevertheless, will the Son of Man find faith upon the earth when he returns?" (Lk 18:8). Christianity and the masses contradict each other one way or another, even if one is not pathetically isolated as an "individual". Instead, simply "fear not, little flock" (Lk 12:32).

91. "I Said, You Are Gods"

Jesus quotes this verse from the Psalms (Ps 82:6; Jn 10:34–35) to demonstrate his more exalted dignity and mission. If God "has already called gods those to whom the word of God came, and if Scripture cannot be abrogated, do you dare say of him whom the Father consecrated and sent into the world, 'You are blaspheming', because I have said, 'I am the Son of God'?" (Jn 10:35–36). To reinforce the point the Psalm added, "And sons of the Most High"—we need to be aware of this as part of Jesus' words too. The Psalm began by asserting, "God takes his place in the divine council; in the midst of the gods he holds judgment." This Old Testament image of a council of the gods is rather ambiguous. Does it refer to the debilitated Gentile gods—to what Paul would call the "principalities and powers", the gods that the same Psalm understands to have fallen into mortality because of their unjust judgments (82:7)? Or does it have to do with the judges in Israel who are elevated to a quasi-divine status as mediators of the law that proceeds from God alone (see Ex 21:6; 22:27, which probably refer to judges)? The question can remain open—what is astonishing is that there is any talk at all of participation in God's Divinity within the context of Israel's strict monotheism. Jesus does not limit this participation to the magistrates, who give judgment as God's representatives, but extends it to all "to whom the word of God is addressed". Since Israel is referred to as a people "chosen" by God "for his own", "consecrated to God", and thus a "holy people" participating in God's unique holiness (Ex 19:6; Dt 7:6, etc.), Israel as a whole is elevated by God to his own realm. Israel is "deified" in the sense given that word by the Fathers of the Church. The meaning of the Covenant given at Sinai is far-reaching: because God—and God alone!—is holy, so also Israel is sanctified on the basis of her election (Lev 19:2; 20:7, 26). Only when one has glimpsed this incomprehensible term can one begin to grasp what exile and "rejection" (Rom 11:11) truly imply.

Yet Israel's *"theiosis"* (deification) is but a symbol (*figura* [1 Cor 10:6]) of what would become reality in Jesus. Unlike Israel, he is not exalted from below to the realm of God; rather, he is "sent into the world" bearing God's most intimate holiness (Jn 10:36) so that the world might "be consecrated in truth" (Jn 17:19). This consecration takes place through the One who calls himself in a special sense the "Son of God", while only the evangelist calls him "God" (Jn 1:18; 20:28). The Jews understand his claim very well (10:33; 5:18).

One need not reject the patristic concept of "deification" as a dangerous exaggeration, provided that human creatureliness is left intact, something the Church Fathers always take care to preserve. The term can be approached more vividly from the work of Jesus Christ than from Israel, for despite the exalted dignity that may seem to be exclusive, Christ's work is essentially an inclusive activity. The Church truly is Christ's body, something one can affirm without thereby saying that the Church is Christ. Thus the Prison Epistles lift him up above the body, as its Head, so that his fullness can pour itself into the body from the Head. All of this gives us access to the central mystery: that the unique God exalted above all else can communicate himself as an inclusive Person yet does not need the world in order to be who he is. Like Jesus himself, the Apostle Paul understands that the interpersonal relationship between a man and a woman offers access to a mystery: humanly it is incomprehensible that two bodies can become "one flesh"—yet the resulting child is a tangible proof of the fact.

Today tendencies from all sides blur the boundary between God and mankind. It matters little whether such supposed unity is described and pursued atheistically or pantheistically, whether one speaks of a cosmic Christogenesis or theogenesis or simply of anthropogenesis. All these paths clearly lead away from what both Old and New Testaments describe as "deification": the free, grace-filled embedding of creation's eternally personal character, with its climax in man, in God's triune love. Both Trinity and Incarnation (including the Cross and the Resurrection) are prerequisites for such an embeddedness, which can only be based on the twofold truth of "birth from God" and "the creature's childhood toward God". The tension between the two remains forever sharply delineated yet reconciled in Christ, the eternal Child of the Father: *filii in Filio* (sons in the Son).

92. "With Him Two Others on Either Side, but Jesus in the Middle"

John puts it in this summary fashion (19:18), while Luke takes the trouble to call them "criminals" (23:33), and Mark and Matthew refer to them as "robbers" (Mt 27:38; Mk 15:27). "So must the Scripture be fulfilled in me: 'He was reckoned among the transgressors'" (Lk 22:37; inserted into Mk 15:28).

This undeniable fact is merely the final realization of Jesus' solidarity with mankind. To be human essentially means to identify with one's fellowmen, and Jesus' entire life was lived together with real lawbreakers, regardless of whether they were of the pious or impious sort. That all his disciples abandoned him during his Passion, having found themselves unable even to share an hour of his vigil in Gethsemane, that people preferred a murderer named Barabbas to Jesus, that he was crucified between two thieves—all of these are merely variations on the same theme.

Jesus' substitutionary atonement must be taken completely seriously: he stands in precisely the same place before God as the sinner. This vicariousness means "standing in for", "answering for"—not displacing but standing among the others, standing in a line with them. It applies especially to all that seems difficult, painful, intolerable, incomprehensible in life on this earth. He does not simply take away whatever gloom human existence spreads over his fellowmen; rather, he places himself under the same dark cloud. And he does this, as he does everything, in the name of the Father and by making the Father present: God does not gaze serenely down from heaven upon earthly suffering; rather, he enters into it and helps carry the load. Without that help humanity and the world would never make it to the end of the road intact. How else could the world's Creator be expected to act toward his creation?

Yet at the same time that he mingles "incognito" (Kierkegaard) among creatures, he is the Totally Other who bears responsibility for all creation. A tangled intertwining of vicariousness and solidarity, of being for and being with, thus develops. Both tighten around each other until the end of the drama: because all have abandoned him, he must stand alone for everyone, and since two are crucified with him, he demonstrates his solidarity to the very end, whether those who suffer with him realize it or not. Luke is the only one who makes a distinction here—one of them curses him along with the crowd while the other points toward him and glimpses a bit of the vicariousness in the solidarity—not merely a sense of Jesus' innocence, as his prayer to the Lord indicates, but also a glimpse of his power to bring even the guilty into his "Kingdom". The one who blasphemes wishes for release from his suffering: "Are you the Messiah? Save yourself and us" (Lk 23:39). The one who prays seeks not to escape his torment but looks beyond its limits toward death. For the first there can be no more theology after Auschwitz. The other belongs among the martyrs (who already experience "well-deserved reward") who glimpse even in the extermination camps a God who suffers with and therefore for.

It is true that the evolving cosmos pays a price in pain and death for all of its blooming life—from bottom to top. But it is equally true that pain and death have a special virulence at the top of nature's ladder, where human free will kindles rebellion by saying "No" to God. The only answer given to that rebellion is God's entry into solidarity with what is cosmically incomprehensible ("Why have you forsaken me?" receives no answer): God suspended with and between insurrection and prayer, hanging in "unspeakable groaning" (Rom 8:22). And Jesus also prays, receiving no answer— the incomprehensibility of the created world at its own summit is a reflection of God's incomprehensibility, which does not float above the created world's incomprehensibility but is present in its midst as the "Not Other". God's incomprehensibility is not absorbed by the world's, for beyond God's solidarity there is the vicariousness; yet the marvelous thing is that the vicariousness functions not above the solidarity but right in its midst. Thus religion does not consist in the unconditional desire to avoid suffering, something one could at most pity; rather, it consists in clinging in the midst of suffering to the unconditional will of the One who suffers out of love and outlasts suffering through love.

93. "Instead, Take Last Place"

The "host may come and say, 'Friend, move up to a higher seat'", which would be "an honor to" the one involved. But one should not seek the last place (Lk 14:7–10) for the sake of subsequent honors but rather because of the instructions that "each should consider the other better than himself" (Phil 2:3) and "outdo the other in showing honor" (Rom 12:10). This should be done without scheming, in the realization that the other person has not abused God's grace as badly as I have. I have no right to judge the way he has used grace ("judge not" [Lk 6:37]), but I am certainly right to judge the way I have employed it. And, if I had applied what I have been given differently and better, the world would be a better place as far as both those I know and those I do not know are concerned. Thus the "humility" that Jesus and the apostle insist on is no "virtue"; rather, it simply recognizes the truth. "He who thinks he is something when he is nothing deceives himself" (Gal 6:3).

Certainly we should put ourselves in the last place in imitation of Christ, who took the sins of the world upon himself and placed himself behind the worst sinner. But in doing so we are not innocents who bear the guilt of others; rather, we are indeed that worst sinner whose guilt is being carried. Certainly we should sit in the lowest seat in imitation of Paul, who said, "It seems to me that God has placed us apostles in the lowest place, like criminals condemned to death, for we have become an [entertaining] spectacle for the world, for angels, and for men" (1 Cor 4:9). But Paul portrays himself with bitter irony as a contrast to the congregation: "You are honored; we are despised"—the congregation really should be occupying the place that Paul has taken up in its place. Thus I find myself once more on the side of the "well-endowed", "dominating" congregation rather than on the side of the apostle who suffers "hunger and thirst, nakedness, and stripes". I must therefore be careful, when I take up the place that belongs to me, in talking about imitating Christ and Paul. I dare not convince myself that, in my relative innocence, I am taking the place of the guilty ones. I must take my place not with a piously "humble" wink or with the calculating thought that God "will not despise a contrite heart"; rather, as the same Psalm (51:4) confesses, "Against you alone have I sinned and done what displeases you. You must be justified in your sentence and be blameless in your judgment."

Many people find this impossible. It seems to them that others have committed worse crimes than they, that others may indeed merit ultimate penalties but they themselves should get off lightly. But in thinking thus they expose themselves to judgment: "Judge not, condemn not" (Lk 6:37). Paul says, "I do not even judge myself . . . my judge is the Lord" (1 Cor 4:3–4). He is not speculating about whether he will hear, "Friend, move up higher".

For a sinner like me nothing is left but to look up at the Crucified One, for I know for certain that he is taking my place in the worst possible place. I know equally well that I cannot rest easily in this knowledge as if it were a cause for rejoicing that someone has spared me the "embarrassment" of being taken down a notch (Lk 14:9). The fact is obvious, and it would be arrogant for me to wish it away, to say to the one suffering for me: "Climb down from the Cross and let me do the suffering." It would be pointless simply because, as the robber rightly says, "Don't you fear God, since you are under the same condemnation [*in eadem damnatione*]? Yet we are justly so, for we only receive what our deeds deserve" (Lk 23:40–41). A penalty that is deserved cannot be endured for someone else.

All grace is completely free—something that people find most difficult to comprehend in its ultimate consequences. We always think that we have earned something different and are entitled to move a few seats higher. May we learn to leave that preference to others—we are, after all, supposed to consider them higher than ourselves. Seated at the end of the table, may we learn for ourselves to recognize the complete gratuitousness of love.

94. "In Him Are Hidden All the Treasures of Wisdom and Knowledge"

The treasures of wisdom and knowledge are hidden (Col 2:3) so that they might be sought and found. The preceding verse expresses the Apostle's desire that believers' hearts may be strengthened and, united in love, attain to the fullness of understanding, to knowledge of the mystery of God found in Christ. Being fortified in faith and united in love mark out the path by which one penetrates God's mystery, which is there for the finding in Christ. In no sense is there any talk of secret knowledge by which an initiate might take possession of knowledge about God. The words *mystery* and *secret* or *hidden* are not surpassed and set aside through the words *wisdom* [understanding] *and knowledge.* They are valid simultaneously; indeed, one could say that each increases the other. The more wisdom deepens, so much more profound is the revelation of the mystery.

This is hard to grasp, since in human terms increased knowledge seems to eliminate the mysteriousness of what becomes known. Admittedly one cannot always be certain about that. For lovers can grow in their knowledge of being loved even though the depth of the mystery of being loved does not diminish. On the contrary, they can even rejoice that superficial knowledge opens up to its full mystery only as love is lived out. One cannot simply call this self-revelation a surrendering of the mystery, for precisely in the attempt to let go, that which is opened up reveals its mysteriousness. A genuine "I love you" is both open and closed, because in being entrusted to someone it can be taken only on faith, not as knowledge.

This opens a path to uncovering the hidden riches of God in Christ. The parable of the treasure found in a field first points the way to this truth, for it appears to say that the buyer of the field can simply open the locked treasure. But in reality he must first "sell everything he owns" in order to buy the field—he must get rid of all his material and intellectual possessions and approach the field in complete poverty of spirit (Mt 13:44). Since this is a divine treasure, he is "in heaven", where one can store only one's heart (Mt 6:21), not any tangible possessions.

Yet God's treasures hidden in Christ are given to us, not taken from us. This is what the apostle tries to express with the puzzling word *arrabōn* (down payment), in which what is already paid out obligates subsequent payments. The real, not merely promised, down payment in our hearts is the Holy Spirit (2 Cor 5:5; 1:22). Poured out as God's love into our hearts (Rom 5:5), he makes us know what God has given us (1 Cor 2:12), he teaches us with his unction about all things (1 Jn 2:27), he permits us to experience in advance the dynamics of the world to come (Heb 6:5), but he does all of this under the veil of faith that sees not (2 Cor 5:7) and of hope that cannot hold that for which it hopes (Rom 8:24). It is veiled revelation, transparency in a puzzling mirror (1 Cor 13:12).

We can be sure that what is called "earnest money" here is a genuine promise of a face-to-face vision (1 Cor 13:12) of God as he is (1 Jn 3:2). But who is he "who dwells in inaccessible light, whom no man has seen or can see" (1 Tim 6:16)? Is he not the eternally greater, unsurpassable One knowable only in the unsearchableness of his unbegottenness, knowable only as the Source whose origin is unattainable? All the treasures of wisdom and knowledge burst forth eternally from the depths and flood us with inexhaustible riches without ever letting us grasp the hiddenness of the absolute love from which this exuberance flows.

95. "Whoever Receives One Sent from Me Receives Me"

If "many have entertained angels unaware" (Heb 13:2), so all the more have many played host to the Lord in receiving his messengers (Jn 13:20). Anyone who addresses a word from the Lord to me, whether he realizes it or not, is an ambassador for the entire Word, and his message is both a gift and an obligation, a sign and an assignment. Therefore the messenger has a simultaneous right to a reply, and the Scriptures can thus instruct Christians again and again to "admonish each other" (Rom 12:8; 15:14; 1 Th 5:11; Heb 3:13; 10:25). The term *admonish* (*parakalein*) covers the entire range from an insistent request or appeal to a consolation. But it also connotes a warning, which is understandable when one hears the Lord himself warning pleadingly, comfortingly, challengingly through the people he sends to us.

The Lord's most insistent admonition to us comes through those whom he calls the "least of my brethren" (Mt 25:40). What we do to them we do directly to him. In the hungry he is the one who hungers; in the thirsty, foreigners, homeless, naked, sick, imprisoned it is he who begs for help, who makes demands even in his pleading, who warns. When someone listens to him, he it is who consoles and gives. Thus the "each other" becomes a reality here. Only apparently does one help and the other receive, for the helping one is helped profoundly in his act; the one who liberates is set free by Christ. An apparent foreigner and stranger, the Samaritan, becomes one's neighbor, a neighbor not merely to the person lying at the side of the road but also to Christ himself.

But is the message any less insistent when it comes from the one of whom the Lord says, "Whoever hears you, hears me" (Lk 10:16)? Often we think it is, especially if we fail to perceive the needs of the one who has placed himself under an obligation to pass Christ's words along: "Woe is me if I do not proclaim the gospel" (1 Cor 9:16). This proclamation includes a duty to "admonish", for it is part of the task of pasturing Christ's flock. One entrusted with an office cannot legally command, for the law is fulfilled in self-sacrificing and suffering love, just as Christ never forced anyone but merely presented the intensity and persuasiveness of his love. The Apostle too can do nothing except admonish by pointing to this love: "In light of the mercy of God, brethren, I urge you" (Rom 12:1); "if there is any encouragement in Christ, any incentive of love, . . . then complete my joy in being of the same mind" (Phil 2:1-2). The admonition of office takes place only "in the Lord" or "through the Lord" (Rom 15:30; 1 Th 4:1), in other words, in the same manner and the same spirit as the Lord spoke words of admonition that were simultaneously consoling and warning. It would not be amiss to see both messengers—the starving one and the one holding office—as sharing the same task. The life of the Apostle Paul shows how the two missions coinhere, for as he endured earthly hardships Paul used his messenger ministry to firm up the validity of his insistently official calling.

In the end is not each person who approaches me also a messenger of Christ, someone in whom we receive Christ in receiving him? Does this not make it possible for Christ's words to echo throughout the entire week instead of remaining nice sounds during Sunday worship? Even if someone approaches me with an intention that seems to have nothing to do with the Lord's purpose, it does not mean that I can dispense with listening for a message from the Lord that requires an answer in the same spirit. All the sayings about love of enemies belong in this context, because Christ's sun of grace rises on the good and the bad alike in imitation of the Father.

That is why Christ says at the end of his admonition, "Whoever receives me receives the one who sent me" (Jn 18:20). An "imitator of Christ" (1 Cor 4:16) is simultaneously an "imitator of God" (Eph 5:1), which brings us even more mysteriously back to where we started: to the hungry, the thirsty, the one pleading for help and assistance in every possible way.

96. "Remember, Then, from What You Have Fallen, ..."

...namely, from the heights of your "first love" (Rev 2:4–5). And the fall is a fact despite the Judge's recognition that the church still can point to many good works. "I know your works, your toil and patient endurance, and how you cannot put up with evil men, for you have exposed the supposed apostles as liars" (2:2–3). (Presumably these are the ones the writer later calls "Nicolaitans" [2:6].)

Is it not astonishing that a church that does so many good things has nonetheless lost its first love? How can so much that is positive be quashed by an apparently greater, decisive deficit? The Judge's verdict probably comes as a complete surprise to a church that can boast of such great Christian accomplishments. Their orthopraxis is indeed beyond reproach, and the Lord himself admits as much. Yet that practice does not adequately prove to him the presence of ortho-agape. Confidence in one's own works, that is, Pharisaism, apparently extends to much deeper and more hidden levels than a church sure of its praiseworthiness realizes. Furthermore, we have to do here with more than just a few degrees of cooling off—the Lord talks about a real plunge from the top to the bottom, a fall that is all the more dangerous because the real damage it causes goes unnoticed.

What could be involved here? Simply that we have grown accustomed to God's love for us and our love for God. We take both for granted as the foundation, the norm upon which everything else—all our marvelous good works—can be constructed. This love is, as it were, the origin and the goal of the entire natural order, of the world, and of history. This makes the so-called cosmic Christ a natural, even if indispensable, building block for social and personal existence. One deals with and counts on the givenness of this existence with great certainty, and thus with equal certainty takes for granted its causal and theological presuppositions. If one is forced to differentiate between the natural order and the order of grace, the assertion that Christ is Alpha and Omega of the entire natural creation seems to provide a way to bypass the effects of that differentiation. If one insisted on an unbridgeable chasm between both realms, then the entire cosmic order would be deprived of its foundation and destiny, and it would be impossible to keep the run-of-the-mill citizen of earth from falling into atheism and nihilism.

Of course one can retain a certain piety even while overcoming the gap between the natural order and the realm of grace. Ephesus was a center of the emperor cult and of worship of the Great Artemis (Acts 19), as the Acts of the Apostles informs us. Why shouldn't Christian worship take its place as one among many? Wasn't the Roman Empire basically rather ecumenical at heart? Certainly the Christians of the city had not wanted to mingle their religion with the others, but if they had held onto their own worship firmly, how is it that they have "fallen from such a height"?

Yet there can be no protest against the Lord's word of judgment. Not only does he exalt himself to a unique height above all the other deities, but he also lifts his own to the same height. "Your life is hidden with Christ in God" (Col 3:3)—which means "up there", since we have died and have been raised with Christ. The height on which Christians live is "Jerusalem above", and we must make our way of living conform to its way of living. It should not surprise us that this is psychologically incredible. It can be attained only through the "incessant prayer" that Paul requires of Christians, through that yearning walk that knows it has not yet reached its Goal but instead has been embraced by it (Phil 3:12–13). Restless in ourselves, we rest in God.

97. "And Fetches Seven Other, Worse, Spirits"

From where does the danger come that threatens a person whom Jesus has delivered from an evil spirit? Restless, the evil spirit strives to reenter what he calls "his house", which now stands clean and spruced up but empty. Therefore he fetches "seven other spirits, more evil than himself", and moves back into his old haunts. "And at the end that man is worse off than he was at the start" (Mt 12:43–45; Lk 11:24–26). The word *empty* is found in Luke as well as Matthew but only in a few manuscripts. Matthew applies the imagery to "this evil generation", the unconverted Jews.

Is it dangerous to be delivered by Jesus from an evil spirit? Perhaps not dangerous, but it certainly brings some responsibilities with it. "Behold, you are healed", Jesus said to the man at the pool near the Sheep Gate. "Sin no more, lest something worse happen to you" (Jn 5:14). Someone who has been healed has lost something to which he was accustomed—what the devil refers to as "my house"—and this means that, despite all his joy over being healed, something will seem to be missing. Perhaps the demonic in him was located in an addiction to criticizing, in his need continually to make himself into a judge of everything. Now his disease is suddenly gone. He certainly feels clean and freshly swept but also as if he has been robbed of something familiar. Instead of criticizing he is simply supposed to believe. Or perhaps he was accustomed to being in charge of all aspects of his life, able to arrange his affairs as he pleased, flushed with freedom. To be healed from this supposed absolute autonomy is at the same time to be placed in the Lord's service: his calling may seem like dishonorable servitude. What kind of vocational options are available to him now? When he does all he can he is still supposed to consider himself a "good-for-nothing slave".

Sinners are often like addicts—having gone through a "detoxification" program does not mean that one will not relapse. The examples cited show that such relapses can be worse and harder to heal than the original problem. Those who believe only for a time can become fanatical and cynical persecutors of the Church when they become disgusted with faith. Those who genuinely recognized their calling yet turned away from it subsequently make fun of every personal calling and keep many others from following a divine call. According to John, the "Antichrists" "have gone out from among you, but they were not a part of us" (I Jn 2:18–19). Outsiders have no reason or opportunity to betray the cause of Christ. Instead the branches of the vine that bear no fruit are the ones that burn in demonic fire after having been hacked off and left to dry (Jn 15:6–7).

Thus, in Jesus' parable, the condition of having been "swept out" is not the goal but a grace that is offered—yet must be freely grasped and incorporated into one's own life. The house may well be "spruced up" yet still be empty, since it remains for the cleansed person to fill it with new life. Jesus' words to the man he healed basically apply equally well to anyone who has received absolution for his sins—here too something has been removed from the person, something that had become part of himself as he consented to sin. One might view absolution as an amputation, since the amputee may still "feel" sensations in the part of his body that is no longer attached. When that happens, psychology wins out over faith. One says to oneself, "I am just as bad as I always was." In God's eyes I may be *justus* (righteous), but in my own mind I know I am a *peccator* (sinner)—in other words, I know better than God. When we trap ourselves in this sort of dialectic, we also find ourselves thinking *pecca fortiter* (sin all the more), which directly contradicts Paul's teaching. "Why should we not do evil so that good might come of it?" (Rom 3:8). "Should we remain in sin so that grace might abound?" (Rom 6:1). Does that not make good sense, if one concedes that "where sin abounded, grace overflowed all the more" (Rom 5:20)? Yet Paul forcefully rejects such a logical conclusion, insisting that it is a trick of the Enemy (Rom 3:8). "How can we who died to sin still live in it?" (Rom 6:2).

To be sure, such points of logic and their refutation carry little weight with those whose end is worse than their beginning. Still, Jesus' warning remains: he who is peace will divide mankind (see Mt 10:34). The Lie becomes aroused only when Truth is on the scene. The book of Revelation is a commentary on Jesus' question: "Will the Son of Man find any faith on the earth when he returns?" (Lk 18:8).

98. "Owe No One Anything, except Mutual Love"

This is a paradoxical statement, since the word *owe* changes its meaning in midsentence (Rom 13:8). In the first half of the sentence it has to do with a legally payable debt; in the second half, with something that cannot be carried out legally—in the first place because love surrounds and surpasses the legal realm and furthermore because the "debt" involved here, if one wishes to use that language at all, is a mutual one.

Even on the level of natural relationships things are paradoxical: a child has a right to his parents' love if he is to become a genuine person, yet this love must be given freely—if it were coerced it would not be love. All this only illustrates the truth that justice, as solid as it may be, can never be the ultimate norm in human relationships. The only exception might be if one meant by "justice" that which is right and fitting, in which case, as in Plato's philosophy, justice can govern all relationships. More important, God's justness can then be the norm for all relations between God and mankind and between men, as is the case in covenantal "justice". What is called "justice" (righteousness) in the Old Testament always coincides with the constancy of God's faithfulness as well as with his mercy—when Israel was unfaithful to its side of the Covenant. Even when most stern, when exiling the people, God's strictness is an instrument of his faithfulness, serving to restore Covenant righteousness.

In the New Covenant the assurance of divine faithfulness is, as it were, over-fulfilled by establishing an indestructible mutual faithfulness between God and man in Jesus Christ. Here God's right to enjoy his people's loyalty because he has freely chosen to choose and guide them finds reciprocity in the Son of Man's obedience (for himself and for everyone), which is also an expression of his absolutely free love. Therefore everything that might be called justice in the Church of Christ rests without the slightest exception on the mutual love between God and the believing Person that was completed in Jesus Christ. In the Church's sacramentality God has a right, based on his incarnate grace, that the truly believing Christian is ready to recognize freely. Likewise, God is prepared to recognize the believer's right to be a son of God, together with all its consequences, based on his incarnate Son's inclusive act of love. If a believer wanted to withdraw from the Covenant, he would not only fall from the love of God into mere "justice" but would also transform God's love into judgment upon himself. That is what Jesus meant when he said, "I am come not to judge the world but to save the world. Whoever rejects me and refuses to accept my words, he has his own judge—the word I have proclaimed will judge him at the last day" (Jn 12:47–48). Love cannot be forced on someone who despises it.

This sheds light on Paul's statement that Christians always owe each other love. The indebtedness stems from the very name "Christian", which they possess only because they want to live in God's Covenant of love with mankind, a Covenant of love that takes concrete form in the Church's sacraments. No one forces them to believe, but if they believe they "must" love "voluntarily" and unconditionally, just as one cannot believe conditionally. And being conformed to Christ, they "must" "voluntarily" love their enemies as well as their friends, for this is the only possible way to move their enemies into mutual love or to commend them into the mutuality of the New and eternal Covenant. In this they are no more powerful than Christ, who did not convert his enemies into voluntary friends within the mortal side of his life.

In the world the mutual love that Christians "owe" to each other remains a model for the wise, showing how to avoid even the subhuman borderline approach of merely punitive justice. "The law does not exist for the righteous but for the lawless and disobedient, the godless, . . . liars, perjurers, . . . and whatever else is contrary to sound doctrine" (1 Tim 1:9–10). Even here it can be said that "those who resist will incur judgment" (Rom 13:2). That all personal human love is voluntary, even where required, means that men can understand the "obligatory freedom" of Christian love.

99. "Created in Christ Jesus to Do in Our Lives the Good Works God Prepared for Us, So That We Might Walk in Them"

The new creation in Christ to which Paul refers here (Eph 2:10) is the same as the new birth together with the Son from the Father (Jn 1 and 3). Birth or creation is a radical beginning, with the life appropriate to it stretching out into the future. A new person cannot simply proceed with the old, predetermined future. Instead we have done away with the old person, "together with his works" (Col 3:9). We no longer even need to suffer the consequences of the old person, for these apparent implications are shattered, and the remnants of what has been discarded can be incorporated into the wholeness of the new future. This future is no vacuum, for we do not stand before God as "newborn children" (1 Pet 2:2) devoid of means and direction. Our birth results from the "imperishable seed, through God's word", which we have believed (1 Pet 1:23–25) and which places before our eyes a plan for our lives.

This plan comes to fruition in the unity of God's Providence and the new freedom for which Christ liberated us (Gal 5:1). The freedom is truly, not merely apparently, given to us as our own. God does not lead us by the nose—he expects us to plan and to act from our own resources given us by God. Thus our freedom can never be separated from our giftedness.

That children are both free and yet obey their parents poses no problem so far as natural children are concerned, although tension between the two can arise. We who are newborn children of God and newly created in Christ are "not childlike in our thinking but rather childlike in regard to evil. In our thinking we are mature adults" (1 Cor 14:20). Thus we can understand that the obedience God expects from us does not contradict our freedom but is the realization of our freedom and fits us into the framework of absolute freedom. What freedom could be freer than that which moves within the space of endless freedom, and what could be more worthy and fantastic than to have the horizons of God's imagination opened up to us? Even to catch a glimpse of God's breathtakingly sublime plans and to achieve them in bits and pieces is to exceed by far the boldest projections of our created freedom.

Perhaps we must learn our lessons first in elementary school, beginning by tracing out the letters written on the blackboard one by one before being able eventually to write an essay on a particular theme. In the process human consciousness grows aware of the possibilities of its freedom, but that does not mean that God, who assigns the essay, has lost any of his freedom. Human freedom unfolds and expands from letter to spirit, but for God the letter always was spirit. "My words are spirit and life" (Jn 6:63). "The Lord is Spirit, and where the Spirit is there is freedom" (2 Cor 3:17). In this passage Paul continues by contemplating the Lord without the Old Testament veil of the letter, permitting us to live in the increasing radiance that emanates from the Lord of the Spirit (3:18). Our autonomy increases to the same degree that it becomes conformed to God's rule, to the degree that it becomes *theonomous*.

This applies to all believers to the same degree—whether they order their own lives in the world, or as members of an active order are subject to ecclesial obedience, or as contemplatives surrender the ordering of themselves entirely to God. The first of these three is no less spiritual than the others, and the last of them is no less literal. All of them live to the same degree within the pattern that God prepared for them in advance. And this living is truly a personal and responsible way of acting. Of course it is a way of acting that is surrounded by and caught up in Jesus Christ's activity, for we are expressly told that we "are created in Christ Jesus to good works". The word *in* reveals both the entire expanse of the redeemed creation and, within it, the concrete co-activity intended for us and expected by us that the Redeemer of the world considers necessary to the completion of his own work. Right here, where our own works are so much emphasized, the whole matter is placed within the framework of grace and faith: "For by grace you are saved through faith. And this is not your own doing—it is God's gift—not by works, so that no one can boast. For we are his workmanship" (Eph 2:8-9), and only and exclusively as such are we created in Christ Jesus to good works.

100. "My Father Is the Vinedresser"

In the parable of the vineyard the Son merely carries the fruit. He does not bear the blame when certain vines connected to him, the trunk, bear no fruit. He is not the one who cuts off these nonproductive branches, so that they dry up and are thrown into the fire. He leaves that task to the Father. Since he is our advocate with the Father, he might correspond more closely to the farmer in Luke (13:6–9) who begs a reprieve for the unproductive fig tree. "Lord, let it alone for this year yet. I will cultivate and fertilize the ground around it, and thus it may yet bear fruit. If not, then you can have it chopped down." Everything that belongs to the Son also belongs to the Father; therefore, he sees to it that the Son's fruitfulness reaches its full potential: "Every branch of me that brings forth no fruit is cut off, and every branch that bears fruit he prunes so that it produces more" (Jn 15:2).

Both the discarded and the cultivated branches endure suffering, but their sufferings have contrasting purposes and meanings. Some members of the body of Christ must be removed for the welfare of the whole, since a "bit of leaven leavens the whole lump" and the congregation therefore should not associate with "someone who calls himself a brother but is immoral . . . or a blasphemer". Paul calls the whole congregation to accountability for its own discipline ("Is it not those inside the Church whom you are to judge?" [1 Cor 5:6, 9, 11–12]). With approval from the congregation he separates the spoiled member from the community (1 Cor 5:4–5). He does this in the hope that the sinner will thereby be brought to repentance, something not mentioned in the talk of being "cut off" by the Father. We are simply not told whether the withering up and burning of the cut-off branches is a temporary or a final process. It is not our responsibility to decide this.

In contrast, the pruned branches should know that it is the Father who goes to work on them "in order that they might bear more fruit". God, not they, decide what is expected of them, for God certainly can "begin judgment with the house of God" (1 Pet 4:17) so that the harvest might be as plentiful as possible. From the Old Testament we know that God can make use of an iron broom as harsh as that of Assyria or Babylonia, and thus persecutions of the Church in the New Covenant may likewise represent God's grace, no matter how cruelly they may rage. Such may be the only way to carve a committed and constructive minority out of a lazy and indolent majority. To resort to such measures is God's responsibility alone, and we should neither wish for nor resist them. God alone can judge whether a small number of well-pruned vines will produce more fruit than a large number of ancient and half-impotent vines.

It may also be better to leave the purifying of the Church of Christ to the Father and his efficacious methods than to hack around at her with human and all-too-human means. To be sure, the Church always needs to be reformed (*Ecclesia semper reformanda*), but she needs to remember how much and in which ways she has lost the fruitfulness she received from God (not from herself), in the process looking back to the unique Lord who has given her precise instructions in the Gospel regarding fruit bearing. His example shows the degree to which one should accommodate oneself to human conceptions and also the degree of resistance one should expect from human conceptions. The ambiguous reception of Jesus' parables makes this clear: he told parables so that people might understand yet also to expose clearly his listeners' basic lack of comprehension. In this respect the parables are not so different from the law: God sets forth his gracious requirements, yet at the same time it becomes obvious that men are unwilling to live in accord with them. If the Church's efforts to cleanse and prune herself by means of a council can produce such contradictory results, no one should be surprised that God's more radical measures are more far reaching and, in ways obscure to us, more effective.

A fruitful tree, according to Augustine's imagery, has its roots in heaven and grows with its foliage hanging down toward the earth. The source of fecundity is hidden in God and cannot be grasped; her earthly produce for a heavenly harvest is God's concern. He pours out his Spirit into human hearts copiously enough (Rom 5:5) to ensure his harvest in ways that he alone knows.

101. CHARISM

In general terms, charism is a gift God gives to a man, yet a gift that does not remain in the possession of the one to whom it is given but rather somehow benefits the entire ecclesial community. Paul yearns to be able to give the Romans "a spiritual gift" (*charism*) but with a view toward a mutual exchange in which both members are strengthened (Rom 1:11–12; *charis* can mean the same thing [2 Cor 1:15]). The "gift" that God gave the apostle in saving him from death (2 Cor 1:11) benefits the churches. Charism can also mean a vocation to a particular status in the Church (1 Cor 7:7) that is supposed to bear fruit for the entire community. It can simply be equivalent to the word *calling* (*klēsis* [1 Cor 7:17–24]). Both words occur side by side in reference to Israel's election: "The gifts [*charisma*] and the calling [*klēsis*] of God are irrevocable" (Rom 11:19). Thus it makes sense that the distribution of various gifts for the Church in 1 Corinthians 12:4–6 proves identical to the ministries and abilities required: "There are varieties of gifts but only one Spirit; varieties of ministries but only one Lord; varieties of abilities but one God who enables all of them in every one." The gift assigned to each is given for service and carries with it its required equipment. That the gift of the Holy Spirit, the ministry of Christ, and the necessary enabling are all attributed to the Father shows clearly that we are dealing with giftedness from a single God for an undivided task.

Charism also exists as a giving of "God's grace" (*charis tou Theou*) that contrasts with the human fall into sin (Rom 5:15) as well as "God's bestowing of eternal life" in contrast to the "wages of sin, which is death" (Rom 6:23). *Charis* also refers to the charity inaugurated by the collection taken for the poverty-stricken church at Jerusalem (2 Cor 8:4, 6–7, 19)—described as "grace" and "commonality" and "service" (2 Cor 8:4). This illustrates how closely related are the grace given by God (as pointing to a task) and human reception and commissioning of that grace. As in

1 Corinthians 12, God's assignments are inseparable from an ability to carry them out and an awareness that the Church is being served. However, the gift of grace (*charisma*) can also be a unique, or, as Paul hopes, repeated rescue from death in which the Church assists only through prayer (2 Cor 1:11). Finally, each member of the Church can receive various aptitudes of both natural and supernatural character that presuppose an underlying grace (*charisma*) in order to be employed for the good of the whole community (Rom 12:3-8). Among these aptitudes, service to the congregation (*diakonia*) receives specific mention. The list of various gifts in 1 Corinthians 12:8-10, based on the situation at Corinth, includes those that fall within the scope of common Christian experience: wisdom, knowledge, discernment of spirits, faith. But others are more unusual and unique: knowing how to heal and the gift of healing, working miracles, speaking in tongues and interpreting such speech; above all, the ability to describe the will of God in a specific situation (*propheteia*).

If one wishes to describe the charismatic life Christians encounter, one needs to keep in mind this entire range of meanings. It reaches from a unique demonstration of grace in unusual circumstances to special gifts of God that sometimes take the form of special callings, tasks, and ministries yet sometimes have to do with individual ecclesial enterprises. This colorful collection is delimited along two sides—they all come from God, and they all are intended for the Church, or, put more broadly, for eternal life. Graces given to an individual are never exclusive. Someone who can expound God's word can also participate in discerning spirits, and the same applies to someone who has been given the office of teaching. The gift of leadership or pastoring (Eph 4:11) also includes ability to teach (Eph 4:11), and the latter involves "knowledge" and "wisdom". Those who are "compassionate" or "hospitable" or "generous in giving alms" (Rom 12:8, 13) will strive to express other Christian attitudes as well. Charisms are anything but specializations. "Apostolate" (probably in a broad sense [1 Cor 12:28]) presupposes many gifts of grace. When the Pastoral Epistles speak of the charism of a Church office (1 Tim 4:12; 2 Tim 1:6), they mean the entire cluster of graces needed to exercise the office properly. A charismatic quality crops up throughout all of Christian life, and no vital Christian will attempt to tie himself down to a single charism. To do so would be to impede the vitality and adaptability of the Divine Spirit who leads him.